About This Book

Why is this topic important?

Over the past decade, human resource (HR) functions, large and small, have been expected to play an ever-expanding role in the strategic direction of their organizations. Whereas at one time HR was seen primarily as an enforcer of policies, it is now considered among top performing organizations to be a key strategic partner in driving and supporting critical business objectives. HR's ability to contribute to the organization's bottom line involves more than aligning its talent management accountabilities with the mission and vision of the organization. It means continually evaluating and strengthening these accountabilities to ensure value, meaningful impact, and competitive advantage. Given this changing role and the fact that HR costs are major expenses in all organizations, improvements in HR program effectiveness and efficiency should be a strategic priority for organizations of all types, including private-sector companies; local, state, national, and international government bodies; and not-for-profit agencies. HR program evaluation offers a well-established set of methods that are directly applicable to meeting these challenges and to supporting the evolving role of HR as a strategic leader in the organization.

What can the reader achieve with this book?

This book's three primary objectives are to increase readers' understanding of, knowledge of, and ability to use HR program evaluation in organizations. More specifically, it provides:

- Understanding of:
  Techniques and strategies for evaluating and improving HR programs
  Major steps and primary considerations when conducting an HR
    program evaluation
- Knowledge of:
  How to lay groundwork and develop milestones for effective HR program
    evaluation
  How to construct measures of effectiveness within the context of HR
    program evaluation

- Ability to:

  Identify and lessen or avoid the effects of potential pitfalls when evaluating HR programs

  Identify appropriate analyses based on evaluation design

  Organize and document findings so that results have impact and are actionable

  Implement results of the evaluation to enhance the effectiveness of the HR program

How is the book organized?

This book divides the HR program evaluation process into six easy-to-follow phases:

1. Identify stakeholders, evaluators, and evaluation questions
2. Plan the evaluation by identifying resource needs, milestones, and evaluators' roles
3. Collect the data in ways that balance the need for high-quality information against costs
4. Analyze and interpret data in meaningful ways for future stakeholder audiences
5. Communicate findings and insights to diverse stakeholder groups
6. Utilize the results by implementing recommendations that will improve or replace the program

Within each phase, the authors provide concrete steps, examples, and illustrations for evaluators to follow.

About Pfeiffer

Pfeiffer serves the professional development and hands-on resource needs of training and human resource practitioners and gives them products to do their jobs better. We deliver proven ideas and solutions from experts in HR development and HR management, and we offer effective and customizable tools to improve workplace performance. From novice to seasoned professional, Pfeiffer is the source you can trust to make yourself and your organization more successful.

Essential Knowledge Pfeiffer produces insightful, practical, and comprehensive materials on topics that matter the most to training and HR professionals. Our Essential Knowledge resources translate the expertise of seasoned professionals into practical, how-to guidance on critical workplace issues and problems. These resources are supported by case studies, worksheets, and job aids and are frequently supplemented with CD-ROMs, websites, and other means of making the content easier to read, understand, and use.

Essential Tools Pfeiffer's Essential Tools resources save time and expense by offering proven, ready-to-use materials—including exercises, activities, games, instruments, and assessments—for use during a training or team-learning event. These resources are frequently offered in looseleaf or CD-ROM format to facilitate copying and customization of the material.

Pfeiffer also recognizes the remarkable power of new technologies in expanding the reach and effectiveness of training. While e-hype has often created whizbang solutions in search of a problem, we are dedicated to bringing convenience and enhancements to proven training solutions. All our e-tools comply with rigorous functionality standards. The most appropriate technology wrapped around essential content yields the perfect solution for today's on-the-go trainers and human resource professionals.

Pfeiffer *Essential resources for training and HR professionals*
www.pfeiffer.com

Pfeiffer™

Evaluating Human Resources Programs

A 6-Phase Approach for Optimizing Performance

Jack E. Edwards

John C. Scott

Nambury S. Raju

John Wiley & Sons, Inc.

Library of Congress Cataloging-in-Publication Data

Edwards, Jack E.
    Evaluating human resources programs : a 6-phase approach for optimizing performance / Jack E. Edwards, John C. Scott, Nambury S. Raju.
        p. cm.
    ISBN 978-0-7879-9487-7 (cloth : alk. paper)
1. Personnel management—Evaluation. 2. Human capital—Management. I. Scott, John C. (John Carlson), 1955– II. Raju, Nambury S. III. Title.
    HF5549.E415 2007
    658.3'01—dc22   2007008709

Acquiring Editor: Matt Davis
Director of Development: Kathleen Dolan Davies
Developmental Editor: Susan Rachmeler
Production Editor: Dawn Kilgore
Editor: Rebecca Taff
Composition and technical art: Leigh McLellan Design
Manufacturing Supervisor: Becky Carreño
Printed in the United States of America

Printing   10   9   8   7   6   5   4   3   2   1

This book is dedicated to
our friend, mentor, and co-author, Nam Raju,
who died shortly before we finished our book.
While his absence will leave a void that can't be filled,
his presence truly made the world a better place and
provided many wonderful memories for all who were
lucky enough to have known him.

CONTENTS

Phase 1: Identify Stakeholders, Evaluators, and Evaluation Questions

Phase 2: Plan the Evaluation

Phase 3: Collect Data

Phase 4: Analyze and Interpret Data

Phase 5: Communicate Findings and Insights

Phase 6: Utilize the Results

List of Tables, Figures, and Exhibits

Tables

Figures

Exhibits

Preface

Why We Wrote This Book

The path to deciding to write this book was circuitous.

Around six years ago, we began editing *The Human Resources Program-Evaluation Handbook*. In our preface for that book, we noted the lack of information about program evaluation as it pertains to human resources (HR). Our goal was to supply practitioners and researchers with insights into key criteria, potential pitfalls, and general guidance in assessing *specific* HR-related programs. We determined that the best way to do this was to ask two or more authors—typically a practitioner and an academic—to write about a single HR program such as performance appraisal or diversity. This allowed us to seek insights from content matter experts for each reviewed HR program.

Midway through the preparation of the *Handbook*, one of our chapter authors asked us to conduct a workshop at the 2002 Society for Industrial and Organizational Psychology convention. When we were allotted only three hours for our workshop presentation, we decided that the time could best be used with an orientation different from that of the *Handbook*. More specifically, we prepared the workshop materials so that they walked participants through the steps found in a typical program evaluation, regardless of the specific HR program being evaluated.

The enrollment for the workshop and the comments that we received from attendees suggested that, while our *Handbook* might fill part of the earlier identified void, practitioners and academics also needed a hands-on, practical guide to HR program evaluation.

We concluded that the additional guide should lead HR specialists in a step-by-step fashion from the beginning of a program evaluation to its conclusion. We hope this book provides that guidance.

Objectives of This Book

We have three primary objectives for this book. They are to increase readers' understanding of, knowledge of, and ability to use HR program evaluation in organizations. Those objectives can be further broken down as:

- Understanding of

  Techniques and strategies for evaluating and improving HR programs

  Major steps and primary considerations when conducting an HR program evaluation

- Knowledge of

  How to lay groundwork and develop milestones for effective HR program evaluation

  How to construct measures of effectiveness within the context of HR program evaluation

- Ability to

  Identify and then lessen or avoid the effects of potential pitfalls when evaluating HR programs

  Identify appropriate analyses based on evaluation design

  Organize and document findings so that results have impact and are actionable

  Implement results of the evaluation to enhance the effectiveness of the HR program

Obtaining an understanding of the information contained in this book will provide internal organizational members and consultants with a foundation for deciding what needs to be considered in their roles as part of an evaluation team. Likewise, this book can act as an introduction to HR program evaluation for graduate students who are preparing for careers in HR. On the other hand, more experienced HR program evaluators will benefit from new perspectives on HR program evaluation as well as from our reminders of traditional concerns.

We believe that the most effective way to use the information in this book is to read the whole book before the HR program evaluation starts and then refer back to a particular phase as it approaches during the actual evaluation. While we have attempted to warn readers about future pitfalls before they become an issue, having as much knowledge as possible about what lies ahead during the entire process can add peace of mind and limit rework, especially for those new to HR program evaluation. In the way of analogy, it's like driving down a curvy, mountainous road. If you routinely drive the road, you will be aware of every stop sign or other place where there is likely to be an accident, but you must still be alert for the unexpected obstacle waiting around each bend. If you have only been down the road a time or two, signs 200 yards before a stop sign or dangerous intersection will allow sufficient time to take appropriate action. Finally, if you have never been down the road, a navigator giving you timely warnings and other advice can help to avoid sudden swerves or crashes.

A Few Words of Thanks

We wish to express our appreciation to the many people at Pfeiffer who helped us see this book to its completion. Matt Davis, senior editor, supplied early encouragement to us as we refined our overall message. Samya Sattar provided excellent editorial assistance, improving our ability to convey a clear message. Also, Kathleen Dolan-Davies, Julie Rodriguez, Dawn Kilgore, Rebecca Taff, and others ably handled the many other tasks that were required to transform our manuscript into a book and get it out to our audience. We would also like to thank the four reviewers who provided invaluable feedback on earlier drafts of our book.

Last but not least, we'd like to thank the following people who received less of our time and attention while we worked on this book. Those people are Deborah Edwards, Mary Edwards, Harold Edwards, Susie Hoke, Patti Groves, Bill Lawson, Willie Mae Lawson, Kimberly Scott, Justin Scott, Jeremy Scott, Marijke Raju, Indira Hanley, Kevin Hanley, Colin Nambury Hanley, Marijke Kathleen Hanley, and Saroja Raju.

Jack, John, and Nam

Overview

HUMAN RESOURCES (HR) PROGRAM EVALUATION

"Trust but verify."
—*Ronald Reagan*

Chapter Objectives

- Detail the context for human resources evaluation and show how it can be leveraged to support HR's evolving role as a strategic leader
- Highlight the difference between HR metrics and HR evaluation and demonstrate how they should be integrated to enhance HR program effectiveness
- Prepare program evaluators for the potential excuses that they will hear for why an evaluation should not be performed
- Help program evaluators recognize three different evaluation strategies
- Introduce program evaluators to a six-phase approach for HR program evaluation

Over the past decade, HR functions, large and small, have been expected to play an ever-expanding role in the strategic direction of their organizations. Whereas at one time HR was seen primarily as an enforcer of policies, it is now considered among top-performing organizations to be a key strategic partner in driving and supporting critical business objectives. This paradigm shift has been the result of an evolving realization that, when HR and line leadership collaborate on the achievement of organizational goals, the result is a significant competitive advantage. HR's ability to contribute to the organization's bottom line involves more than applying best practices to its talent management accountabilities. It means closely aligning these accountabilities with the mission and vision of the organization and continually evaluating the outcomes to ensure value and meaningful impact.

HR professionals have long understood their value in helping line organizations achieve their goals by offering critical services in the areas of recruitment and retention, compensation and benefits, assessment and evaluation, training, performance management, organizational development, and succession planning. What has been lacking over the years, however, has been a systematic process for (a) quantifying the economic contribution of these services and (b) evaluating how well these services meet the expectations of the clients or stakeholders served and using that information to make improvements.

A number of metrics are now available to help HR organizations quantify their worth and support their role in driving the business. Some excellent strides have been made in quantifying the "intangibles" associated with HR services (Fitz-enz & Davison, 2002; Sullivan, 2002). For example, through research conducted by the Saratoga Institute, we now have a good handle on the costs of turnover and the economic impact that a well-designed talent retention program can have on the bottom line. Similarly, we are now able to calculate credible return on investment figures for a valid selection system based on studies that show the relative worth in dollar terms of high-, average-, and low-performing employees. Metrics are available for most of the service areas provided by HR, including staffing, training, compensation, performance management, employee engagement, and organizational effectiveness. Metrics are also available for deciding whether outsourcing any or all of these services makes economic sense. Any HR function, large or small, should be taking advantage of these and other resources to establish relevant metrics to quantify the value of their HR services and link these metrics to their organization's objectives. The establishment of metrics is a fundamental first step in demonstrating HR's contribution to the organization's bottom line.

While metrics are critical and serve as the baseline criteria for HR program success, they alone are not sufficient for establishing a best-in-class HR organization that meets the compelling needs of its stakeholders or helps ensure the competitive advantage of its organization. What is needed beyond the metrics is a disciplined process for gathering, reporting, and acting on data that show why a particular HR program or function is not performing as efficiently as it could and how it can be improved to meet the established criteria. A decision to adjust, replace, or even outsource an HR program, or the entire HR function, needs to be driven by an accurate assessment of key stakeholder needs, business objectives, cost, and quality considerations, as well as any associated risk factors such as litigation exposure that should not be guessed at or inferred. The consequences are too significant to leave these sorts of decisions to chance or guesswork. What is needed here is a systematic methodology for establishing the appropriate metrics of success for an HR program and then determining how this program can be improved, replaced, or outsourced to meet these success criteria.

The good news is that the field of program evaluation offers a well-established set of methods that are directly applicable to meeting these challenges and to supporting the evolving role of HR as a strategic leader in the organization. Program evaluation is a specialty area that gained prominence in governmental and educational institutions as a process for ensuring program accountability and continuous improvement. It is an outgrowth from the commonsense belief that programs should produce demonstrable benefits (Berk & Rossi, 1990). Program evaluation as a discipline overlays nicely onto the HR field because it entails a systematic process for determining both overall program worth and for building continuous course corrections and realignment strategies. HR organizations hoping to improve or become best-in-class providers of talent management solutions with demonstrable economic contributions to the organization's bottom line would do well to make the evaluation of their functions and programs an ongoing activity and priority. This means developing a thorough understanding of what is required to meet the organization's business objectives and strategies to evaluate and enhance each HR program.

All types of organizations need to evaluate their HR programs to determine how benefits can best be realized, assets leveraged, and potential consequences from poorly administered programs minimized. The consequences of poorly administered HR programs are not insignificant. They can range from loss of credibility within the organization to such extreme outcomes as death resulting from an inadequate safety training program or extremely expensive class-action litigation resulting from poor HR practices. Today, class-action employment litigation presents a major risk to the bottom-line health of organizations. Unfortunately, even an accusation of improprieties in an organization's HR processes can lead to lengthy, costly, legal action. Employment litigation is a threat to every aspect of business. The best defense against litigation is a fair, balanced, and reasoned approach to talent management and HR processes. The evaluation of these programs is critical to ensure that they are not only meeting the needs of the organization's stakeholders, but that they correspond to the various legal guidelines and professional standards.

Given that their people play a major role in the success of all organizations and that HR costs are major expenses in all organization, improvements in HR program efficiency and effectiveness should be a concern for organizations in both industrialized and developing countries. Similarly, HR concerns are relevant to all types of organizations: private-sector companies; local, state, national, and international governmental bodies; and not-for-profit agencies. Moreover, it is hard to image any type of endeavor—education, health care, public policy, and so forth—that has an HR component and could not function more effectively and efficiently. Therefore, we believe that all organizations should *incorporate* HR program evaluation as part of their strategic and tactical plans.

Use the Approach That Best Addresses Your HR Program Evaluation's Objectives

In this section, we review three general strategies that we have found to be particularly useful when conducting an HR program evaluation. The three strategies differ based on the primary focus of the evaluation: goals, processes, or outcomes. Table 0.1 uses a performance appraisal program to illustrate various aspects of the three strategies. More specifically, Table 0.1 provides a definition, an example, and an evaluation question for goal-, process-, and outcome-based strategies for HR program evaluation. While some academics or practitioners of program evaluation might strongly advocate use of one strategy to the near exclusion of others, it is likely that multiple strategies will be useful for most HR program evaluations. For example, the processes used in the day-to-day administration of a program will likely need to be examined, even when an evaluation team emphasizes outcomes or end results in its assessment of the program's levels of success in reaching its mission goals. Let's explore each of the three approaches shown in Table 0.1 further.

Use Goal-Based Evaluations to Focus on Program Objectives

Hopefully, the design and implementation phases of an HR program included development of a specific statement about what the HR program was meant to achieve. Such a mission statement, along with any subsequent modifications, would help in the identification of the primary criteria for assessing how well those goals had been met. Using a recruitment program as the example, the program's goals might include statements such as (a) 90 percent of the positions will be refilled within sixty days of someone leaving the organization, (b) no more than 5 percent of the new hires will leave voluntarily within the first two years after starting work, (c) the experience-level mix of the new hires will be approximately 75 percent new college graduates and 25 percent experienced talent, and (d) the demographic

Table 0.1 Distinguishing Characteristics for Three General Strategies to HR Program Evaluation

Characteristics	Three General Strategies for Conducting a Program Evaluation		
	Goals-Based	**Process-Based**	**Outcome-Based**
Description of the strategy	The evaluation assesses how well an HR program accomplishes objectives that have often been identified before the program evaluation begins. For example, this type of evaluation might assess the degree to which the actual benefits of the program matched those predicted in the business case developed for the implementation of the program.	The evaluation analyzes workflow and procedures used to accomplish HR program tasks. Those tasks may include activities of program staff, users, vendors, and others involved in the HR program. Examples of process analyses might include comparisons of earlier versus current procedures, and prescribed versus actual procedures.	The evaluation results in statements about how effectively or efficiently a program influences individual and group performance. The evaluation might include examining returns on investments or other metrics related to the organization's bottom line. Common criteria for this type of evaluation include changes in productivity, absenteeism, or employee turnover.
An example question for a performance appraisal program	How well does the performance appraisal program achieve the objectives outlined for it in the HR strategic plan?	How do the actual performance appraisal procedures compare to those prescribed in the performance appraisal handbook?	How well does the performance appraisal program promote and reward higher productivity?
An example of an assessment task by the evaluation team	Evaluate the extent to which various aspects of the program address each relevant objective laid out in the HR strategic plan.	Examine the step-by-step appraisal procedures used throughout the organization for consistency.	Determine whether individuals who receive more awards are producing at a higher level than lower-performing peers.

mix of new hires will meet the organization's equal employment opportunity utilization targets.

While the cited level of detail and quantification for the example recruitment program is desirable, the goal or mission statement for many programs may be much less specific or even non-existent. Regardless, a secondary benefit of goal-based evaluations might be the refinement or establishment of statements specifying the HR program's goals.

At the end of the evaluation or possibly before, findings may suggest that the program accomplishes all of its goals because the goals are set too low. In such cases, the evaluation team may offer insights into the development of more appropriate goals and desired performance levels for those goals. Conversely, the goals for another program might be unrealistic and set too high. For example, one of the authors recently evaluated a program that is used to develop professional employees during their first two years in the organization. The originally stated goals suggested that the program was responsible for many functions that were under the control of other organizational units. As a result of the unrealistic goals, the initial attempt at evaluating the program was shelved until the program administrator and his staff identified which functions were solely theirs, which were accomplished with assistance from other units, and which were outside the purview of the program.

Use Process-Based Evaluations to Focus on Workflow and Procedures

An evaluation of the workflow, procedures, communication patterns, forms integral to the program, and other process-oriented information that an organization uses to implement its HR program may reveal inconsistencies and inefficiencies. Descriptions of various aspects of the processes used to implement and administer a program can be found in the organization's HR policy manuals, in the instruction manuals for using software that is central to the program, and through verbal step-by-step accounts or demonstrations of the steps that program staff and users perform to accomplish the required program tasks. For example, a recent evaluation of a company's sexual harassment program examined the following process-based components: (a) formal policy, (b) training practices (content and datedness related to the law and policies, attendance tracking, retention evaluation, extent of tailoring to work context, and availability of refresher modules), (c) approach for conducting harassment investigations, (d) accountability mechanisms for employees and managers, (e) communication practices, (f) procedures for linking harassment polices and practices to business outcomes and the organization's code of conduct, (g) appeals and dispute-resolution practices, and (h) processes for ensuring consistency in the application of the policy. This evaluation was conducted through interviews with HR and organizational leadership, reviews of written policies and practices, and archival survey data that had been used to assess the organization's culture.

Often, differences will be revealed when the process descriptions are presented or demonstrated by different stakeholders. This is especially true when the program *staff's* step-by-step descriptions are compared to those from program *users*. For instance, in a performance appraisal, the individuals being rated might emphasize certain features of the process that they think are important and de-emphasize steps that those in the HR department who are responsible for overseeing the program believe are critical. For example, in one company, the program staff's primary concern was having the performance appraisal ratings completed and returned on time so that compensation decisions could be implemented at the beginning of the first quarter. However, the employees being rated felt that the written comments section was the most valuable part of the appraisal process and that, without it, the ratings were essentially meaningless. A different set of the program users—the managers—indicated that implementation of the compensation decisions would need to be delayed if they would be required to write the comments while preparing the ratings. Identifying and reconciling the discrepancies in processes or misperceptions about a process are the first steps to determining the best set of processes for effectively and efficiently accomplishing an HR program's objectives. In some instances, effectiveness and efficiency can be increased relatively easily with training, reemphasis on proper procedures, process re-engineering, or other interventions.

Use Outcome-Based Evaluations to Focus on Results

The emphasis for this approach to program evaluation is examining the end result of the HR program. Caution is needed to make sure that the evaluation team is focusing on outcomes rather than simply the outputs of the program. This confusion is particularly likely to occur in the evaluation of training programs. For instance, the *outcomes* of a sales training program might include the number of new clients developed and the increase in dollars or units of sales over a specified period of time. In contrast, example *outputs* of training might include the number of people trained, as well as the number and types of courses offered. The reason for making the distinction is to emphasize that an output may not translate into a desired outcome. Again using the training example, a four-hour course on sales techniques could be attended by the organization's entire sales force, but the elementary level of the course materials could have resulted in no increase in sales because no new knowledge or skills were acquired.

In our experiences, top-level stakeholders have typically emphasized outcome-based evaluations more than any other general strategy for HR program evaluation. Having said this, it is, however, common to look at goals, processes, or other strategies as part of an evaluation in order to gain an understanding of the outcomes. In fact, the mission statement for an HR program may (a) contain goals that are stated as outputs or outcomes and (b) emphasize the processes that are necessary in providing high-quality service to internal and possibly external stakeholders. Common types of outcomes include decrease in cost, change in time required to accomplish a task, and enhanced quality or service.

Integrate Ongoing and Periodic Program Evaluations into the Operation of HR Programs

Our discussion throughout this book emphasizes conducting a periodic, large-scale evaluation of an HR program, but much of our book can and should also be applied to the continuous monitoring and improvement activities that play important roles in maintaining efficient and effective HR programs. At the same time, readers can readily downscale our prescriptions and apply our recommended courses of actions to smaller organizations or to smaller HR programs in large organizations. Our use of the larger-scale examples helps prepare HR program evaluators or evaluation teams to perform any size evaluation, regardless of the complexities they may encounter. As a convention in the book, we frequently refer to evaluation teams when describing the phases in our recommended approach. However, we certainly recognize that in many cases the evaluation team may be a single individual. Even when a single individual comprises the evaluation team, that individual may obtain help from one or more other employees in the organization. For example, the evaluator might work with the organization's accountant in order to graph the quantitative findings from the HR program evaluation. The concepts presented in this book apply equally to large- and small-scale evaluations that are conducted by teams or an individual evaluator.

Program evaluation specialists often refer to the ongoing assessments as *formative* evaluations and the periodic assessments as *summative* evaluations. Finer distinctions between formative and summative evaluations are noted in Table 0.2 and the following subsections.

Enhance HR Program Performance Through Ongoing Formative Program Evaluation

As Table 0.2 indicates, the focus of formative evaluation is continuous improvement through taking full advantage of the program's strengths and correcting weaknesses. From an HR program evaluation perspective, the formative program evaluation may occur at every stage in the

Table 0.2 A Contrast of Typical Characteristics Found in Formative and Summative Program Evaluations

Characteristics of the Evaluation	Formative Program Evaluation	Summative Program Evaluation
Aim of the evaluation	Obtain prospective, frequent feedback to diagnose interim performance levels and foster continuous improvement	Provide retrospective, one-time or infrequent evidence to key upper management about continuing or discontinuing a program
Rigor underlying evaluation findings	Conducted by program staff who may • Have little training or experience in evaluation methods and • Use more limited data as the bases for their improvements	Conducted by an evaluation team that • Contains staff with evaluation training/experience and independence from the program and • Uses more methodologically sound procedures and larger samples or populations before providing recommendations
Examples of events that might lead to an evaluation	• Standing requirement to evaluate the program • Suggestions from users about program weaknesses that need to be corrected • Need for adjustments after program modifications (e.g., adoption of a new time-and-attendance system)	• Class-action or high-profile legal challenge to an HR program • The methods for administering an HR program have not kept pace with those used by the rest of the industry • Merger of organizations and a need to determine which program will remain
Example questions that could be answered for a healthcare program	• What steps should be taken to decrease the time and paperwork required to receive healthcare reimbursements? • What are the major obstacles to decreasing the overhead costs associated with the healthcare program?	• How long would the alternative healthcare program take to pay for itself? • What are the relative advantages and disadvantages of replacing the current healthcare program with Option A?

See Center for Effective Teaching and Learning (2005), Sonnichsen (2000), and Worthen, Sanders, & Fitzpatrick (1997) for additional distinctions between the two types of evaluations.

program's lifecycle. Ideally, formative program evaluation would have been a concern during the planning for implementation of the program, and monitoring would have been performed on a frequent basis thereafter. Continuing with the performance appraisal example in a formative evaluation context, an organization attempting to introduce a new appraisal program might start with a pilot test, even trying it out within the HR department. Participants in the pilot would take the appraisal through its paces in an abbreviated timeframe and complete a structured questionnaire or participate in a structured interview at the end of the pilot. The evaluation at this point might focus more heavily on processes such as ease of use, clarity of instructions, and interpretability of the rating scales. Changes to the process could be expected at this point; some may be significant, others insignificant. There may also be questions related to goals and outcomes, but they would be more focused on whether the appraisal would *likely* meet the stated goals and achieve the desired outcomes (with potential barriers identified) given the participants' experience with the appraisal processes (more so than the outcomes) in the pilot. The point here is that, before formally rolling out the program, it is evaluated by a knowledgeable or representative group who could then provide the feedback necessary to help ensure a seamless implementation company-wide. Once the program is implemented throughout the company, a follow-up survey can be administered to gauge users' reactions, which could then be followed up by targeted interviews or focus groups with the key users and stakeholders. Other follow-up evaluation activities could include gender and race/ethnicity analyses of ratings, quality review of performance objectives, and determination of the extent of help desk or HR support needed throughout the process. The nature of the evaluation activities will follow from the stakeholder goals for the program. In addition, ongoing evaluation can be used to adjust the program throughout its lifecycle and help the program better meet its objectives.

Even if HR program evaluation is an afterthought that came about once the program was up and running, program administrators can benefit greatly from an empirical, data-driven improvement process. If the formative evaluation comes after a major periodic evaluation or as the result of an evaluation designed to determine whether to keep or replace an existing program (usually referred to as a summative evaluation), program administrators can use the criteria, methods, and assessment-related aids that were developed by the team conducting the summative evaluation to assess and improve their program on an ongoing basis.

Worthen, Sanders, and Fitzpatrick (1997) suggested other characteristics typical of a formative evaluation. For example, they noted that formative evaluations are typically carried out by program administrators and staff, are used for diagnostic purposes, and often are performed with small sample sizes. This may take the form of a pilot test before a program is formally implemented or periodic "lessons-learned" focus groups involving key stakeholders at selected intervals in the program's cycle.

Enhance HR Program Performance Through Periodic Summative Program Evaluation

Returning to Table 0.2, it shows that summative evaluations take a look backward to see what the program has accomplished during its existence or since the last major periodic program evaluation. This overall or summary evaluation can have important implications in answering questions about whether an HR program will be continued, replaced with a new in-house HR program, or outsourced to an external firm that will handle all aspects of administrating the HR program. The evaluation will likely examine data from multiple years in answering those questions before coming to a bottom-line assessment of the program's effectiveness and continued viability.

Mohr (1995, p. 32) noted that summative studies may be "enormously complicated by measurement concerns." Because the monetary and disruption costs of replacing an HR program could be significant, organizations will want to ensure that accurate answers are provided with any recommendation to retain or replace an existing HR program.

Consider Our General Philosophy
of HR Program Evaluation

Although formal education in program evaluation, statistics, and other disciplines can provide a firm methodological basis for conducting an evaluation, they are merely starting points. Our abilities to pick up useful approaches from others and learn from our own mistakes supply additional important perspectives about optimally structuring and carrying out an HR program evaluation. As a result, two evaluators could propose very different ways for evaluating a program, with each evaluator's proposal having strengths and weaknesses.

While we would all like to know that an approach has been used successfully before we apply it in our own organization, we should be concerned about the fit of a previously developed approach to the current HR program evaluation, situation, and organization. The evaluation of a program is not a stand-alone activity that occurs in a vacuum. Instead, the program is continuing to operate during the evaluation. As such, evaluation team members can engender a more amicable relationship with the program administrators if, when possible, they give due consideration to working around the program staff's required duties.

It is important to recognize that the very act of evaluation may cause some parts of the program to operate differently during the time when the evaluation is occurring. For example, some program tasks may take longer because program staff are being diverted to assemble data for the evaluation team. Conversely, program staff may perform some of their duties exactly as described in program manuals while they are being observed as part of the evaluation, even though that is not their usual manner of operating.

An evaluation runs more smoothly, can be more comprehensive, and can be completed more quickly when the evaluation team approaches its tasks as a collaborative effort. Members of the evaluation team must work together, but they must also work well with the program's internal and external stakeholders, who may have competing reasons (for example, fear that their program will be made to "look bad") for not wanting to cooperate. Getting off to the wrong start with top management or with the staff who administer a program can doom the evaluation or make it very difficult to complete. The evaluation team can lessen the odds of this undesirable outcome occurring by, among other things, establishing a collaborative environment with non-team members and taking the time to let the others know the purpose of the evaluation and evaluation timelines. In addition, the evaluation team can encounter ill will and passive resistance if program staff are constantly reminded that they have to supply the requested data because someone higher in the organization said that the evaluation was going to be performed. At the same time, it also must be recognized that higher-level intervention is sometimes required if needed data are not provided in a reasonable period of time.

Be Prepared to Address Potential Excuses for Not Conducting an HR Program Evaluation

Although HR program evaluation is not a panacea for all organizational ills, it offers organizations a systematic, objective means for identifying steps to self-improvement. Despite offering potential improvements in important organizational outcomes, conducting a program evaluation may be a tough sell within the organization. As Worthen and his colleagues (1997) noted, an idealistic desire to evaluate everything ignores practical realities such as the program is too small to warrant the effort, a program is too new for a comprehensive evaluation, or sufficient time may not be allotted to complete the evaluation.

While it may seem counter-intuitive to admit the following at the beginning of a book on HR program evaluation, we too have questioned or discouraged some organizations from doing large-scale investigations for the previously mentioned reasons, as well as others. Poorly planned evaluations can result in needless monetary costs and disruptions to an organization. Furthermore, providing results and recommendations that are of limited use to the organization could discourage top management stakeholders from conducting subsequent program evaluations when other evaluations would have had a greater probability of being successful and resulting in sizable benefits to the organization.

Bearing in mind Worthen and his colleagues' cautions about avoiding program evaluation when it is not warranted, we have assembled five potential excuses that program evaluation advocates may encounter. While we added the first one from our experiences, the other four potential excuses derive from McNamara's (1998) explication of various "myths" surrounding the usefulness of conducting program evaluations. The latter four were further extended to HR program evaluations and discussed by Rose and Davidson (2003). We are re-labeling the five myths reviewed here as potential excuses to emphasize that there may sometimes be factual bases (real reasons) for not conducting an evaluation. In our description of the potential excuses provided below and throughout the book, we refer to program sponsors, program administrators, and program staff. The *program sponsors* are those individuals who have ultimate accountability for the HR program and its outcomes, and for funding the evaluation. These individuals typically fall within the upper management ranks and are often at the officer level. We refer to *program administrators* and their *program staff* as those who are responsible for managing the day-to-day operations of the program and who direct the program staff. It should be noted that the program administrator may also be the program sponsor or even the sole program staff, depending on the size and other characteristics of the program and organization.

Potential Excuse 1:
The Resources Required to Conduct a Program Evaluation Are Better Spent on Administering the Program

The resources argument is a common objection to conducting a program evaluation, particularly with large-scale HR programs when significant time and resources have already been invested in the program's development and implementation and when significant accountabilities rest with the program's success. Unless the system is clearly broken or has been challenged, program sponsors often have little desire for investing additional resources to properly evaluate a new or existing HR program. Many times, the program sponsors' perspective is that, if resources are available, they should be invested in the program itself.

While program goals are often specified when new HR programs are designed and implemented, there is often less discipline when it comes to establishing the procedures that will ensure that these goals are monitored and evaluated against clear criteria. The internal, and possibly less formalized, evaluation components may therefore be conducted in a haphazard manner or relegated to the back burner as other organizational exigencies and new projects take precedence. Program evaluation needs to be conceptualized as an integral part of an HR program's design and implementation. By incorporating evaluation as a key activity in the implementation plan, with an associated budget, it is treated as a seamless exercise that must be performed in order to optimize HR program performance.

Throughout this book, our emphasis is on *optimizing*, rather than *maximizing*, outcomes, regardless of whether we are talking about HR programs or the steps and tools used to evaluate the programs. Without constant vigilance, HR program evaluators can design evaluations and propose HR program improvements that are not feasible on a one-time basis or sustainable over the life of the HR program. In such a case, the extra resources required to maximize outcomes can result in investments that would outstrip the return that an organization could expect.

To the extent that program evaluation is treated as a separate, independent activity, it may be difficult to convince program sponsors to later allocate resources for this effort, particularly when these resources could be used to support other aspects of the program (for example, add a new software module or help fund additional staff). To overcome this potential excuse, program sponsors need to be educated on the value of a program evaluation, in terms of the bottom-line impact on the organization. Among other things, this education could include demonstrating whether the program is operating as intended and ensuring ongoing quality improvement.

Potential Excuse 2:
Program Effectiveness Is Impossible to Measure

Another potential excuse provided by HR program sponsors for not conducting a program evaluation is the assertion that the impact or effectiveness of the program is too complicated to measure. HR program evaluators must work with HR program staff to provide upper management with answers to questions such as, "How can you tell that the new selection system is resulting in better hires overall or that the revised compensation system has increased employee morale and ultimately retention?" There are clearly challenges involved in measuring the effectiveness of HR programs and human behavior; however, most measurement challenges can be addressed through systematic analyses of the program's goals against well-developed criteria.

If the evaluation team has been asked to conduct a truly unfeasible evaluation, the team can provide a beneficial service to the organization by identifying an evaluation that is feasible and useful in addressing some of the concerns at hand (Prosavac & Carey, 2003). Other times, the impact of this potential excuse can be allayed by either explaining to top management stakeholders the sorts of assessment tools that might be applied to the particular evaluation or describing the evaluation team's former successes with similar problems and its measurement expertise. We have also found that a give-and-take discussion with the program sponsors can lead to creative ideas on how to measure a program's effectiveness and has the side benefit of engaging important stakeholders in establishing a collaborative relationship.

Potential Excuse 3:
There Are Too Many Variables to Do a Good Study

A related, but slightly different, potential excuse proffered by program sponsors against conducting a program evaluation is that there are just too many outside or contaminating variables to be able to isolate the impact of a specific HR program.

This type of argument is frequently heard when evaluating promotion and performance management programs with sales organizations. Those discouraging the use of program evaluation might maintain that there is no real way to isolate an individual sales representative's performance in order to make a fair assessment for either promotion or compensation purposes. Variables such as the economy, emerging competition, changing markets, the weather, new legislation, new products to learn and sell, and team versus individual accountabilities are but some of the factors that can contribute to sales performance. There is no question that these factors do indeed influence performance. At the same time, other factors such as expected behaviors or competencies that are important to overall performance can be assessed and do fall under the control of the sales representative. One way to tease out this multiple of extraneous conditions is to convert sales targets to a ranking system and track results over a longer timeframe (for example, six to eight quarters). In this scenario, a sales representative would be considered an exceptional performer if he or she ranked in the top 85 percent of peers in the same region for five out of the last six quarters. A region-based ranking approach limits the vagaries of the marketplace and ensures a fairer comparison across the sales representatives' peers. If the marketplace is depressed, all sales representatives would be impacted by this fact and a relative ranking places everyone on the same scale. By extending the measurement over six quarters, short-term fluctuations are also accounted for. The critical job competencies that are under the direct control of the sales representative can be combined with the regional rankings and the two sets of data weighted to reflect the performance expectations for the job. In this way, we have optimized the performance appraisal program by focusing on critical aspects of performance, while teasing out those factors that are less under the sales representative's control.

While these and other such variables clearly need to be taken into account when evaluating an HR program, the evaluation can be designed in such a way as to help isolate the impact of the targeted program. Again, these issues can often be addressed with a discussion of the general evaluation approach that provides examples of how the many variables will be taken into account, along with a solicitation of the program sponsors' input.

Potential Excuse 4:
No One Is Asking for an Evaluation,
So Why Bother?

This potential excuse may be openly stated by program sponsors, but more frequently it is exhibited as a generalized attitude against conducting an evaluation. This attitude takes the form of "If it ain't broke, don't fix it." The underlying assumptions are that the program left unevaluated will meet its goals as intended and that, unless there are complaints, an evaluation leads to nothing more than over-engineering the process. These possibly erroneous assumptions can be short-sighted views that are very challenging to overcome. The key is to identify for the program sponsors the sorts of value that will accrue from conducting an evaluation. Also, the sponsors and evaluation team should come to an understanding about the goals of the HR program evaluation: whether the goals are to demonstrate how well the overall program is working, identify efficiencies that can be realized, both, and/or some other goals.

We have found it is useful in these situations to facilitate a discussion with the program sponsors about how well they believe the goals established for the program are being met and what criteria make sense for confirming these results. This dialog leads to a natural exploration of an evaluation study where the value and return on investment of the evaluation are generally proportionate to the significance of the HR program within the organization.

Potential Excuse 5:
"Negative" Results Will Hurt My Program

The implementation of an HR program is often a long process that requires extensive planning, resource leveraging, networking, political maneuvering, and overcoming sometimes substantial organizational resistance. It is therefore not surprising that, once a program is finally in place, the sponsor would be reluctant to expose it to the possibility of a negative evaluation. Accepting less-than-positive evaluation findings does not come easy to most people, particularly when those results are made public and could undermine gains that have been achieved in some hard-fought battles.

As with the other potential excuses for not conducting a program evaluation, this argument may be based on the short-sighted view that feedback is harmful and can only result in a losing proposition. This belief may result from the program sponsors' previous experiences within the organization or from the potential for loss of credibility due to the high status or exposure afforded by the target program.

HR program evaluations are frequently conducted at the request of an organization's legal department. Occasionally, these evaluations are short and targeted to specific issues, while other times, they can be wide-ranging and span every HR program. Regardless, by the time the need for an evaluation has reached the legal department (unless they are being proactive), a certain level of anxiety has likely already surfaced among program stakeholders. It is not unusual in these cases to find that the program sponsors and other stakeholders are somewhat resistant to drilling into programs for which they have invested considerable time and resources and now feel as if they are on the firing line. For example, consider a selection system that took two years of developing and modifying the business case to get budgetary approval from top organizational leaders, six months to develop, and three months to implement. Shortly after implementation, the legal counsel requested a review of the selection system because of her concern that it may be screening out a disproportionate number of protected group members. As a result, the organization asked an outside expert to review the system and make recommendations.

It is no surprise that this fairly common scenario would be met with some resistance, particularly given the time and resources spent putting the selection program in place. An approach that frequently works in these situations is to frame the evaluation as a chance to further improve upon what is there and to create an opportunity to more clearly link the system or the overall program to valued organizational objectives. The evaluation activities should include the input of key stakeholders, particularly the program sponsors and administrators, because they will be living with the outcome and will need to support it. Additionally, a process should be set up for ongoing monitoring so that program sponsors and other interested parties (in this case the legal department) will have metrics, should additional program adjustments be needed.

Program evaluation should be positioned as a support tool for the continued usefulness of HR programs. This is a proactive process that is designed to bolster, rather than weaken, the program by providing constructive feedback that maximizes the chance of success over the long run.

A Look at How the Remainder of the Book Is Organized

The remainder of this book is devoted to helping readers understand and use our six-phase approach to HR program evaluation. Figure 0.1 shows that each of the six phases has multiple steps, and the steps and phases overlap one another. While taking prescribed small steps, HR program evaluators will be led up the stairs until they reach the end of their project. Throughout the book, doable tasks with appropriate cautions are outlined to provide readers with a step-to-step guide to

Figure O.1
Our Six-Phase Approach to HR Program Evaluation

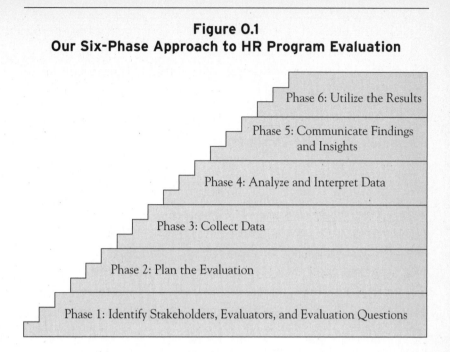

Phase 6: Utilize the Results

Phase 5: Communicate Findings and Insights

Phase 4: Analyze and Interpret Data

Phase 3: Collect Data

Phase 2: Plan the Evaluation

Phase 1: Identify Stakeholders, Evaluators, and Evaluation Questions

conducting HR program evaluation and reaching the ultimate goal of enhancing the performance of the HR program.

Phase 1: Identify Stakeholders, Evaluators, and Evaluation Questions

Phase 1 deals with the three basic identification steps that will have implications throughout the HR program evaluation. The identification of stakeholders is a critical first step toward ensuring that the evaluation is appropriately targeted and that the results will be utilized. Upper management, the HR department, and other internal groups readily come to mind as important stakeholders; but the perspectives of external stakeholders such as stockholders and customers might also need to be considered. Other decisions involve the identification of the evaluators. Using an evaluation team, rather than a single individual, helps to both speed the evaluation and increase the likelihood that the right skills are present to generate valid findings and recommendations. Finally, we cover the identification of well-focused, answerable questions and how essential this step is to valid findings and recommendations.

Phase 2: Plan the Evaluation

Phase 2 focuses on budgeting and anticipating the steps and timeline that will be required to accomplish the later tasks of data collection and analysis, feedback of results and recommendations, and transitioning to the implementation of program changes. With organizations asking their employees to do more with less, development of a reasonable budget may be a key to working effectively with top management stakeholders. Among other things, the evaluation team's budget should consider staffing, travel, special equipment, and space requirements. The depth of the plans for accomplishing tasks can vary markedly, depending on factors such as how large the organization and HR program evaluation are, the methods that will be used in the data collection and analyses, and the team members' familiarity with the evaluation process.

Phase 3: Collect Data

Data collection will likely require more time than any of the other phases. Our review of more than twenty-five methods and sources provides readers with a checklist of where and how to collect potentially important data. The methods and sources must be considered with due regard for selecting an evaluation design that addresses practical constraints that are faced when conducting a program evaluation in an organizational setting. Another area that is discussed pertains to enhancing data quality through procedures such as pretesting data collection instruments, training data collectors, and verifying information. Finally, cautionary notes are added to remind evaluation teams to avoid excessive data collection and monitor data collection schedules closely.

Phase 4: Analyze and Interpret Data

Because databases serve as the basis for organizing and analyzing the stacks of data gathered in the HR program evaluation, creation and modification of a database is the first topic covered in the chapter on analyzing and interpreting data. We discuss three types of tasks: designing data codes, designing the database, and deciding how to handle missing data. Another set of concerns that should be addressed before data analysis starts is then presented. Those concerns include the potential for error that accompanies conclusions about what is and is not statistically significant, as well as distinguishing between practical and statistical significance. Other parts of the chapter provide overviews of the types of quantitative and qualitative analyses that evaluation teams commonly use.

Phase 5: Communicate Findings and Insights

The overall success of an HR program evaluation may well hinge on how effectively the communication plan is designed and executed. Phase 5 focuses on strategies for ensuring that evaluation results are meaningfully communicated. With all of the information produced by an evaluation, the evaluation team needs to be able to differentiate between what is essential to communicate from what is simply interesting and then identify the most effective medium for disseminating information to each type of stakeholder group. While each stakeholder group may have a preferred means for receiving communication regarding the evaluation's progress and its findings, the bottom line is that the information must be conveyed in a way that engenders ownership of the results and motivation to act on the findings.

Phase 6: Utilize the Results

Putting evaluation findings and recommendations to use is an important but challenging hurdle for organizations. A basic premise of Phase 6 is that an HR program evaluation should produce useable findings and recommendations. Useable findings and recommendations tacitly imply that information from the evaluation team can lead to meaningful action that directly addresses the stakeholders' interests and concerns and the evaluation findings. This outcome may be accomplished with either a full-scale replacement of, or targeted adjustments to, an HR program. The evaluation team must be aware of and be prepared to address the organizational obstacles that can undermine the full use of the HR program evaluation findings and recommendations. These steps can be facilitated by the application of multidisciplinary approaches to organizational change, full engagement of key stakeholders throughout the process, and effective removal of organizational barriers to change.

Deviate from Our Approach
When It Makes Sense for Your Evaluation

Our six-phase approach is designed to provide a set of general guidelines for the activities that are performed in most HR program evaluations, but deviations from our approach are to be expected. Actual program evaluations may over- or under-emphasize some of the steps within our phases or accomplish a step in an earlier or later phase than that specified in our approach. Deviations from our approach may be related to the characteristics of the organization, the HR program being evaluated, the evaluation team or single evaluator, time limits imposed on the evaluation team, or available resources.

Each organization has a unique culture that influences how most things are accomplished, and HR program evaluation is no exception. For example, very large organizations that emphasize continuous improvement may have designated units devoted to internal audits and program evaluation. In those cases, the units may accomplish the same steps in a slightly different manner than will evaluators in other organizations. Other organizations may use outside consultants whenever they perform their evaluations because their culture values external perspectives. In addition to organizational culture and size, other organizational factors that could result in some deviation from our approach include concerns such as the geographic dispersion of the company (including international locations), type of industry, and whether or not some organizational members are unionized.

Evaluating large or traditional HR programs (for example, selection or performance appraisal) may result in using a slightly different approach than when evaluating a smaller or non-traditional HR program (for example, child care or flexi-time). Likewise, the types of clients for whom the program is targeted may require flexibility within the phases of our approach. Perhaps an evaluation that looked at executive succession planning would rely on different assessment strategies, timelines, criterion development, and so forth than would an evaluation for an HR program (such as salary and benefits) that affected the entire organization.

Characteristics of the evaluation team will also have an impact on how our approach is applied. As with any activity, individuals have preferred ways of doing things. Evaluators are no different, and their preferred procedures could be based on their knowledge of the content area of the HR program being evaluated, training and experience with HR program evaluation and methodological techniques, and the size of the evaluation team.

Finally, time and other resources are always an issue in HR program evaluation. If the team has little time, staff, funding, or other resources to conduct its evaluation, many of the steps might need to be abbreviated. Even if the organization is willing to devote sufficient time, money, and other resources to the program evaluation, the program evaluator needs to decide carefully what are required versus what are important but secondary issues. Requiring resources that may be of questionable need could (a) deter top management stakeholders from conducting program evaluations or (b) lead the same stakeholder to incorrectly believe that future program evaluation proposals need to be cut because they could be similarly done with less than what the program evaluation team proposes.

Suggested Resources

Berk, R.A., & Rossi, P.H. (1990). *Thinking about program evaluation*. Thousand Oaks, CA: Sage.

Fitz-enz, J., & Davison, B. (2002). *How to measure human resources management* (3rd ed.). New York: McGraw-Hill.

Prosavac, E.J., & Carey, R.G. (2003). *Program evaluation: Methods and case studies* (6th ed.). Englewood Cliffs, NJ: Prentice Hall.

Rossi, P.H., & Freeman, H.E. (1993). *Evaluation: A systematic approach* (5th ed.). Thousand Oaks, CA: Sage.

Royse, D., Thyer, B.A., Padgett, D.K., & Logan, T.K. (2001). *Program evaluation: An introduction*. Belmont, CA: Brooks/Cole.

Worthen, B.R., Sanders, J.R., & Fitzpatrick, J.L. (1997). *Program evaluation: Alternative approaches and practical guidelines* (2nd ed.). New York: Addison Wesley/Longman.

Phase 1

IDENTIFY STAKEHOLDERS, EVALUATORS, AND EVALUATION QUESTIONS

"Chance favors prepared minds."
—*Louis Pasteur*

Chapter Objectives

- Remind the evaluation team of the many types of stakeholders whose views might need to be considered during the assessment
- Review important considerations that must be addressed when assembling an evaluation team
- Offer evaluators general methods that can be used to generate effective program evaluation questions

The recommendations that derive from an HR program evaluation will be driven by the nature of the questions that are posed and the stakeholders involved. For example, in evaluating a succession planning process, the chief executive officer may have expressed concerns about the organization's current mix of leaders and how the upcoming retirements of key players could limit achievement of strategic business objectives and depress shareholder value. He wants immediate answers as to how the organization's succession program can be positioned to populate the talent pool for all fifteen critical leadership positions within nine months of implementation. The outcome of this evaluation will likely focus on what enhancements need to be made and resources need to be allocated to the current succession program to achieve this high exposure and aggressive goal. On the other hand, a directive from your manager to evaluate all of your training programs and make recommendations for cutbacks will result in a different series of questions related to the overall worth of each program and their differential impact on the organization's bottom line. The outcome of this type of evaluation would focus on which of the training programs should be dropped based on its relative contribution.

In many cases, stakeholder groups, evaluators, and evaluation questions will be evident from the content area of the program and the events that led to the program evaluation. Any number of events could have precipitated the start of an HR program evaluation. These events can vary from a periodically scheduled review of a program that seems to be running smoothly (a review of the compensation system every five years) to the need for a program to be certified (safety in a nuclear power plant) to a major revamping of a program caused by a catastrophic (a death in the workplace) or a high-visibility (publicized race-based incident in one restaurant for a chain) event.

Regardless of the reason for the evaluation, three key types of identification activities must occur, before even planning to carry out the evaluation. Specifically, the first phase of our HR program evaluation focuses on the identification of stakeholders, the evaluation team or evaluator, and the questions that need to be answered. This chapter examines factors that can help HR professionals systematically determine each of the three.

Identify Stakeholder Groups

A stakeholder in an HR program evaluation is any person potentially affected by the HR program being assessed or the subsequent decisions (for example, to leave a benefits program unchanged) that result from the assessment. Stakeholders can provide important perspectives about the various aspects of an HR program. With in-depth knowledge about some parts of the program or the total program, stakeholders are well-suited to help evaluators focus on the most critical issues to be addressed in the assessment. In addition, they may be able to identify some of the criteria for judging how efficiently and effectively the HR program is operating.

The evaluation team should involve as many types of stakeholders as possible in initial discussions. Expanded involvement enhances buy-in to the evaluation processes, takes into account the many different perspectives among stakeholder groups, and lessens potential resistance to change. It is also sometimes wise to include a representative group of stakeholders as an advisory panel for the evaluation, or even as part of the evaluation team of content and program evaluation specialists. Rossi and Freeman (1993) maintained that evaluators must understand both their relationships with the stakeholders and the relationships among stakeholders in order to conduct their evaluation effectively.

A convenient way to identify stakeholders for a specific evaluation is to think of three general categories of such individuals: internal, unionized, and external stakeholders. Figure 1.1 shows some of the more common types of groups that we have encountered in each category. Those groups will be discussed in the remainder of this section.

Decide on Internal Stakeholders First

Because HR programs generally affect everyone in the organization, nearly all the organizational members will have vested interests in any changes that result from a program evaluation. Some internal stakeholders might resist such change. For example, an evaluation examining possible workplace redesign could result in an organizational unit being moved to another area of the headquarters and that unit's middle managers having smaller offices, less privacy, and less opportunity to interact with upper management. To minimize the apprehension resulting from possible change, selection of the advisory stakeholders (spokespersons for each stakeholder group) should be made apparent to all stakeholders and progress as quickly as possible. People often deal better with change when they are involved in the process, and the selection of recognized leaders from the key

Figure 1.1
Common Stakeholders in HR Program Evaluations

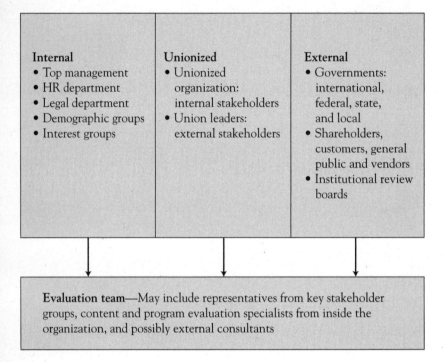

Stakeholder—Any person potentially affected by the HR program being assessed or the subsequent decisions that result from the assessment

Internal	Unionized	External
• Top management • HR department • Legal department • Demographic groups • Interest groups	• Unionized organization: internal stakeholders • Union leaders: external stakeholders	• Governments: international, federal, state, and local • Shareholders, customers, general public and vendors • Institutional review boards

Evaluation team—May include representatives from key stakeholder groups, content and program evaluation specialists from inside the organization, and possibly external consultants

stakeholder groups offers an opportunity for those groups to have input into the evaluation.

Membership in one internal stakeholder group typically over-laps with membership in other internal stakeholder groups. The net result of the overlapping membership with regard to organizational change is that members may lose in one way and gain in another way. Using the redesign example again, members who drive to work now have the post-redesign benefit of having parking spaces next to the entrance to their office rather than much farther way. But the net result of the change varied according to other types of group membership. At one extreme, lower-level employees' office spaces remained much like before, and those employees got better parking. At the other extreme, up-and-comer middle managers who took mass transit lost informal face time with upper management and will have to walk farther to get to their office from the mass transit stop.

The prior paragraphs hinted at the composition of some internal stakeholder groups. Let's look at five types of internal stakeholder groups that will be important in all or almost all HR program evaluations in larger organizations. These internal stakeholder groups are (1) top management, (2) staff in the HR department and (3) the legal department or outside counsel, (4) different demographic groups, and (5) special interest groups. Figure 1.1 schematically shows these and other types of stakeholder groups. Smaller organizations may not include all of these stakeholder groups, such as legal or union representatives.

Recognize the Value of Top Management Stakeholders. Organizational leaders constitute one of the most valuable and readably recognizable stakeholder groups for an HR program evaluation. In some critical program evaluations, top management stakeholders (the vice-president level) could be on the evaluation team. Their inclusion would depend on factors such as the visibility of the HR program being evaluated, cost and scope of the program evaluation, and the impact of the program on other units in the organization.

While inclusion of a top management stakeholder on the evaluation team has advantages, it can also bring concerns such as perceptions that this stakeholder will unduly influence the evaluation's findings and recommendations. The inclusion of a top management stakeholder on an advisory panel is a strategy that allows for upper-level input. At the same time, it could lead to the negative consequence of perceptions that the evaluation team is merely going to recommend changes that top management wanted, regardless of what an unbiased evaluation would have shown.

Top management stakeholders may provide the actual evaluation questions that they want answered or indicate the general issues that are to be addressed. The interactions with top management may include both individual and group meetings. The individual meetings allow each upper-level management member to provide his or her unique insights. In addition, one or more group meetings between these managers and the evaluation team leader might be needed to iron out differences that the various stakeholders have about issues such as milestones, budgets, and researchable questions.

Gain Expertise from the Program Staff in the HR Department. Another easily recognizable group of stakeholders is the HR department, with the staff who deal with the strengths and weaknesses of their programs each day. The HR department staff will be interested because they will be directly affected by any changes that result from the program evaluation. Thus, conflicts of interest can occur for program staff. Moreover, serious negative findings from the evaluation could result in adverse consequences—including replacing an HR program, undesired personnel transfers, and poor performance evaluations—for members who are in charge of or work in the HR program that receives low marks at the end of the evaluation. Although rare and extreme, a program evaluation might result in termination of HR staff if incompetence or malfeasance is found. Conversely, HR staff may wholeheartedly embrace the evaluation as a way to upgrade an out-of-date or ineffective HR program that they have heretofore been unable to change, despite their desire to improve it.

Because at least one member of this stakeholder group will typically be on the evaluation team as either a member or as a liaison, the HR department will probably receive periodic feedback about what is being done and found during the evaluation. Information exchange between the evaluation team and the HR department stakeholders is essential during all stages of the program evaluation because implementation of any changes to an HR program will almost surely require participation by members of the HR department. Besides, if HR program staff learn about the findings and recommendations at the last minute, momentum for implementing changes may be slowed.

Involve the Legal Department to Address Prohibited Practices Proactively. This stakeholder group will have insights into potential contractual and legal limitations that the evaluation team and the whole organization will face during and after the program evaluation. More often than not, the legal department (which could be outside counsel for smaller organizations) will want to be aware of the evaluation's scope, subsequent findings, and the potential impact of recommended changes on employees and the organization as a whole. This last statement is particularly true for HR areas (for example, selection and compensation programs) prone to employee challenges and litigation. Therefore, one of the organization's attorneys should be assigned to the HR program evaluation team as either a full member or liaison. Smaller organizations without internal legal representation may want to engage an outside employment attorney for this purpose.

The legal department should have detailed knowledge regarding the types of changes that might be limited by labor agreements (for example, alteration of the conditions of work) or contracts with vendors (for example, that prevent the customization of HR-related software). Additionally, the attorney should be able to advise top management and the evaluation team on applicable international, national, state, and local regulations that govern an organization's HR practices. More will be said about labor, vendor, and regulatory concerns in later sections on unions and external stakeholders.

Ask Whether Program Participants from Some Demographic Groups Will Be Affected More Than Others. While most program evaluators would consider it a given to include evaluation inputs from participants who belong to various demographic groups, this might not be done in some (for example, paternalistic) organizations. For example, Posavac and Carey (2003) noted that participant input may not occur in situations in which reliance is placed on program staff's opinions to determine what is needed because there is a belief that the participants do not know fully what they need.

The organization's membership is made up of stakeholders from various demographic groups that might perceive either the need to keep the program as it is or to change it. A prime example of this point relates to equal employment opportunity. Some stakeholder groups may feel that any gains made by another demographic group will negatively affect the group to which they belong.

Retirees are a quasi-internal demographic group. While they are not at work in the organization each day, they may be entitled to participate in some of the organization's HR benefit programs. These programs might include subsidized health insurance, retirement income plans, and special company-specific benefits (such as discounted fares for former airline employees and purchase discounts for former store employees). As has been seen in recent high-profile curtailments of retirees' benefits, legal, public-relations, and ethical concerns can be voiced when organizations change longstanding HR programs that affect retirees' quality of life.

Individuals selected to represent demographic groups (for example, as a member of the evaluation team or in individual or focus-group interviews) have much pressure on them. Many of these stakeholders may feel uncomfortable speaking for all organization members who share their demographic characteristic(s). Moreover, others may feel that they are treated as tokens. Therefore, the procedures for selecting demographic group representatives as well as the evaluative role of the representatives should be transparent and objective.

Therefore, the evaluation team should think broadly when identifying demographic subgroups that could be affected by findings and recommendations from its HR program evaluation.

Ask Whether Members of Some Interest Groups Need to Have Their Perspectives Highlighted. Similarly, transparency and objectivity should be present in the identification and roles of representatives for interest groups (for example, parents with day care needs, employees who use mass transit, or people who participate in the company's stock plan). These stakeholders' interests may be tied directly to an HR program being evaluated.

While the stakeholders in some interest groups might willingly identify themselves, others may not. Individuals with drug problems would be an example of those who may fit into the latter category. There is little probability that drug abusers will identify themselves for interviews during a program evaluation to determine whether or not a confidential drug treatment benefit needs to be added to the employee assistance program. As a result, the organization may have little internal information upon which to base the potential need for or benefits derived from changes to some programs. In such cases, where the data central to the evaluation's objectives may be questionable, it is important to identify methodological limitations early in the evaluation process and then determine whether or not an evaluation with sufficient rigor and probability of providing meaningful findings can be performed.

Consider the Perspectives of Unions and Their Members

Unions and their members fall into a gap between internal and external stakeholder groups. Rank-and-file union members are internal stakeholders, but upper-level leaders of the union(s) probably are not. The situation is complicated further because stakeholders from an affected union may receive support from internal stakeholders in other unions that will not be affected by the program evaluation or its findings. An example of such an action is illustrated when pilots, flight attendants, or mechanics unions support each other in negotiations on wage and benefits reductions.

The often adversarial relationship of an organization's management and union officials and their members can cause a program evaluation to be longer and more sensitive than it might be in an organization without a union. Obtaining unionized members' perceptions may require pre-approval of surveys and attendance by a union representa-tive when the members are interviewed. For example, Berk and Rossi (1990) suggested that an evaluation of an educational program would be seriously impeded if the teachers' organization recom-mended that its members not cooperate with the evaluator. Also, recommendations at the end of the evaluation might seek to change conditions of work (for example, safety or compensation) governed by a labor agreement. In such cases, implementation could be de-layed or prevented, especially when bargaining units have not been kept informed throughout the HR program evaluation.

Don't Forget That There Are External Stakeholder Groups

Although the external groups discussed in this section are not in-volved in the day-to-day HR operations of an organization or the pro-gram evaluation, they can exert significant influence on internal HR decisions. Therefore, the evaluation team should cast its net widely to identify external stakeholders who might be affected by the way that an HR program is administered or the decisions that result from an evaluation of such a program. The list of potential external stake-holders includes governmental agencies, stockholders, customers, the general public, vendors, and institutional review boards.

Assess Governments' Positions. An evaluation team would rarely seek direct input from governmental agencies, but the Joint Committee on Standards for Educational Evaluation (1994) cor-rectly noted that laws and regulations are one basis for interpreting program evaluation findings. Consequently, an assessment of com-pliance to applicable rules and regulations needs to be integrated into HR program evaluations. Among other things, governments often influence HR programs by establishing minimum HR program standards that organizations must meet. These minimum standards could be established through laws, executive orders, court cases, and other materials. Depending on how dispersed their operations are, organizations may need to comply with legal standards enforced by international, national, state, and local governmental agencies.

- *International regulations*. With more and more organizations having offices in multiple countries, organizations must be cognizant of international HR regulations. For example, the European Privacy Directive could greatly impact program evaluations for multinational companies because this directive provides common rules for collecting, maintaining, and transmitting personal data about employees, even when the data are transferred to non-European Union countries. The U.S. Department of Commerce's Safe Harbor Provisions aid in the uninterrupted flow of such data for U.S. companies that agree to abide by certain constraints regarding the collection and dissemination of data.

- *National regulations*. Organizations that operate only within the United States still must comply with HR-related regulations from myriad federal agencies. Let's examine three of the many types of compliance concerns that an organization might face during an HR program evaluation. A federal agency like the Equal Employment Opportunity Commission may take legal action to correct a workplace situation that is thought to violate civil rights standards. Another federal agency monitors workplace health and safety, with serious violations potentially resulting in the immediate closure of a work site. Other agencies such as the Bureau of Labor Statistics might require the periodic submission of data on the organization's labor force as part of its efforts to generate national labor statistics.

- *State and local regulations*. State and local governments sometimes issue minimum standards that are more restrictive than those issued by international and federal governments. For example, some U.S. municipalities have established minimum wage laws that provide for a higher minimum wage than that required by federal regulations. Such wage considerations would be of concern during the evaluation of a compensation system.

Consider the Needs and Views of Stockholders, Customers, the General Public, and Vendors. Wood (2005) provided a succinct but thorough list of other types of organizational stakeholders. Among the others that she noted are financial analysts and markets, financial institutions, customers, local communities, environmental and consumer protection groups, and suppliers who provide the input materials for the organization. We have addressed these stakeholders as four groups: stockholders, customers, the general public, and vendors.

Stockholders' expectations of dividends and capital growth indirectly limit the scope of some HR programs in private-sector organizations. In particular, changes in market share, downturns in stock price, and other economic influences may result in expectations that the organization must tighten its belt. That belt tightening might include a rollback of company benefits or the elimination of jobs. Many times, the belt tightening is done without the benefit of a formal program evaluation; rather, it is done when upper management *thinks* that the most money can be saved with the least negative impact.

If the organization receives bad publicity because of events such as actual or perceived racial discrimination against employees or customers or violations of environmental regulations, demographic groups of customers could decide to refrain from buying the organization's goods or services. Similarly, the general public is an external shareholder in a more general sense. For example, various publications provide lists of the best employers. Being named a best organization can make it easier for an organization to recruit and retain top talent. Many of the characteristics used to identify top organizations pertain to HR practices. Program evaluation can make the HR programs more attractive by making them work more efficiently and effectively.

Vendors are important external stakeholders because organizations may have contracts to purchase a vendor's HR-related goods and services across multiple years. Also, the vendors may have contracts that prevent the modification and duplication of HR-related software for such things as an HR information system or an automated 360-degree feedback program. In those cases, HR program evaluations may be constrained with regard to recommendations for immediate improvement and therefore might need to design both shorter- and longer-term strategies for improving a program.

Engage Institutional Review Boards When They Are Present in the Organization. In some organizations, internal review boards blur the lines between HR research and practice. While these boards have typically monitored an organization's research using human participants, some governmental agencies have questioned whether all HR-related surveys need board approval. This could be a growing trend for HR programs in academic and healthcare institutions that are required to maintain institutional review boards to protect the rights of human participants in research projects.

Identify the Evaluation Team

When feasible, we believe that HR program evaluations should be performed by teams rather than by a single evaluator. A single evaluator may have limited the choice of evaluation methods to those with which the individual feels most comfortable, rather than to the most appropriate methods for the given situation and program being evaluated. Another problem encountered when using a single evaluator could involve the interpretation of findings. Often, more than one explanation can be given for a finding, but the ability to see patterns and alternative interpretations is probably more limited when a single person performs the whole program evaluation. Because of these and other problems that result when a single evaluator performs an assessment, the remainder of this book assumes that a team will be used for all HR program evaluations. Of course, the size of the organization or program being evaluated may dictate that a single evaluator conduct the evaluation. Successful evaluations can certainly be conducted with a single evaluator. We are simply recommending that, when it is possible, a team-based evaluation brings with it a number of advantages, particularly in large-scale, high-profile evaluations. For example, the evaluation of a compensation system within a large organization that is experiencing gender bias claims would minimally require that the evaluator possess content expertise in compensation, performance assessment, and statistics; have the time and resources to conduct the necessary policy reviews, data collection, and analyses; and have well-developed oral and written communication skills to present the findings, conclusions, and recommendations to key groups and individuals, such as top management in the organization and attorneys inside and outside of the organizations. The required skill sets and diversity of tasks involved with this sort of evaluation are more simply accomplished by a team. We recognize, however, that not every organization will have the luxury of using an evaluation team.

When determining the evaluation team, consideration needs to be given to the team's size, composition, leadership, and charter.

Ask, "How Big Should the Team Be?"

The answer to this question is a very ambiguous "as big as it needs to be." The authors have worked on teams that had as few as one primary member (one of the authors) who examined a very limited HR issue to teams that have had as many as ten members. A team that is too large may have trouble coordinating its activities, even with something as straightforward as identifying times when everyone can meet. Also, if the evaluation team is using consensus as its means for decision making, large teams could use more time than smaller teams. Conversely, a team that is too small may have trouble completing the evaluation in a reasonable period of time. Having a very small evaluation team decreases the likelihood that some tasks can be done simultaneously. For example, the person who is conducting the interviews may be the only evaluation team member who has experience designing surveys. In such a case, tasks must be done serially, rather than simultaneously.

Some of the factors that are particularly important for determining the size of the evaluation team are the size of the organization and program, how long it has been since the program was last evaluated, and how soon the evaluation has to be completed. The size of the team may increase and decrease at different times during the program evaluation if temporary members are used to perform certain activities. While it is important to obtain inputs from a wide variety of stakeholders, those inputs can be obtained during interviews and other data collection efforts. More specifically, the formal evaluation team does not need to include members of all stakeholder groups as part of the day-to-day working group.

Ask, "Who Should Be on the Team?"

Decisions have to be made about where the organization will obtain its evaluation team members. At minimum, most teams will probably include evaluators with skills in the program content area, general program evaluation procedures, and statistical analysis. The need for additional specific skills such as interviewing and survey design will become apparent as the evaluation team starts identifying the data collection and analysis methods that it intends to use. Love (1991) offered six tips for building effective internal evaluation teams. Those tips were to:

- Keep the team small,
- Emphasize the need for high performance,
- Reward team members and the leader,
- Focus on people instead of methodology,
- Inventory team members' skills, and
- Use project management tools to benchmark success.

The need to balance team size considerations against the needs for diverse skill sets suggests that the net should be cast widely to obtain the best combination of evaluators for the team. Fink and Kosecoff

(1978) suggested that, for small evaluations (and therefore, probably small evaluation teams), evaluators should possess a wide variety of skills. For larger evaluations (where more evaluators will probably be involved), they recommended that the team include members with specialized skills in statistics and report writing. The team should also represent all key stakeholder groups. Some of the representation may be obtained by including someone from one stakeholder group on the evaluation team. Other stakeholder groups may be represented indirectly by periodically seeking input from and providing feedback to an advisory panel of representatives from the other stakeholder groups.

According to Berk and Rossi (1990), another important characteristic of evaluation team members is that they should not be people "who prefer to avoid controversy, or who have difficulty facing criticism" (p. 14). They also noted that criticism is often political and that methodological flaws in the evaluation are one way in which the attacks are made. We believe that the best way to ameliorate these often real concerns is (a) through the selection of a team leader—and to a lesser extent, team members—who is well-respected and perceived to be objective throughout the organization (for example, government blue-ribbon panels to study politically sensitive problems) and/or (b) with the addition of external consultants who have expertise in program evaluation in the content area in order to minimize methodological weaknesses. Regardless, the evaluation will go more smoothly if all of the evaluation team members have good interpersonal skills that allow them to be collaborative as well as firm if/when the need arises.

Select Team Members from Three Categories of Evaluators. In general, members of the evaluation team fit into three categories: HR staff, other organizational members (that is, those not from the HR department), and external consultants. Each type of evaluator brings potential strengths and weaknesses to the evaluation process. As might be expected, one category of evaluators might bring strength to the evaluation for one issue, but use of the same type of evaluator for a different evaluation activity could result in a potentially flawed finding.

Members of the HR department constitute one category of potential evaluators. Since they work every day with the various HR programs and HR program administrators, they may have program-related insights that are not available elsewhere. At the same time, their closeness to the program may prevent them from recognizing opportunities for improvement.

Non-HR organization members are another category of potential evaluators. The evaluation team leader might choose other internal staff for a variety of reasons:

- The views of one or more of the five types of previously identified internal stakeholders should be represented.
- A unit (for example, manufacturing) is particularly affected by the quality of the program (for example, safety). Therefore, the evaluation requires a team member with specific content knowledge.
- An individual possesses a desired skill set (for example, an accountant's skill with budgets or a quality control manager's experience with sampling).

External consultants are a third category of potential evaluators. Organizations can contract with external consultants to (a) perform the entire evaluation by themselves, (b) work as part of the evaluation team during the entire process, or (c) complete specified evaluation tasks. If the organization sees implementation of recommendations as a continuation of the program evaluation, an organization may choose to exclude the external evaluators from participating in Phase 6 of our approach. While such a step might result in less biased input from the external evaluators, it could also deprive the organization from using consultants who know much about the organization and the HR program.

Consider the Relative Strengths and Weaknesses of the Three Categories of Evaluators. Worthen and his colleagues (1997, p. 44) noted that "No professional association or government agency has yet assumed or accepted broad responsibility for licensing or certifying the competence of evaluation practitioners. . . . In the absence of certification and licensure, uninformed amateurs and unprincipled hucksters can do much mischief and greatly tarnish the image of program evaluation in the process." While this conclusion should serve as a caution, most organizations should find a wealth of qualified professionals, possibly internally or externally, who can contribute to their HR program evaluations.

Table 1.1 shows eight issues that are important to an evaluation and our general assessment of the relative strengths and weaknesses that each category of evaluator might bring to a program evaluation. Our generalized conclusions in Table 1.1 are designed as guidelines for an organization embarking on an HR program evaluation. The situations considered in our generalized conclusions may, however, differ from the actual situation in an organization because of the particular characteristics of the organization's staff or the consultants. For example, if the HR staff includes a recognized expert for the type of program being evaluated, some of our general statements may prove incorrect. Likewise, our conclusions about external consultants may be incorrect for such issues as frankness if the external consultants sold the HR program being evaluated to the organization and continue to be paid for maintaining the program.

One thing is readily noticeable from the shading in each column of Table 1.1. Each category of evaluators brings certain strengths and weaknesses to the program evaluation.

To aid readers, we have shaded the relative strengths and weaknesses so that the darker shading indicates there is often a major concern, lighter shading denotes a caution, and no shading suggests that the category of evaluator is usually well-suited to handle the issue. For example, relative to the other categories of evaluators, HR department personnel have the advantage in knowing the HR program and the organization, but the evaluation team might want to exercise caution before using HR staff in evaluation tasks for which personal frankness about aspects of the HR program is a primary concern.

The team leader should consider our generalizations for the eight issues, along with potential team members' actual strengths and weaknesses, when choosing team members and the tasks that each member will perform. Such planning can go a long way toward ensuring the validity of evaluation findings by maximizing team members' strengths and minimizing their weaknesses. Introspection of the team's strengths and weaknesses during this initial phase can avoid problems that it will be too late to address in the final phases of the HR program evaluation.

Ask, "Who Should Lead the Evaluation Team?"

The team leader is often an internal person or an external consultant who has the best combination of position power and technical skills, with position power typically carrying more weight—rightly or wrongly—than technical skills. The leader must be someone who has immediate access to top management and other key stakeholders. Having the ability to get onto people's calendars with little prior notice is particularly important when (a) providing periodic updates about the progress of the evaluation, (b) obtaining more time or resources if something unplanned occurs, or (c) negotiating entry into organizational units where managers may not want to provide their subordinates for program evaluation tasks such as surveys or interviews.

The team leader will be particularly important for the planning that occurs during the second phase of the program evaluation and for keeping the team within its timeline and budget. As with other members of the team, the leader may be devoted full- or part-time to the program evaluation.

Ask, "Should the Evaluation Team Write a Charter?"

It is a good idea for the evaluation team to create a team charter that specifies the evaluation team's mission, membership, and general evaluation plan, including milestones and resource needs. In essence, it is

Table 1.1 Assessing Various Types of Program Evaluators Against Numerous Criteria

Criteria Against Which Evaluators Are Judged	HR Staff	Types of Program Evaluators	
		Other Internal Staff	External Consultants
Knowledge of the organization and the organization's HR program	Have in-depth knowledge of both the organization and the HR program being evaluated	Have in-depth knowledge of the organization but may have limited knowledge of HR program specifics	Will lack this initially if it is the first time that they have worked with the organization
Knowledge of industry best practices for specific HR program and program evaluation	May be aware of best practices; but awareness depends on networking, keeping up knowledge of the literature, and other such factors	Are unlikely to know about best practices for an area outside their own areas of expertise	Are probably exposed to the various practices of multiple clients and general practices for program being evaluated
Credibility with decision makers/stakeholders	May have their knowledge, skills, and abilities underestimated by their organizational peers	May partially compensate for their lack of HR expertise by being (a) a high-level stakeholder or (b) a representative of a stakeholder group	Have high credibility at time of entry because the organization formally picked them—supposedly for their expertise with the HR program
Potential constraints to a frank evaluation	May not be totally objective because the program belongs to the HR department, and a negative assessment may reflect badly on the department (or even get them fired)	Have less-direct reasons for biasing the evaluation findings than do the other two types of evaluators	May not be totally objective because they (a) are also focused on building client relationships or (b) helped design the HR program being evaluated

Time and dollar cost of the evaluation	May work on pieces of the evaluation as part of their normal HR program duties, and program familiarity may result in more rapid completion of those pieces	Take time away from their normal jobs to do the evaluation, and doing work outside one's area of expertise probably results in poorer return relative to cost	May be (a) more because consulting rates are high compared to internal salaries or (b) less because expertise decreases the time needed for an evaluation
Design of a practical implementation plan for program changes	Can identify practical concerns better than others, but may attempt to limit the changes because of (a) internal HR turf concerns and (b) a desire to keep expectations low to reach objectives	Probably have limited HR-specific knowledge and thereby have limited ability to design the plan to fit with other HR programs	May wish to add features that result in (a) "Cadillac" version of program or (b) steps that do not fit the organization's culture
Program evaluation and HR-program knowledge left in the organization after the evaluation	Keep some evaluation expertise in-house because a member of the HR staff will have been a member of or a liaison to the evaluation team	Will lose their HR knowledge as a result of disuse, and transfer of new evaluation skills will probably be limited because transfer is to new content domain	Take their knowledge with them when they exit the organization unless additional consulting occurs
Fresh perspective	Could be overly conscious of former constraints that no longer exist	Might consider internal constraints but could stimulate out-of-the box thinking	Are not bound by perceived organizational constraints

Adapted from J.C. Scott, J.E. Edwards, & N.S. Raju's April 2002 workshop, *Program evaluation for human resources: The art and science of measuring success*, and later published and copyrighted (in 2003 by Sage Publications) in D.S. Rose & E.J. Davidson's chapter, Framework for human resources program evaluation, in J.E. Edwards, J.C. Scott, & N.S. Raju's book, *The human resources program-evaluation handbook*.

a contract between the team and top management about how the HR program evaluation will be conducted. Love (1991) provided extensive lists of contract responsibilities and terms of reference that evaluation teams could use. These lists are useful as reminders of potential issues that might need to be included in either a legally binding contract with external consultants or a psychologically binding contract between an internal evaluation team and management.

Steinhaus and Witt (2003) noted that a charter signed by top management lends tremendous influence to the team's efforts in securing the necessary organizational resources. While a key purpose of the charter is to ensure buy-in from top management, a secondary goal of the charter development is to force team members to think through key questions and issues in advance of taking action.

Identify Evaluation Questions

How the evaluation questions are posed has implications for the kinds of data to be collected, the source of the data, data analyses, and the conclusions that can be drawn. Therefore, the evaluation team must arrive at evaluation questions that are doable within the constraints that the team will face. Still, the constraints should not typically be the primary concern at this early stage in the HR program evaluation process. If a sufficient business case can be made for a more in-depth evaluation, top management may choose to devote more resources to the effort and lengthen the timeline.

Berk and Rossi (1990) noted that program evaluation questions can be addressed at varying levels. "When great precision is needed and ample resources are available, the most powerful evaluation procedures can be employed. When the occasion demands approximate answers or when resources are in short supply, 'rough and ready' (and, usually, speedier) procedures can be used. Correspondingly, the answers supplied vary in quality: The findings of some evaluations are more credible than others, but all genuine evaluations produce findings that are better than speculation" (p. 34).

The team needs to be aware of the three general types of evaluation questions as they begin developing the questions. The ability to distinguish among the types is a key to generating and refining questions to meet the information needs of key stakeholders. Also, the team must identify the measures of success—that is, criteria. We discuss desirable characteristics of criteria in the last part of this section, but it is impossible for us to identify in this book the criteria for each specific type of HR program. Our *Human Resources Program-Evaluation Handbook* (Edwards, Scott, & Raju, 2003) contains actual criteria that subject-matter experts identified for evaluating over twenty types of HR programs, including personnel selection, appraisal, and training.

Determine the Types of Evaluation Questions That Match the Evaluation Objectives

Different types of questions lead to different types of answers. And most large-scale HR program evaluations are likely to include more than one of the three types of questions: descriptive, normative, and impact.

Use Descriptive Questions If Simple Information Is Needed. This type of question results in information about the HR program's specific conditions, processes, or contexts. An example of a descriptive question is: "What procedures are used to report the different categories of work accidents?"

Descriptive questions are important in providing key stakeholders with basic knowledge or a context for interpreting more complex information about another part of the HR program. At first blush, it would appear that organizations have already answered such questions with documents such as previously prepared reports and policy or procedural manuals. However, the information in the reports and manuals may be out-of-date or otherwise inaccurate. In evaluating a diversity program, descriptive questions might include the following:

- What topics are covered in the diversity awareness training program, and how is the information conveyed to training participants?

- What percent of the employees have participated in the training program, and does it vary according to organizational level?

- How does the organization track discrimination charges, audits, and lawsuits?

- Has the company collected fairness perception data (administered as diversity climate survey)?

- Last year, how many discrimination complaints were resolved at each stage in the organization's four-stage problem-resolution system?

Use Normative Questions to Compare the HR Program Against Standards. This type of question results in data that identify how the organization's evaluated HR program compares to internal or external standards. An example of a normative question that uses an internal standard is: "How have the organization's injury rates changed during the last five years?" An example of a normative question that uses an external standard is: "How do this organization's injury rates compare to industry-wide averages?"

Continuing with the diversity program evaluation, normative questions may include the following:

- How have the diversity climate ratings changed over the past three years?

- How do the diversity climate ratings compare to those in best-practice companies in your industry?

- How has spending on diversity vendors changed over the past two years?

- For each of the last three years, how many discrimination complaints were resolved at each stage in the organization's four-stage problem-resolution system?

- How have your customer demographics changed since implementation of your diversity training program? How does this change compare to your competitors?

Normative questions that use internal standards let key stakeholders determine whether conditions in the organization's HR program are improving, staying the same, or deteriorating. A major constraint in asking such questions is that the organization may not have (a) the same kind of data from prior years or (b) prescribed standards or procedures. Data from surveys often have the former type of problem. If the items have not been asked before in one of the organization's surveys or have been modified to correct previously detected deficiencies, the organization is left with only baseline data for a future trend analysis. For the latter type of problem, the HR program may never have laid out prescribed objectives or standards (for example, amount of time allowed for issuing a travel reimbursement) such as those commonly found in a program's mission statement. When either type of problem exists, the evaluation team will be unable to answer a normative question that looks at internal standards.

Normative questions that use external standards let key stakeholders determine where their organization's HR program fits relative to programs in other organizations in the same industry or across all organizations. For some HR issues, this type of information is available from the government (for example, Bureau of Labor Statistics), industry clearinghouses/consortia (for example, national associations), or other sources (for example, newspapers to see the prevailing rate of compensation for locally recruited workers). HR issues with readily available external standards include salary, benefits, injury rates, and workforce availability in a given geographic area. Normative data are not readily available for a wide range of other HR issues (for example, per capita expenditures on training). However, certain associations, such as the American Management Association, the Conference Board, and consulting firms, conduct HR benchmarking surveys to provide a context for determining whether aspects of a given type of HR program are above average, average, or below average relative to those for other organizations that the association monitors.

Caution is needed when making comparisons to external standards. Some vendors of surveys, tests, and other HR-related products provide "norms" as part of their product. For example, survey vendors frequently offer clients their national or international norms as part of the survey package. Internal company norms that are developed as part of the survey data collection may be more useful when identifying strengths and weaknesses as well as prioritizing actions; however, the appeal of external norms cannot be denied.

One major problem with external norms is that the organizations included in the normative database are not necessarily representative of an identifiable population, much less representative of the specific workforce against which it is being compared. In such instances, the only population to which an organization conducting the program evaluation can compare itself is the population of other organizations that happened to use the diagnostic instrument. As a result, conclusions about being above or below average on the diagnostic instrument could be an artifact caused by differences in the size, profitability, geographic location, industry, and other characteristics of the organizations in the "norms" and have little to do with the characteristics of an HR program as such.

Likewise, concerns may also arise as the evaluation team attempts to determine how applicable the external norms are when the team compares findings for its HR program against those present in best-practices organizations. Underlying this point is an acknowledgement that what one expert judges as a best practice may not be similarly judged by another expert. For instance, some of the HR procedures by formerly esteemed dot.com organizations in existence around the turn of the century illustrate this point. The dot.coms were recruiting disproportionate numbers of the highly valued talent from more staid organizations and the pool of new college graduates. It would be easy to conclude that the dot.coms had superior recruiting programs, when one of the real reasons for their success in recruiting was probably the high levels of compensation that seemed all-but-certain from the stock options and a variety of unusual perks. A few years later, many of these "best-practices" organizations were no longer in existence, and their state-of-the-art recruiting practices were seen in a less-positive light. In these cases, some of their initial successes may have been less about the recruiting practices and more about the technology buzz that lured this top talent.

Use Impact Questions When Cause-and-Effect Can Be Reasonably Assumed. This type of question focuses on data that reveal whether the observed conditions are attributable to the HR program. An example of an impact question is: "What effects have the organization's new safety program had on injury rates?" In the diversity program evaluation context, impact questions might appear as follows:

- What effect has the diversity awareness training program had on employees' perceptions of fairness?
- What impact has the diversity vendor program had on changing customer demographics?
- How has the leadership development program affected the diversity of applicants for executive positions?

Various degrees of uncertainty will enter into the answers to almost all impact questions used in HR program evaluations. The uncertainty is caused by the myriad factors that could be influencing results. Foremost among the factors is the fact that clear cause-and-effect conclusions require laboratory-type methods (for example, random assignment to intervention and control groups) that are seldom feasible in applied settings. For example, consider the following impact question: "What effects has the organization's new safety program had on injury rates?" A decrease in injury rates could be the result of (a) an improved safety program, (b) a newer, more restrictive definition of what constituted a reportable accident, (c) new pressure from supervisors to not report some types of accidents, (d) a less harsh winter that led to fewer falls due to icy conditions, or (e) many other factors.

When answering an impact question, an evaluation team can try to eliminate alternative possibilities for program-related changes by looking at the central issues from different perspectives. Using different methods and sources to obtain fact-based data allows evaluators to determine with greater certainty (than would a single method or source) whether the program or other factors caused the observed impact on the outcome measure. This technique—sometimes referred to as triangulation—can be illustrated for diversity program evaluation. We could use surveys and individual and group interviews (different methods) to ask a number of the same questions about serving customers to both employees and customers (different sources) throughout the organization's sales regions. Consistent findings across different methods and sources would carry more credence than would findings that surfaced from only one method or source.

Develop and Refine Evaluation Questions

While top management may dictate the program and possibly the general issues to be evaluated, the team is often responsible for translating the general issues into researchable questions that address stakeholders' information needs. A useful two-step process for generating researchable evaluation questions is to brainstorm potential questions and then to refine them.

Brainstorm. Brainstorming is an excellent way to identify a large number of initial questions for each issue. In their book on focus groups, Stewart and Shamdasani (1990) suggested that brainstorming appears to be most useful for generating ideas when there is no single best solution and that creativity in identifying ideas is facilitated by the airing of the different perspectives of the group members. Group members are encouraged to build on the ideas of others as well as generate new ideas. The questions generated in brainstorming sessions can be developed using the framework of the program's goals, processes, and desired outcomes. Including questions suggested by key stakeholders at this time avoids problems of getting near the end of the evaluation and learning that some stake-holders' concerns were not surfaced, much less addressed.

Brainstorming in the development of researchable questions can be accomplished in many ways. We have found the following process to be useful across a wide array of organizational types. The first step is to assemble a group of individuals who represent the key stakeholders' perspectives and are knowledgeable of the HR program under review. Once assembled, the facilitator—usually the team leader or a team member with strong facilitation skills—asks the group to generate an exhaustive list of questions that address the HR program's goals, objectives, roll-out procedures, communication strategies, implementation processes, and anticipated outcomes. The facilitator's goal here will be to maximize the likelihood that all stakeholders' perspectives are heard and that the group agrees that an exhaustive set of questions has been generated.

Refine Questions After Initial Issues Have Been Identified. Now that the team has identified questions that might be used to address the key stakeholders' initially identified issues, it is time to refine the list. A team could begin the refinement process by clustering all of the brainstormed questions into groups of two or more questions that address aspects of the same larger issue. This process might include listing questions on small separate sheets of paper and moving them around on a table until every question is assigned to an issue.

Grouping the questions provides several benefits. The team can eliminate redundant questions and identify evaluation gaps. Also looking ahead to the end of evaluation, it is easier to explain two or three findings within each of one to four major issues than it is to talk about eight to twelve seemingly independent findings. It is not enough to brainstorm and refine the questions; instead, grouping the questions starts the team on a path to developing their vision about how they will present the results, conclusions, and recommendations at the end of the evaluation. Envisioning the end state at each step in the six-phase HR program evaluation will maximize the odds of producing accurate and meaningful findings, conclusions, and recommendations.

Finally, each question should be categorized as descriptive, normative, or impact. This step forces the team to consider again whether it has gaps in the types of information that *should* versus *will* be gathered and analyzed.

The importance of starting with the right question is summed up by an unreferenced quote that is often attributed to the well-known statistician John Tukey: "An approximate answer to the right question is worth a good deal more than an exact answer to an approximate question."

Attend to Desirable Characteristics When Selecting Criterion Measures

A program evaluation will only be as good as the measures that are used to answer the researchable evaluation questions and judge program effectiveness. The ultimate goal for the evaluation team is to deliver the most useful and accurate information to key stakeholders in the most cost-effective and realistic manner possible. Deficient criteria could hamper the evaluation team's efforts to obtain stakeholders' buy-in that the proposed methods will provide valid findings, conclusions, and recommendations when the evaluation is complete.

Although identification of specific criteria for every type of HR program is beyond the scope of this book, many researchers have provided lists of desirable characteristics for criteria as well as recommendations for the specific criteria. We have already referred to the work of the Saratoga Institute and researchers in the field of HR metrics (Fitz-enz, 2002; Sullivan, 2002). These metrics can provide a running start for establishing the criteria against which many HR programs can be evaluated. Obviously they should be checked against stakeholder goals and expectations and adapted as needed for the particulars of the program. Chances are, no criterion will embody all the desired characteristics to a high degree because of the complexities found in human behavior, differences across organizations, legal restrictions, and other factors important to a successful HR program. Therefore, a key to good HR program evaluation is choosing multiple criteria and methods that lessen the shortcomings of any single criterion or method.

The Joint Committee (1994) identified, defined, and gave examples for thirty desirable standards or characteristics for program evaluation criteria. That particularly thorough list of standards is suggestive of important characteristics that should be present in the criteria or measures that will be used in all types of HR program evaluations. Our list of desirable characteristics for criteria overlaps significantly with the list that Steinhaus and Witt (2003) put forth. Like their list, our list of ten desirable characteristics can be grouped into three categories. Our categories are *measurement quality*, *relevance*, and *practicality*. The three categories, the ten desirable characteristics, and a description of each characteristic are presented in Table 1.2. To illustrate these characteristics further, the following paragraphs also describe conditions that occur when the criteria are deficient of the desired characteristics.

Build Measurement Quality into the Criteria. Basic to any successful evaluation is the need to have faith in the quality of the criterion data used to arrive at the findings, conclusions, and recommendations. While individuals in professional fields such as psychometrics and survey development spend years learning techniques to maximize measurement quality, even less experienced members of an HR program evaluation team can help their more experienced colleagues optimize data quality. They would accomplish this by placing due emphasis on using criteria that are reliable, valid, measurable, observable, and unbiased.

Emphasizing the development and use of high-quality criteria could, however, be difficult if no one on the evaluation team has training or experience in the professional field of measurement. Pedhazur and Schmelkin's (1991, p. 3) comment about students is equally applicable to the same people who are later part of an evaluation team:

Table 1.2 Desirable Characteristics for Criteria

Desirable Characteristics	Descriptions and Actions to Increase the Desirable Characteristics
Measurement Quality	
Reliable	• Measures are stable across individuals, time, and circumstances • The focus is on accuracy or precision of measurement
Valid	• Measure must address key evaluation objectives • Lack of validity implies that an area of interest is not being effectively isolated and measured • A valid question (a) focuses on a single issue, (b) is unambiguous, (c) is directly linked to key criteria, and (d) requires little interpretation by respondents
Measurable	• Measurements can be either quantitative or qualitative • "Triangulating" in on an answer by using multiple methods is one way to lessen the uncertainty caused by the measurement limitations for any one method
Based on Observable Events	• Others viewing the same data, events, and so forth should discern the same qualities/levels without relying on assumptions, judgment, or intuition • Standardizing procedures minimizes the influences of unfounded assumptions, judgments, or intuition
Unbiased	• Evaluation questions are reviewed for potential bias • Measures should not be biased toward certain groups
Relevance	
Meaningful to Stakeholders	• The criterion data are credible for key stakeholders • Criterion variables are selected with stakeholder concerns in mind
Focused on Value Added	• Criteria should emphasize how the program contributes to effectiveness or efficiency of the organization • Return on investment estimates are desirable, but questionable estimates can harm the program and evaluation
Actionable	• Criteria should be aimed at facilitating program improvement and structured to reveal improvement opportunities • Data collection should emphasize obtaining information that can result in program changes that are feasible and can be implemented
Practicality	
Practical and Cost-Effective	• Targeted results of program evaluation need to be realistic and not overzealous in their goals • Criteria should be accepted by key stakeholders • Costs need to be balanced with expected benefits
Organizational Politics	• Hidden agenda can derail even the best evaluation • Anticipating all stakeholders' points of view can help a team mitigate the effect of organizational politics

"Many students get the impression that no special competencies are necessary for the development and use of measures. . . . Unfortunately, many readers and researchers fail to realize that no matter how profound the theoretical formulations, how sophisticated the design, and how elegant the analytic techniques, they cannot compensate for poor measures."

Assess How Reliable the Criteria Are. The measures being used to evaluate the criteria must be reliable in order for the team and stakeholders to have confidence in the accuracy of the HR program evaluation results. A reliable measure is one that will obtain consistent results, regardless of who is administering the measure and when it is being administered. Reliability can be built into criterion measures by standardizing instructions, structuring questions, pilot-testing the measure to ensure clarity, training evaluators to gather the data in the same way, periodically testing and calibrating evaluators to make sure they judge the same information in the same way, and collecting data from the population or a representative sample. Phase 3 includes a section that reviews common steps that evaluators can take to enhance the reliability of information during data collection.

There are at least four ways to quantify reliability. One, measurements might be taken with the same instrument at two or more times to see whether there is consistency in the attribute being measured (technically referred to as test-retest reliability). Two, measurements of an area of interest such as job satisfaction may be obtained using more than one instrument (all designed to measure the same variable) to see whether individuals who score relatively high or low on one instrument also score at the same relative position on the other instrument (alternate/parallel forms reliability). Three, we could have two or more raters evaluate the same individuals, processes, or other organizational issues of concern, and then we could determine the degree to which the different raters agreed on the assessments (inter-rater reliability). Four, if multiple raters or instruments are not available, reliability can be assessed through a measure of internal consistency for a single set of homogeneous items on an instrument such as a survey or test.

Ensure That the Criteria Are Valid. Validity refers to the degree to which a score on an assessment reflects what the assessment is designed to measure. In order to ensure that an HR program evaluation produces relevant and meaningful recommendations, it is essential that the criterion measures used to generate findings, conclusions, and recommendations are directly linked to the key evaluation objectives. A criterion measure is valid if it accurately assesses the evaluation design questions. A lack of validity implies that an area of interest is not being isolated and accurately measured.

Careful planning and analysis are positive steps that the evaluation team can take toward ensuring that the criterion measures are adequately addressing the key design questions. Again, pilot-testing is important for ensuring that the criterion measures are providing information that truly answers the questions about the HR program being evaluated. In addition, each of the other desirable characteristics of criterion measures impact validity to varying degrees. For example, a measure can be reliable but have no validity (for example, height can be reliably measured, but is not a valid predictor of employee turnover). However, an unreliable measure cannot be a valid predictor.

Make Sure That the Criteria Are Measurable. Both quantitative and qualitative criteria need to be measurable. The absence of measurable criteria opens an evaluation team's findings to criticism. It is very difficult for an evaluation team to defend its conclusions when the findings were based on general impressions drawn from unstructured interviews and other unsystematic methods. It would be much easier to defend the same conclusions if they were based on measurable characteristics obtained with multiple methods that systematized the data gathering to provide quantifiable information.

Quantitative measures (for example, performance ratings or years with the organization) provide countable information describing an HR program. They yield relatively straightforward measures that are generally understood when presented to stakeholders. In an evaluation of a safety program, a quantitative measure might be the numbers of accidents occurring during the six months immediately before and immediately after a safety awareness program was provided.

Qualitative information (such as attitudes and opinions) can be measured with data collection techniques such as interviews, surveys, and naturalistic observations. Quantification of qualitative information helps the evaluation team understand an HR program and the context in which it operates. Such measurement often involves coding open-ended or narrative answers or observations. For example, team members might code narrative answers from structured interviews by assigning them to different categories based on the issues raised in the answers, or the team members might rate the answers based on how positive or negative the answers were in tone. The evaluation team can then summarize the various aspects of the qualitative data by calculating the frequency with which each category of narrative answer or observation occurred.

Base the Criteria on Observable Events. Different evaluation team members are likely to arrive at different conclusions about the impact of a program if they are relying on assumptions and intuition, rather than on observations or hard data. To arrive at defensible conclusions, criterion data should be systematically observed and collected. In the process, the evaluation team should allow long enough for the full range of behaviors to be observed. Too short an observation period (for example, only the month before the performance appraisal ratings are submitted) may not allow sufficient opportunity to gather information on a process that uses a longer cycle time (for example, a performance appraisal year). Another potential observational problem is the Hawthorne effect—when "group members' knowledge that they are being observed changes the quality and frequency of their behavior" (Zaccaro & Marks, 1996, p. 158). An HR concern like discrimination in promotion may challenge an evaluation team with regard to finding a way to "observe" the behaviors of concern, but accurate conclusions about potential discrimination can only be drawn through a systematic evaluation of the program's various components and an analysis of its potential differential impact on protected groups.

Continuing with an example of possible discrimination, some stakeholders may assume that an organization's performance appraisal program is discriminatory and should be changed if protected group employees perceive the system is unfair. Before drawing such a conclusion about whether discrimination is or is not occurring, it would be necessary to define specifically what discrimination means in this context (that is, how it might manifest itself or be observed). For this type of situation, some evaluation team members might interview protected group members to determine their specific concerns and the observed and perceived discriminatory behaviors that they and others have experienced, while other team members could review hard data (differences in performance ratings, compensation, promotion rates, and tenure) to see whether the perceptions are supported by other data. If differences are found, the evaluation team would also determine whether they are isolated in a particular department or exist organization-wide. These are only a few of the steps that would need to be taken to conduct a thorough evaluation for this HR issue, but they highlight the primary point—criteria need to be operationally defined and conclusions must be based on observable measures.

Make Sure the Criteria Are Unbiased. From a measurement perspective, bias is a consistent type of error that occurs when a data collection, analysis, or interpretation process results in a score that is *consistently* too high or too low. While bias is often discussed in its narrower context of discrimination, the current context uses the broader meaning of bias that includes all types of consistent errors in measurement. A bathroom scale that is out of adjustment is a simple example of an instrument resulting in a biased measure—that is, one that is consistently too high or low. In an HR program evaluation, findings can similarly be biased for/against a total population or some group within the population. Depending on the severity of the bias, a biased finding can alter the conclusions and recommendations drawn from the data. It is therefore important that evaluators who are designing criterion measures be aware of the different types of bias that can impact criterion measures and take the necessary steps to eliminate them during the design phase. The presence of bias should also be specifically assessed during the pilot-test of instruments and procedures.

One type of bias pertains to the use of culturally specific language. At its extreme, this issue would be of concern when a multinational organization wants to solicit information from its members who speak a language other than the one in which the original questions were written and answered. This issue may also be salient when different groups in the same country are asked to respond to written or verbal interview or survey questions. Some questions may be interpreted differently by members of the different groups. To minimize the chance that bias will enter the evaluation, a subgroup—representative of the population—should review the measures for this type of bias, either as part of the pilot-test or as a separate task.

Another type of bias that can impact data accuracy is the influence of evaluators' or stakeholders' assumptions about the criteria under study. This influence can lead to criterion measures being designed to consciously or unconsciously confirm preconceived notions. The end result is a measure that is less informative or accurate than it could be.

Establish the Relevance of the Criteria. Suggesting that criteria need to be relevant might seem like stating the obvious. Much harder is operationally defining the relevance with characteristics that are equally transparent to stakeholders. Steinhaus and Witt (2003) listed and discussed three such characteristics: criteria that are meaningful to the stakeholders, focus on value added to the organization, and result in actionable recommendations.

Consider the Meaningfulness of the Criteria to Stakeholders. Early in the program evaluation, the evaluation team must gain key stakeholder buy-in on what is meaningful to them and will be used as the criteria for judging the effectiveness of the program. To gain that buy-in, the team must find criteria that are transparent and phrased in the stakeholders' language. Stakeholders' buy-in from the beginning of the evaluation will lessen the likelihood that they will later raise questions about whether the "correct" criteria were studied. The buy-in is particularly important when the results do not come out as the stakeholders would have liked.

As we mentioned earlier in our section on identification of stakeholders, different stakeholder groups may hold very different perspectives from those of others about the evaluation, its purposes, and what the outcomes should say. Since the criteria used to conduct the evaluation will influence the eventual evaluation outcomes, arriving at meaningful criteria for all stakeholders can be a challenge.

Evaluations of compensation systems offer an example of how the meaningfulness of the criteria might vary by stakeholder type. For a city government examining whether it provides equal pay for equal work, some stakeholder groups might argue for higher or lower weight to be given to criteria that support how much they are paid. For example, white-collar stakeholders might push for more weight—and therefore more compensation—to be given for post-secondary education and the competing salaries paid to white-collar employees in local private-sector organizations. Other types of workers such as garbage collectors might advocate for more weight to be given to criteria that acknowledge the need to work in very cold and hot environments and perform physically strenuous work. Failure to address all stakeholders' concerns with criteria that all of them agree are meaningful can doom the credibility of the program evaluation findings, conclusions, and recommendations.

Focus on Value Added. Value can be measured in many ways, but monetary value is typically the preferred metric for top management. While it is desirable to put a dollar value (for example, return on investment) on every HR function, that is sometimes not possible. When an HR department or program evaluation team tries to put a questionable dollar value on a function, the questionable estimate can sensitize those receiving the information to other assumptions that were made. And this additional sensitivity can result in criticisms of other findings and conclusions. A whole field of study has emerged in utility analysis, which explores ways to quantify the effect of different HR interventions and actions.

A good way to couch findings is to phrase the results in terms of the goals and outcomes stated for the HR program. For example, an on-site day care center's performance might be judged by looking at the turnover and absences of parents who used the center versus the turnover and absences of both parents who do not use the organization's center and non-parents. While it would be possible to place a dollar value on the avoided costs such as those for recruiting and training a new employee to replace departing employees, it may be sufficient to merely report other meaningful metrics that still show value to the organization without requiring the involvement of accountants and others to arrive at the dollar-valued metrics. Making assumptions about the dollar-based replacement costs for departing employees can result in the evaluation team opening its evaluation up to criticisms that could have been avoided by sticking with a different value metric.

Determine Whether the Criteria Will Result in Actionable Recommendations. A key to determining whether many HR program evaluations are deemed to be successful is to look at whether the evaluation resulted in the organization taking actions to make the program more efficient and effective. Information for information's sake is often not useful, and in some cases may be harmful. Among other things, the harm may be a denial that anything can be done to improve the program because the evaluators could not or did not identify alternative actions to improve or replace the HR program. Also, data collected without concern for how the data can be used in a subsequent action could set up those supplying information with unrealistic expectations that changes will be made based on findings.

To illustrate, if most organization members indicate on a survey that they are dissatisfied with their pay, the respondents might expect increases in pay. If respondents do not see changes, an additional adverse effect could be decreased response rate on subsequent surveys. In past applied organizational research, focus group participants told one of the authors that they do not send back surveys any more because no one ever does anything with the information when a problem is identified. Our advice: Don't gather the data if you don't (a) *really* want to know the answer to what you asked and (b) hope to take some action based on the data.

Focus on the Practicality of the Criteria.

Teams will face many hurdles in the course of an evaluation, and they must arrive at practical means for dealing with such obstacles. Common hurdles addressed by our third category of desirable characteristics for criteria are the needs to select cost-effective criteria and to minimize the effects of organizational politics.

Emphasize Practical and Cost-Effective Criteria. With organizations emphasizing efficiency and cost-consciousness in all of their functions, it stands to reason that the criteria used in an evaluation must be practical and worthwhile relative to the resulting expense required to obtain the information. Attempts to gather perfect data can result in excessive time or monetary costs. For example, moving from an 80 percent response rate to a 100 percent response rate for an organizational survey may require more resources (for example, evaluator time as well as respondents' goodwill and time) than the additional data will be worth. Answers very different from those already obtained would have only minor effects on the *overall* organization findings. The remaining 20 percent could, however, be important if the non-respondents fell disproportionately into the same *subgroup* and findings for that *subgroup* were to be examined and reported separately.

Phillips (1997, p. 3) similarly noted that, at a more global level, the question, "Is it worth it?" should be asked before undertaking an evaluation. He cited an example in which a training course for ten supervisors cost $5,000 and an evaluation of the course could easily cost $50,000. He concluded that the evaluation might not be of merit for a training program that cost $5,000, but a $50,000 training evaluation might be a worthwhile investment for a training program that cost $750,000.

Beware of Organizational Politics.   To some extent, the information for this issue has been alluded to when we discussed obtaining key stakeholder buy-in; but because of its importance to the success of an HR program evaluation, a few more words about this issue are warranted in this section on desirable characteristics for criteria. The effects of organizational politics on the choice of criteria and the ways that those criteria are defined conceptually and operationally can greatly impact the outcome of an HR program evaluation.

Royse, Thyer, Padgett, and Logan (2001, p. 326) stated, "agency directors, managers, employees may have strong motivations to present their programs or organizations more favorably than might otherwise occur in an unbiased program evaluation. The actions of these individuals can seriously affect treatment fidelity and make a complete mess of evaluation efforts." In contrast to this desire to make a program appear favorable in an evaluation, many of us in the HR program evaluation field have also encountered situations in which key stakeholders have wanted evaluation results to show that a program should be dropped or some aspect of the program should be greatly modified.

Conclusions

While we have dealt with the identification of stakeholders, evaluators, and evaluation questions as three discrete tasks in order to limit confusion, the tasks are interrelated. Moreover, the steps required to accomplish one of the identification tasks can be performed at the same time that steps for another of the identification tasks are being performed. The next chapter on planning the evaluation will address some of the specifics that will start the team on its journey toward a successful HR program evaluation.

Suggested Resources

Berk, R.A., & Rossi, P.H. (1990). *Thinking about program evaluation*. Thousand Oaks, CA: Sage.

Edwards, J.E., Scott, J.C., & Raju, N. S. (Eds.). (2003). *The human resources program-evaluation handbook*. Thousand Oaks, CA: Sage.

Joint Committee on Standards for Educational Evaluation. (1994). *The program evaluation standards: How to assess evaluations of educational programs* (2nd ed.). Thousand Oaks, CA: Sage.

Love, A.J. (1991). *Internal evaluation: Building organizations from within*. Thousand Oaks, CA: Sage.

Steinhaus, S.D., & Witt, L.A. (2003). Criteria for human resources program evaluation. In J.E. Edwards, J.C. Scott, N.S. Raju (Eds.), *The human resources program-evaluation handbook* (pp. 49–68). Thousand Oaks, CA: Sage.

Phase 2

PLAN THE EVALUATION

"Planning without action is a daydream; action
without planning is a nightmare."

—*Japanese proverb*

Chapter Objectives

- Provide guidance on determining the timelines, milestones, responsibilities, and steps for the remainder of the project
- Identify factors that must be considered in determining the resources and budget for conducting the HR program evaluation
- Highlight significant issues that need to be resolved before actually planning the particular steps that will be used in the next four phases of the evaluation
- Provide specific guidance and details for planning the data collection and analysis steps
- Identify planning strategies for communicating with program stakeholders and building their commitment to the outcome of the evaluation

The strength and credibility of an evaluation's findings hinge largely on how well the evaluation is designed and planned. A good evaluation design ensures that the correct questions are being asked, the methodology is appropriate and defensible, the organization's resources are used efficiently, and stakeholders can make meaningful use of the results. A well-executed evaluation requires much front-end planning to ensure that the factors likely to affect the quality of the results and recommendations can be addressed. Conversely, a hurriedly developed plan or a plan with few details frequently leads to one or more of the following adverse consequences: rework of previously completed tasks, missed milestones, unmet expectations, and other problems that make the findings and recommendations difficult to "sell" to top management and other stakeholders.

A successful HR program evaluation requires planning throughout the life of the project. Rossi and Freeman (1993, p. 27) noted that "evaluation is a practice almost always requiring revision and modification of the initial evaluation plan, making compromises in the types, quantity, and sometimes quality of the data collected, and responding to shifts that occur in the conduct of the program and in the composition and interests of the stakeholders involved."

Effective planning for an HR program evaluation should address at least five issues, some of which may result in iterative adjustments as the plan gets fleshed out. These issues are listed below:

1. The evaluation team should prepare a preliminary list of the resources—including time—that will be needed in order to complete the HR program evaluation.

2. A data collection plan should be formulated that anticipates and addresses potential obstacles so that the team can deliver the best possible information for the level of resources provided.

3. An analysis plan should be developed that ensures that the evaluation questions are answered with appropriate data, research methods, and statistical procedures.

4. Before the findings and recommendations are available, the team should decide how to package them for feedback, with

due consideration given to both the content being communicated and the stakeholders' preferred methods for receiving such information.

5. The team should plan the steps that it will take to obtain top management's buy-in for accomplishing the steps outlined in this paragraph, as well as lay the groundwork for the buy-in that will be required to implement any recommendations that develop from the evaluation.

The American Evaluation Association's website (www.eval.org/resources.asp) identifies thirty texts that are available entirely online from government resources, foundations, universities, and other organizations. For each, it lists the organization sponsoring the book, the scope of issues covered, the audience for whom the book is appropriate, and the web link to the site. In addition to accessing the online handbooks and text, the association has provided a list of universities that have major programs in evaluation; these may be useful to small companies that do not have in-house experts on program evaluation or need to find free or low-cost program evaluation advice and assistance.

Determine the Resources Needed to Conduct the Evaluation

A team cannot optimally complete its program evaluation without adequately planning its resource needs. Resource planning requires deciding what will be needed and when it will be needed. In some situations, having the resources too late can be equivalent to not having them at all.

The program evaluation budget and milestones should be realistic, and provisions should be made for changing the required resources and deadlines should the need arise. This is not a blanket excuse for later changes or even a suggestion that it is useless to prepare a plan. Instead, it is an acknowledgment that even the best-laid plans can go awry when dealing with the complexities of people, organizations, and their environments.

Develop a Preliminary Budget

While different organizations structure their project budgets in different ways, all program evaluation teams need to consider some core types of resources. Five types that are commonly found in HR program evaluation budgets are staff, travel, communications, equipment and supplies, and space.

Account Fully for Staffing Costs. The most readily apparent staff costs are the salary and benefits of the evaluation team, be they internal staff or external consultants. A full and conscientious accounting of all staffing costs is particularly important if an organization is comparing the evaluation-related expenses of using in-house staff versus external consultants. Leaving out some of the costs for in-house staff could result in the organization making an apples-to-oranges comparison and possibly choosing a non-optimum solution for completing the evaluation. While monetary cost is not the only factor to consider in determining whether internal or external staff should be used in the HR program evaluation, it is important to use accurate information when making that decision, even if the organization considers in-house staff time as a sunk cost that must be paid anyway.

In-house team members may work around their normal job tasks to perform their evaluation tasks. Nonetheless, the evaluation tasks still have in-house staffing costs associated with the evaluation. The personnel assigned full- or part-time to the evaluation team have other, normal job tasks that are not being done or must be done through paid or unpaid overtime. Some organizations that closely monitor all costs of doing business will want to have a full accounting of the program evaluation costs, even when the relative cost of having the evaluation done externally is not an issue. In contrast, other organizations may consider some or all of the salaries and benefits for HR staff and other internal evaluators to be sunk costs that should not be separately calculated.

External consultants may be hired to perform or assist with the entire program evaluation or discrete pieces of the evaluation. Given that the consultants should have superior content-area and program evaluation skills, they will probably be able to complete some discrete tasks much faster than internal staff. This time-based savings may, however, be at least partially offset by three other factors: the time required to learn about the organization's culture and HR program, possibly higher salary costs for the external specialist, and the need for the consulting firm to show a profit.

In addition to the direct costs of internal and external evaluators, there are often indirect staff costs. Many evaluations fail to take into account these often substantial costs, which can take employees away from their normal work activities. For example, these costs are incurred for surveys, interviews, and other special data collection efforts. If the program evaluation includes a twenty-minute survey administered to six thousand employees, the total time required for members to complete the survey equals two thousand hours, approximately one person-year of work. Other internal staff may be used for additional tasks without becoming part of the formal program evaluation team. The additional time required of individual interviewees, focus group participants, HR staff to extract data from electronic or paper files, and other data collection can also increase indirect staff costs. In such cases, indirect staff costs can exceed direct staff costs if the need for scientific rigor is not balanced against practicality concerns when doing real-world program evaluation.

Project Travel Costs That Might Be Encountered. Travel is primarily an issue for organizations with multiple locations. With more and more organizations spanning international borders, travel expenses—including the costs of staff time to get to and from the locations—could add significantly to the cost of carrying out an HR program evaluation. While these expenses can be easily seen in an itemized proposal from a consultant, these evaluation costs are less often considered separately for internal staff travel associated with a program evaluation. For example, collecting data in another country or traveling from one part of the United States to another may require three days of expenses for a single day of data collection. Thus, unless internal staff can combine the travel for the data collection with other tasks that had to be done at the other office, the costs of a single day of data collection are much more than the cost of a flight and rental car for a day. The budget will have to include transportation costs, multiple days of food and lodging, and other travel-related expenses. The personnel time during travel and data collection would probably be expensed as part of the staffing costs reviewed earlier.

In a somewhat extreme example of how data gathering can impact resources, a large pharmaceutical firm flew over fifty sales personnel to a centrally located city for one-hour interviews at a hotel beside an airport and flew most of them home the same day. In this case, the need to collect information as quickly as possible was judged to be more important than the costs of the flights and the undeterminable lost opportunity cost for the more than fifty days of sales contacts that were not made.

Use Communications Advances to Minimize Staffing and Travel Costs. Innovations in video telecommunications are another way that some organizations minimize the travel costs for their HR program evaluations. Again, some organizations will view the use of the communications equipment and telephone line charges as sunk costs, while other organizations will want the program evaluation team to account for any equipment and line usage separately. Moreover, other employees' use of communication resources for normal organizational functions might make it more difficult or less convenient for the evaluation team to access those resources at the specific times required to complete evaluation tasks.

In addition to video telecommunications, software and other advances in communications can be used still other ways when conducting program evaluations. For example, a U.S. federal government agency recently used the Delphi technique and regular email with a panel of subject-matter experts who were located throughout the United States. The experts received a series of questions and returned their answers within a couple of days. Answers were collated and fed back for a second round of responses. Similarly, the answers from the second round were fed back again for a third and final round of responses. This process allowed the experts to communicate through facilitators and come to a consensus without being physically located together.

Determine What Equipment and Supplies Might Be Needed.
The increasing affordability of computers, software, projectors, and other technology has greatly increased the likelihood that these types of aids will be available when an evaluation team needs them. Moreover, advances in versatility through greater compactness and portability provide program evaluators with capabilities that were not available a few years ago.

Similarly, obtaining printing and other supplies are not the problems that they once were for evaluation teams. Many of the printed materials that were formerly required by program evaluation teams are no longer required in the same way. For example, more and more organizations are using web-based surveys instead of the more traditional paper-and-pencil surveys. Likewise, reports about findings and other such communiqués are distributed using websites, videotaped telecasts, and other methods that expand the communication possibilities for evaluators.

When there is, however, a need for printing, color graphics, and other functions that will be supplied from outside of the evaluation team, it is imperative that the evaluation team coordinate its needs well in advance with the relevant offices. The team's need for large-scale printing can be waylaid by higher priority jobs, such as printing and mailing the organization's annual report, that are due to be printed at the same time. The key for the team is to plan its milestones with dates and then pre-arrange the availability of the equipment and supplies for those specific dates.

Don't Forget to Assess Space Requirements.
A team might need to arrange for short- and long-term use of conference rooms and other spaces in the organization. While evaluators might be able to conduct individual interviews in their own offices or in the office

of the interviewee, larger gatherings (for example, for meetings of focus groups, the full evaluation team, and stakeholder representatives) will require finding meeting space. Other space reservations may be needed periodically by members of the program evaluation team who are at the site for data collection or to confer with other evaluation team members. Also, it is useful but sometimes not feasible to reserve a room for storage of the team's records and other materials. Where possible, long-term reservation of the space facilitates greater sharing of information among evaluation team members and can limit the access to sensitive information to team members only.

The HR program evaluation team might need to work with the information systems group to set up shared computer space that would have its access restricted to evaluation team members or even subgroups of the team with a need to know particular types of data. The ability to access one another's work should help the team complete its tasks more quickly, particularly if some of the evaluation team members are located in other cities. At the same time, care must be used with shared directories because they could compromise pledges of confidentiality or allow personnel access to financial and other types of data that should have restricted access. The issue of limiting access to restricted-use data may be a particularly important issue if external consultants are a part of the evaluation team.

Set Milestones with Dates— Making a Commitment Is Hard to Do

The effort required to develop milestones with dates can pay large returns. Developing milestones forces the team to examine evaluation tasks that will need to be performed concurrently, the availability of resources at the needed time, critical paths in the evaluation, and how long each phase and the whole program evaluation will take. In situations in which a program must be completed by a given time (for example, to achieve certification or to determine the amount of funds needed in the next budget to modify the program), it is often useful to work backward from the date when the evaluation results are needed. The backward look can reveal that some potential steps in the planned HR program evaluation are not feasible within the allotted timeframe.

Be Specific When Setting Milestones. Many computer-based software programs are available for planning a project. A team can decide how much detail is necessary for its project plan. At one extreme, one of the authors worked with someone who had over three hundred steps in a plan for conducting large-scale, complex surveys. That level of detail is rarely needed for most HR program evaluations. Table 2.1 shows a few steps and elements from an actual evaluation plan for a performance management program.

In part, the level of specificity provided in the evaluation plan will be evident from the specificity that the organization required for prior projects, including HR program evaluations. Additionally, the expertise of the team with regard to program evaluation could be an important determinant in the specificity of the plan. We believe that greater specificity is desirable when either the team leader or a large proportion of the team has little experience with program evaluation. In such situations, operating without a detailed plan would make it more likely that the team would forget to anticipate key concerns for some steps or otherwise underestimate the time required to arrange interviews, develop and conduct a survey, or complete some other step in the HR program evaluation. Relative to a more general plan, a detailed plan allows the leader and team to detect deviations from the schedule earlier and take catch-up steps sooner.

The specificity provided in timelines will vary by the size of the evaluation team and the complexity of the evaluation itself. A large evaluation or one with a large number of evaluators will benefit from increased timeline specificity because the plan acts as a surrogate for some of the person-to-person communication that would occur within a smaller team. For example, team members can consult the plan to see what others are currently doing, what tasks are approaching, and the date when tasks must be completed. Also, the plan presents the leader of the evaluation team with a tool for keeping the HR program

Table 2.1 Example of Milestone Information Found in a Project Plan

Project Steps and Activities	Resource Requirements
Step 1—Project Planning and Identification of Steering Committee (Timeline Week 1) Identify internal Project Liaison to serve as a day-to-day contact for the project and assist in gathering company information (for example, policies and procedures, employee performance rating data), coordinating logistics, and so forth. Identify Steering Committee members from key constituencies (senior management, Human Resources, and Legal) who represent system stakeholders. The Steering Committee will review and approve the evaluation questions, project methodology, work plan, timeline, and resource requirements and review the results of the evaluation.	Internal Project Liaison; six to eight Steering Committee members
Step 2—Review Performance Management System (Timeline Weeks 2 to 5) Review performance management system (for example, instruments, policies and procedures, and training materials) against relevant professional and legal guidelines. Examples of the review criteria include: • Are the employees rated against job-related dimensions/content? • Does the instrument include behaviorally based performance evaluation standards? • How is employee performance appraisal information used with other HR systems and processes (for example, determination of merit increases/bonuses, promotion decisions, employee development, and downsizing)? • What type of rating scale format is used (for example, graphic rating scale, behavioral checklist, Likert rating scale, and number of rating points)? • Do procedures exist to ensure rater accountability (for example, next level review and evaluation of managers in carrying out their performance management responsibilities)? • Is there a formal appeals process employees can use when they disagree with their performance ratings?	Assemble information on performance management system, including instruments, training materials, policies, and procedures
Schedule meeting with Performance Management Process Owner and System Users to review and confirm preliminary observations. Document results of review.	Meeting time with Process Owner and System Users

Table 2.1 continued

Project Steps and Activities	Resource Requirements
Step 3—Evaluate Statistical Differences and Adverse Impact (Timeline Weeks 3 to 6) Assemble electronic data file. Examine and ensure the integrity of information in the data file(s) by checking data (for example, consistency of coding schemes, missing or duplicate information), performing relevant statistical analyses, and summarizing results. Examine and summarize statistical differences and adverse impact of performance management system by key organizational (for example, pay grade, FLSA exemption status, function) and demographic (for example, gender, ethnicity) variables. Table the statistical results and document relevant issues for review by the Steering Committee.	Statistical/ Data Specialist assembles appropriate data for statistical analysis, conducts analyses, and tables results
Step 4—Meet with Steering Committee to Discuss Findings and Present Recommendations (Timeline Week 7) Present findings and recommendations to Steering Committee. Document evaluation methodology and findings.	Meeting time with Steering Committee members

evaluation on schedule. Weekly review of the milestones can reveal where slippage is occurring. When slippage begins to occurs, the leader can consult with the evaluators to determine whether

- They will be able to catch up within a reasonable time if they are not given additional support,
- The milestone can be slipped because the task is not part of a critical or serial path (that is, the start of other tasks is not contingent on the completion of the delayed task),
- Additional staff will need to be devoted so that the task can be finished on time,
- The task or some other part of the evaluation will need to be cut back in scope, or

- Top management stakeholders must be informed that the team is experiencing a delay that will cause the evaluation to be completed later than promised.

Another common planning mistake for evaluators is to over-commit themselves. While evaluators with can-do attitudes are always valued, there are limitations on how much each team member can do at any phase in the evaluation. If the plan includes linking evaluators to the specific tasks and timelines for which they have responsibility, the likelihood of over-commitment of staff is reduced. Concern about over-commitment becomes especially important when evaluators come from within the organization and the organization expects the program evaluation to be done in members' "spare" time. Milestones tied to specific evaluators can reveal that the only evaluator with the requisite skills to accomplish an evaluation task also has the majority of her time during the same period reserved for a major milestone on her regular job. If such a situation were detected during the planning, the team leader could determine whether one or more milestones could be moved. If not, the evaluator could be replaced with someone else who possesses the requisite skills *and* has spare time available when the program evaluation task is projected to occur.

Update Key Stakeholders   The team leader will probably need to provide periodic updates to top management and possibly other stakeholders. This is especially true for a long evaluation or one dealing with a very sensitive issue. For example, a recent inquiry about a selection system by the Equal Employment Opportunity Commission brought about an urgent request for a formal evaluation by a company's legal counsel. The selection program was screening out a disproportionate number of females, and there were questions about the datedness of the test items and supporting documentation. As would be expected, the company's attorney was keenly interested in the progress and results of the evaluation and required weekly update meetings. In addition, the chief executive officer, who is also an attorney, was also following the evaluation and expected frequent updates. These update meetings were generally brief and concentrated mainly on the approach being used to conduct the evaluation. The evaluator resisted the urge to present preliminary findings due to the chance of them changing, but was able to discuss progress and possible solutions given worst-case scenarios. These meetings helped establish the credibility of the evaluator and served to facilitate the implementation of the evaluation team's recommendations.

The feedback provided during meetings with key stakeholders may involve a briefing or a short write-up such as a one-pager. Either way, a plan with specific milestones can provide structure for such an update and minimize the preparation time required to prepare the feedback. Additionally, informal communication between the team and stakeholder representatives should be used to keep groups current on the status of the evaluation. No one likes surprises in a program evaluation, particularly when the surprises entail missed major deadlines, the need for large additional commitments of resources, or the curtailing of previously promised work.

Lay Out Plans for Data Collection

Once the evaluation questions have been formulated and the general scope of needed resources has been defined, the team can concentrate on the procedures that will be used to collect information. "Planning information collection for an evaluation requires finding the most efficient techniques to answer questions about a program's merit, setting the time and place for collecting information, and deciding who will participate in the evaluation and be responsible for the collection of data" (Fink & Kosecoff, 1978, p. 24). In making decisions about which methods and sources might be most cost-effective for evaluating a particular HR program, the team would do well to consider the quality of existing data and the importance of the not-yet-obtained information to the overall evaluation.

In the remainder of this section, we discuss five methodological issues that the team will face while planning data collection. For the first two issues, we review desirable attributes of data and the wide range of methods available for HR program evaluations. Third, our discussion of anonymity and confidentiality warns evaluators about concerns that may not be apparent until much later in the program evaluation. Next, we review some common types of data errors, with the hope that sensitizing the team to the errors will be the first step toward mitigating their adverse effects. Finally, we raise questions and give guidelines about when a census or a sample would be preferred in a program evaluation.

Determine Desirable Attributes for the Data That Will Be Collected

A program evaluation team will collect data that vary across many attributes. Figure 2.1 identifies twelve such data attributes that HR program evaluation teams should consider when planning their assessments. The list is particularly noteworthy because it distinguishes how each of the twelve attributes differs along a continuum that varies from strategic planning to operational control. This explicit consideration of both long- and short-term issues forces the team members to plan more fully how they will eventually want to couch their findings, conclusions, and recommendations.

The management control continuum underlying the twelve data attributes suggests that different organizational levels may view, describe, and judge the quality of an HR program from very different perspectives. In turn, this almost certainly means that some differences in perspective will be obtained during the data collection phase of the evaluation. The team will need to recognize the differences when synthesizing the information, feeding back findings, and implementing program changes. In other words, Figure 2.1 shows that one size does not fit all when it comes to collecting and analyzing data, interpreting findings, feeding back results, and making recommendations.

An HR program evaluation will require that attention be paid to both ends of the twelve continua because the team must consider both (a) the current and longer-term efficiency and effectiveness of an HR program and (b) how the program contributes to the organi-

Figure 2.1   The Interplay of Strategic Planning and Operational Control in Data Collection

Data Attributes	Management Function		
	Strategic Planning	Management Control	Operational Control
Type of question	What if?	←———————→	What is?
Time horizon	Future	←———————→	Current
Information sources	External	←———————→	Internal
Measurement	Qualitative	←———————→	Quantitative
Level of detail	Aggregate	←———————→	Individual
Level of analysis	Synthesis	←———————→	Descriptive
Frequency of reporting	Periodic	←———————→	Continuous
Scope of reporting	Summary	←———————→	Detailed
Accuracy of reporting	Approximate	←———————→	Exact
Mode of reporting	Graphics	←———————→	Numerical/text
Number of people possessing the data	Very few	←———————→	Many
Organizational level possessing the data	Highest level	←———————→	Each level for its own operations

Figure adapted from *Internal Evaluation: Building Organizations from Within*, by A.J. Love, 1991, p. 29. Copyright 1991 by Sage Publications, Inc. Adapted with permission of the author. The final two rows were added to the table by the current authors.

zation's overall functioning must be considered. Chances are, stakeholder groups at different levels will pay more or less attention to the tactical and strategic implications of any recommendations that result from the evaluation. The interests of some stakeholders might be on the shorter-term effects of recommendations and actions (for example, job losses in the next year as automation is added), whereas other stakeholders might focus on the bigger-picture or longer-term effects of the HR program evaluation (for example, automation changes paying for themselves within five years).

Remind the Team of All the Sources and Methods They Might Use

HR program evaluators are fortunate to have so many data sources and data collection methods from which to choose. Moreover, many of the sources contain data that are readily available to the HR program evaluation team because the organization has already assembled the information for other purposes. Other methods such as individual interviews will require the collection of new data and be used for most types of HR program evaluations.

During this portion of the planning process, evaluators may suggest using methods that they have used successfully in other data collection efforts. A problem will occur if evaluators try to force a "square method peg into a round data-need hole." For example, focus groups might have worked well for a program evaluation that included identifying enhancements to the safety program, but their ability to gather truthful data on a sensitive, personal issue like workplace drug and alcohol abuse might be very limited. In other words, a data collection method appropriate for one project may not be very useful for the HR program evaluation being planned.

> Taking a few extra moments to remind all of the evaluators of the wide range of sources and methods available to them could result in more efficient data collection and better information to answer the evaluation questions. Succumbing to the pressure to get started immediately with the actual data collection might result in the team's forgetting to consider some of the less common, but possibly more applicable sources and methods.

In the next chapter, more than twenty-five data sources and data collection methods are briefly reviewed. It might be useful to the team, especially if the evaluators have little prior experience in program evaluation, to go through the list and individually discuss whether each source or method would be useful, and why or why not. After this preliminary review, the team is better prepared to begin in-depth planning about how the data collection will be undertaken.

Decide Whether Pledges of Anonymity or Confidentiality Will Be Needed

An issue that has to be considered when deciding on which data collection methods to use is whether individuals supplying information will be promised anonymity, confidentiality, or identification. Anonymity exists when it is impossible to connect specific answers to the individual who provided the answers. In contrast, confidentiality exists when a data collector or data analyst can connect answers to the specific individual who provided the answers, but the organization and data collector/analyst pledge to limit access to the data and not to reveal the links to anyone. Finally, an identified condition exists when there is an explicit link (for example, name or employee identification number) between the answers and the organizational member, and the answers may even be attributed to the specific person during briefings or in the report.

While the very nature of true anonymity prevents the linking of responses to a specific individual, providing a pledge of confidentiality to interview participants, survey respondents, or others can also restrict the specificity of information provided at the end of the HR program evaluation. If confidentiality is promised, the evaluation team should develop an explicit statement that details the steps being taken to protect members providing the information. Then the statement needs to be vetted through top management and the legal department before it is incorporated into the data collection instruments and processes. Vetting the anonymity or confidentiality promise before data collection can avoid potential problems later should key top management stakeholders want to know "Who made that promise? I didn't." In such cases, the evaluation team can remind those asking for the link that they agreed to anonymity or confidentiality.

Divulging identifying information may also be governed by the ethical standards of evaluation team members. In addition to their own personal ethical standards, professionals serving on an evaluation team may need to comply with standards established by their societies. For example, one of the American Psychological Association's ethical standards states "(a) Psychologists discuss with persons and organizations with whom they establish a professional relationship . . . (1) the relevant limitations on confidentiality, including limitations where applicable in . . . organizational consulting, and (2) the foreseeable uses of the information generated through their services. (b) Unless it is not feasible or is contraindicated, the discussion of confidentiality occurs at the outset of the relationship and thereafter as new circumstances may warrant" (see Ethical Standard 5.01 in Lowman, 1998, p. 104). Another standard reminds psychologists that the maintenance of confidentiality could also be specified in laws and institutional rules. We briefly alluded to both of these requirements in Phase 1 when covering the identification of stakeholders such as governmental bodies and institutional review boards. These issues should be fully explored with the organization's legal counsel before deciding how to proceed with pledges of anonymity or confidentiality.

Evaluate the Advantages and Disadvantages of Using Anonymity and Confidentiality. For many data sources and methods (for example, external documents and most types of internal documents), deciding whether to offer anonymity or confidentiality will be a moot issue. This is because either (a) no answer is being solicited directly from an organization member or (b) there is no potentially harmful or embarrassing information to be revealed about or associated with an organizational member. For methods such as surveys and interviews for which personally or politically sensitive answers may be solicited, concerns about anonymity or confidentiality could result in either a refusal to answer some or all questions, or answers that are less than honest.

Also, anonymity—and sometimes confidentiality when no demographic data are gathered—will prevent the evaluation team from linking information in one database (for example, survey responses) to information in another database (for example, personnel file information). The lack of a link can severely limit the types of analyses that can be performed. For example, the absence of a link like a name or employee identification number would make it impossible to see whether dissatisfaction reported on a prior survey was related to members' leaving the organization during the subsequent year or two.

In some situations, the evaluators may decide that it will be important to identify the organizational members who supply answers, and therefore the evaluators would not promise anonymity or confidentiality. This would be done when it is important to link responses from one database to another or when it may be necessary to follow up on prior responses. If responses to surveys and interviews are collected under an identified condition, evaluators should be prepared for two outcomes: fewer responses from those being asked to answer and respondents being less willing to answer honestly.

Eliminate Confusion About When Anonymity Versus Confidentiality Will Be Promised.   Evaluators conducting surveys are particularly likely to confuse the two conditions. They may indicate that the respondents' answers are anonymous because no name or identification number is requested on the questionnaire. Often, that condition is not sufficient for ensuring anonymity in organizational settings when data collection methods such as surveys are used. During subsequent data analyses, simultaneous cross-tabulations on a variety of demographic variables could allow team members to identify the specific answers of many—if not all—members of the organization. For example, there may be only one female vice president, and any analyses that looked at survey responses in a simultaneous breakout by gender and organizational level might reveal that individual's specific answers. In this case, it might be more appropriate to note that the survey responses are being collected confidentially rather than anonymously.

Focus and discussion groups are a place where a pledge of anonymity or confidentiality is sometimes inappropriately given. While the facilitator may promise to not identify who specifically said what during a group session, it is impossible for the facilitator or other evaluation team members to prevent the focus group participants from telling what other participants said. Therefore, confidentiality—much less anonymity—should *not* be promised to focus and discussion group participants.

Deliver What Is Promised. If an organization is interested in conducting *anonymous individual interviews*, it must (a) hire an external consultant to collect and analyze the data and (b) agree that the raw data would never be released to the organization. The organization would receive only summarized data from the interviews. Some organizations may find this too high a data-loss price to pay. Also, the organization and the external consultant need to indicate in the contract how long the contractor will store the data in case the information needs to be accessed again.

If an organization wants to conduct an *anonymous survey*, it can limit the number of demographic questions (for example, organizational unit and possibly a gross measure of whether the respondent is a white- or blue-collar employee). This, however, may prevent the use of web surveys if there would be a link back to who returned each survey. Alternatively, the organization could conduct a confidential survey with more demographic questions by using in-house staff or a consultant. Either way, the confidentiality pledge on the survey would detail why the respondents should believe that their responses are confidential. Anonymity and confidentiality conditions also extend into the data analysis and feedback. It is typical to protect respondents by not reporting any subgroup findings that have fewer than eight to ten people in them. As the number of respondents in a subgroup gets smaller, it becomes easier to identify members who may have given particular types of answers.

One very important caution should be noted. Confidentiality *must* be preserved once it is promised. If anonymity or confidentiality is ever promised and that pledge is subsequently broken, even inadvertently, it could seriously damage subsequent data collection efforts. It takes a long time to regain members' faith in the organization once they have seen or heard of a member's anonymous or confidential answers being discussed, with the answers being attributed

to specific individuals. More will be said on the negative consequences of violating anonymity or confidentiality pledges when we
discuss Phase 5—Communicate Findings and Insights.

Avoid or Minimize Common Data Collection Errors

An evaluation team must be concerned about errors that can result
during data collection because inaccurate information can undermine
the quality of the evaluation's results, conclusions, and recommendations. (*Note:* Error can connote either consistent or random error, but
bias refers to consistent error only.) Salant and Dillman (1994) identified four types of errors—sampling, non-response, measurement, and
coverage—that occur with sample surveys. Except for sampling error
that only occurs when sampling from the population, the other three
errors can be present in data gathered from either a census or sample;
and all four types of error can be found with data collection methods
other than just surveys. Using those four types of errors as a starting
point, we present information on them and other types of errors that
may be present in the data. Rating errors is added as a fifth category of
error; and acquiescence, socially desirable responding, yea- and nay-
saying, and order effects are discussed as special types of measurement
error. Although Table 2.2 provides an example, a cause, and steps to
lessen the errors, a little more will be said about each type of error.

Sampling error is an acknowledgment that our findings would
vary somewhat if we drew relatively larger or smaller random samples from a population or even other samples of the same size from
the population. Everyone has seen or heard sampling errors mentioned in newspapers, popular magazines, and nightly televised
news programs. Therefore, stakeholders should already have some
understanding of the concept before it is time to explain the findings. More will be said about sampling error in the next section on
deciding when to use a census or a sample.

Non-response error is a problem that results from missing data, most
typically with entire surveys or selected responses from surveys not

Table 2.2 Five Types of Error That Should Be of Concern During Data Collection

Type of Error	Example	Causes	Steps to Lessen the Error or Its Effect
Sampling error[1]	Population estimates from a survey or data extracted from personnel files are projected with ±4 percentage points of error	A randomly drawn, representative sample is used instead of the population	• Increase the sample size to reduce but not eliminate sampling error • Cannot estimate sampling error if the sample is not randomly drawn and representative of the population
Non-response error	Someone who received a survey did not return the survey or returned it with some questions left unanswered	Some of those selected to participate did not do so or provided incomplete information	• Repeat attempts to solicit information from non-respondents • Obtain missing data to supplement information contained in surveys, interviews, file extractions, or other data • Compare characteristics of non-respondents with those of respondents to see whether the two groups differ from expected population distributions (for example, for gender, race, or unit)
Measurement error[2]	A respondent is forced to choose only one racial category, but her parents are from different races	Responses do not reflect "true" opinions or behaviors because questions were misunderstood, appropriate response alternatives were not provided, or the respondents chose not to tell the truth	• Conduct careful pre-testing of instruments to revise questions that are misunderstood, leading, threatening, or inadequate in terms of alternatives • Use skilled interviewers to reduce bias in interviews

Coverage error	Organization's employee theft-identification system does not catch all employees who steal	The organization theft-identification system cannot be focused on each employee for the entire shift	• Use multiple methods for detecting theft and triangulate in on the rate of thefts by looking at the overlap and unique persons identified with each system
Rating error	Evaluators engage in rating patterns that do not accurately reflect behaviors or dimensions being rated	Lack of rater training and conditions to support accurate ratings	• Use multiple methods for rater training based on purpose of evaluation, along with behaviorally based rating methods • Ensure presence of conditions that support accurate ratings (for example, trained assessors, appropriate criteria, valid and reliable instruments, and culture that values accurate ratings)

[1] All but sampling error may be present for both a census and a sample.

[2] This type of error might include acquiescence, social desirable responding, yea- or nay-saying, and order effects (that is, primacy and recency). The qualitative measurement error discussed in this context should not be confused with "standard error of measurement," a quantitative measure. Robie and Raju (2003) defined the standard error of measurement as the variation in test, attitude, or other types of scores that would be found if an individual provided answers on multiple occasions or to different sets of items from the same content area.

being answered. Another source of non-response error occurs when questions are added to a data collection instrument after it has already been used to gather information from some interviewees, survey participants, or personnel records. It is frequently not possible to go back to the original sources and obtain information to the questions that were added after the initial data collection began. Evaluation teams often address this problem by assuming that the missing data would have been distributed much like the information from the individuals or records where the data were actually collected. As the percentage of cases with missing data on a given variable (for example, satisfaction with pay) grows higher, this assumption becomes more tenuous. A large percentage of cases with missing data on a variable could lead to concerns about how well the findings reflect the population to which the findings are to be generalized.

Measurement error often occurs when evaluators fail to sufficiently pretest their data collection instruments. As a result, different evaluators as well as people providing the information might interpret questions differently. Or respondents may actually answer the question that we posed to them, rather than answer the one that we meant to ask! Other times, organizational members providing the answers may understand the question but choose to provide a less-than-honest answer because of fears that their answers could have adverse consequences for themselves or others. Measurement error is most common with surveys, interviews, and questionnaires that are used to extract and code information from various types of files. Edwards, Thomas, Rosenfeld, and Booth-Kewley (1997) noted four types of response error that could be included under the rubric of measurement error:

- *Acquiescence* is a type of error that occurs when individuals provide answers based on what they think the questioner wants to hear.
- *Socially desirable responding* is a tendency for individuals to fake or say things that are socially appropriate, rather than candidly express their true beliefs.

- *Yea-saying* and *nay-saying* occur when individuals tend to agree or disagree with survey or interview items regardless of their content.

- *Order effects* occur when individuals tend to choose their answers from the initial items (a *primacy effect*) or the last items on a list (*recency effect*).

Coverage error is probably the error that evaluation teams think about least, often because they cannot get a good handle on how much coverage error there is in identifying a population being studied in an HR program. Coverage error is the uncertainty that results when the evaluation team is unable to identify *all* the cases (such as personnel records, organization members, or security violations) that fit into a typically hard-to-recognize population. That is, the evaluation team does not know how adequately it has covered all possible instances or people who fit the population definition. Examples of situations in which HR coverage errors would be found would be in identifying the populations who take actions such as cheating on urine analysis tests, using illegal drugs in the workplace, stealing from the store inventory, or padding travel claims. All of these examples of coverage errors have two things in common: (a) a portion of employees in each situation is going undetected and (b) those who are caught may not be representative of those who go undetected. As a result, the extent or incidence of the behavior cannot be accurately estimated. While it may be impossible to achieve a precise estimate of some behaviors, it might be possible to collect data from multiple sources and triangulate toward (or narrow in on) a general conclusion about whether the problem is small, moderate, or widespread.

Rating effects refer to certain evaluation patterns that may or may not lead to measurement error. These patterns include range restriction (using only the top, middle, or bottom of a scale), leniency (using only the top end of a scale—a specific type of range restriction), and halo (letting an evaluation for one dimension bleed over onto the evaluations for other dimensions). While a rating effect may actually be a correct reflection of performance (that is, all members of an experienced, high-achieving team receive high ratings across all performance dimensions), it is important to be aware of how these patterns can impact measurement accuracy. Although performance ratings may be an important source of data for assessing HR programs such as the administration of merit-based compensation or the internal promotion or reassignment system, ratings are a key assessment procedure for a wide variety of HR program issues (for example, level of employee engagement and customer satisfaction). Rating format and conditions have an impact on rating accuracy, as does the nature of training that raters receive.

Decide When a Census or Sample Should Be Used

Program evaluators are often faced with a question of whether they should collect data from every person, file, or some other element in an HR population (conduct a census) or from a selected subset of that population (use a sample). We look at reasons to use a census, a representative sample, and a purposeful sample.

Conduct a Census When Benefits Outweigh Costs. Even though a sample is typically less disruptive and costly than a census because a sample uses information gathered on or from fewer individuals, the evaluation team might still choose to conduct a census. This decision could be based on a number of important considerations:

1. There might be little cost or time savings in sampling. If an organization had ninety-eight managers and it wanted an assessment of managers' opinions about the 360-degree performance feedback system that was implemented the year before, eighty-five or more of the ninety-eight managers might have to be sampled and interviewed or surveyed to reach a desired level of precision.

2. The utmost precision is needed in some cases. For example, an organization facing a class-action lawsuit for age discrimi-

nation might have to have data available on the population in order to support its position. While sampling personnel records might save some time, imprecision associated with sample-based findings—not to mention the complexities of explaining sampling and weighting during legal proceedings—may result in significantly greater financial and public-relations costs in the end.

3. The evaluation team does not have the needed sampling, weighting, and analytic skills. Although it would be possible to obtain these skills under a contract, the lack of skills would make it difficult for the evaluation team to understand, explain, and defend their findings, conclusions, and recommendations. Losing credibility with key stakeholders in Phase 5 or 6 of our HR evaluation approach could doom any advantages that would be derived from the sampling.

4. Sometimes, it is important to assure all organization members that their opinions count. This point should be emphasized as the stakes go up in a program evaluation (for example, how the pay-for-performance system will be implemented). Moreover, sampling can lead to suspicion of why someone is selected for participation and someone else is not.

Use Probability Sampling to Minimize Costs and Disruptions. Large organizations can often cut the costs of program evaluation by using probability-sampling-based data collection and analysis procedures: identifying the population of interest, selecting a random sample for the data collection, weighting the sample-based information so that it reflects the population, and computing the population estimates along with their estimated levels of precision. Because data are being collected from a portion of the population, it can typically be collected more quickly and at lower cost than can data collected from the full population. Sampling can also have non-monetary benefits. For example, surveying samples might result in more potential respondents returning completed surveys because they would not feel surveyed to death.

The wide array of available probability sampling techniques only hints at (a) the complexities involved in choosing an optimum sampling design and (b) the fact that the evaluation team may be limited to using simple random sampling if the team members have little prior experience or training with probability sampling. Incorrectly drawn samples or miscalculation of the weights applied to each case in the sample can result in inaccurate findings. Therefore, team members should not attempt to learn about and use probability sampling techniques as part of the ongoing evaluation.

If, on the other hand, someone on the evaluation team has the needed training and experience with sampling, the HR evaluation team should review the tradeoff between the increased precision that comes with a larger sample size versus the greater number of cases (and cost) that the team will have to include in the sample. Other things being equal, sampling saves relatively few cases when it is done in a smaller—rather than larger—organization or organizational unit like the marketing department. For example, if the evaluation team desires 5 percentage points of precision on an employee satisfaction survey and they anticipate that 90 percent of the organization's one hundred employees are satisfied, the team would need to sample about seventy of the one hundred members in the population and obtain data from each person. In contrast, other evaluation teams would need to sample much smaller portions (but a larger number) of the population in larger organizations to obtain the same amount of precision.

Employ Purposeful Sampling to Target Particular Subgroups. Unlike probability sampling, *purposeful* (also sometimes called *purposive*) sampling does not involve the selection of cases based on the probabilistic representation of cases in the population. Instead, an evaluation team using purposeful sampling chooses a subgroup of organization members, files, or some other population of interest based on judgments that those cases share characteristic(s) that are particularly relevant to a purpose addressed in the program evaluation. Royse and colleagues (2001) noted that purposeful samples sacrifice breadth for depth of information. They listed several purposeful sampling techniques—deviant case sampling, typical case sampling, maximum variation sampling, snowball sampling, convenience sampling, negative case sampling, and politically powerful sampling.

Some methodological purists may say purposeful (that is, judgmental) samples should never be used because such samples do not provide findings that are generalizable to the population with a specific level of precision. Taking this constraint at face value suggests that many HR programs can never be evaluated because it is impossible to manipulate people's lives and careers as easily as it is to manipulate conditions in a laboratory. Time limitations, organizational and economic constraints, ethical issues, and other concerns found in dynamic workplaces make it impossible to use random selection and assignment to experimental and control groups for many HR program evaluations. This being said, it is imperative that evaluation teams alert information users to the limitations of the findings obtained from a purposeful sample and the rationale for using the sample. Worthen and his co-authors (1997) noted that, despite risks in generalizing to a population, purposeful sampling can be helpful for describing a subgroup and gaining a better understanding of the program as a whole.

Purposeful sampling is often appropriate in qualitative evaluations. In such cases, evaluators choose their samples to provide maximum information from each person, file, incident, or other type of unit in the sample. In such instances, the primary objective is often to obtain rich, in-depth information about deviant issues with the smallest cost/sample possible. For example, if a police department is examining the use of potential lethal force during investigations of domestic disturbances, the HR program evaluation team might select its sample from only those cases in which police officers drew their weapons. Although valuable additional information might be obtained in a contrast of potential lethal force and non-lethal force cases, the budget for the program evaluation might not permit such an evaluation design. The risks to generalizability that result from using purposeful sampling may be somewhat ameliorated by using other methods to confirm non-projectible findings.

Identify the Data Analyses
Before the Data Are Collected

To a large extent, the type of data collected will determine the data analysis procedures. Therefore, a team must simultaneously plan how it will collect and analyze the data. Otherwise, a team may find that certain data analyses cannot be conducted because inadequate attention was paid to how these data should be treated when the data collection strategies were being planned.

As a part of the analytic planning, the team must allow time for ensuring that data are as free from errors as possible. Otherwise, the trite, but true, saying, "Trash in, trash out," becomes a reality. Enhancing data quality should be factored into the planning of every step in the data collection and data analysis phases. Enhancing data quality before and during the data collection can be ensured by allowing time for actions such as training data gatherers and developing and using structured data collection instruments. Assessing and cleaning the data after it has been gathered requires that sufficient time has been allotted for the data analyst to look for such anomalies as out-of-range values and odd patterns of data. If the planning and implementation of data quality steps in the collection phase were effective, few data quality problems should be identified in the data analysis stage.

While it will be important to plan many of the basic analyses that will be performed, it is unlikely that the team will be able to identify every analysis before the data are gathered. Identifying the initial set of analyses starts the team toward scoping the size of the analytic effort, determining whether team members can do the analyses or special technical assistance will be required, and looking to see where multiple methods are used to investigate the same issue. Additional analyses will almost always be needed as the team tries to explain unanticipated findings and reconcile conflicting findings that were obtained with different data. Therefore, the team's analytic plans must allow for more time than just that needed to conduct the initially identified analyses.

Reporting findings from both quantitative and qualitative data provides stakeholders with a richer understanding of the HR program than does reporting only quantitative- or qualitative-based findings. In planning both types of analyses, the team may want to keep a few practical points in mind. First, a program evaluation is probably not a good time for the data analysts to try using a new statistical procedure that they have never performed before. While they may be able to obtain output from the computer without error messages, the printed results may not be meaningful. Second, even if the data analysts are very adept with complex statistics, complicated statistics will not be appropriate if key stakeholders do not understand them. Key stakeholders who are asked to accept recommendations based on findings they do not understand are probably not going to buy in to the findings, conclusions, or recommendations. Third, systematically analyzing qualitative data (for example, comments from surveys, focus groups, or individual interviews) often requires much time. Therefore, taking the time to plan who will extract and code the information and then allowing sufficient time to complete these tasks will lessen the likelihood that the team will be spending long, unanticipated hours performing the analyses on qualitative data as the briefing time looms close.

Plan the Procedures for Supplying Feedback

The leader of the program evaluation team will need to negotiate a variety of feedback issues with top management before the HR program evaluation begins. Difficulties finding times to communicate with top management and other stakeholder groups can result in misunderstandings. Moreover, failure to ensure the transparency of the HR program evaluation team's actions and to communicate effectively with the stakeholders can begin to disintegrate the goodwill that the team has built in earlier phases of the evaluation. Therefore, early planning for minimizing potential problems can have a good cost-to-benefit ratio.

"Without careful consideration of the process of communicating, even well-crafted evaluations will not be understood, and if not understood, they cannot be utilized" (Posavac & Carey, 2003, p. 253).

Some of the issues involved in establishing an effective communication process include identifying how often the key stakeholders will be updated on the progress of evaluation and the preferred communication format. Each stakeholder group involved in an evaluation will likely have its own preferences that are tied to evaluation questions that are most salient for the group. It is important to establish an agreed-on communication plan, with timelines and milestones, to follow throughout the evaluation so that there are no surprises for the team or the stakeholder groups. In addition, a commitment to ongoing dialog with stakeholders will increase ownership of the process and will also help the evaluation team to make any necessary interim refinements to the evaluation design, questions, methods, and interpretation of results.

Three interim feedback procedures must be addressed before data collection begins. These procedural issues are (a) how often the evaluation team will be expected to brief top management, (b) who will be included in the update briefings, and (c) the form of the updates. It might be assumed that each update would add little time to the evaluation timetable, but this assumption may be wrong. Substantial time commitments can result from (a) the need to do analyses over and over for each findings update, (b) disruptions caused by taking team members away from other activities to synthesize an emerging message, and (c) a desire to look good before top management. Interim briefings with other key stakeholder groups will probably be less frequent than those with top management.

Royse and colleagues (2001) noted another feedback issue that should be addressed at the beginning of the evaluation. They suggested that the astute evaluator would want to negotiate the feedback of findings to diverse stakeholders at the end of the program evaluation. While this issue may be months away from the beginning of the evaluation, it must be addressed early. At some point during most evaluations, individuals who are providing information to the evaluation team will ask what—if any—feedback they will receive about the program evaluation findings and follow-on actions that result from the findings. Therefore, it is important for the leader of the evaluation team to have discussed this issue with top management before the evaluation starts and the questions are voiced. Top management's commitment to share both findings and steps to correct deficiencies will do much to help an evaluation team during data collection. As with the issue of anonymity and confidentiality in surveys, breaking a promise to give prompt findings and recommendations feedback after the completion of the program evaluation could result in harm to future data collection efforts. Therefore, the leader of the evaluation team and top management need to clarify what information providers (for example, interviewees and survey respondents) will be promised and subsequently provided.

Enhance Buy-In from Top Management

Before finalizing the evaluation plan for presentation and sign-off by top management, it is a good idea to refine the overall design and resource requirements. Specifically, the evaluation team should review and adjust elements of the plan based on new information that has come to light since the original elements of the plan were developed. Some of the central concerns of the review are

- The appropriateness of the design with regard to key stakeholder needs,
- The extent to which stakeholders agree with the evaluation team on the evaluation questions and design,
- Direct and indirect costs associated with the resources needed for the evaluation,
- Whether all of the information that is being proposed for collection actually needs to be gathered, and

- How stakeholders will be briefed throughout the evaluation and what final reports will be required.

By examining and ultimately aligning these facets of the evaluation with stakeholder and management expectations, the evaluation team will greatly increase its chances for both buy-in and ongoing success in the evaluation.

Now that all of the planning has been completed, it is time to obtain top management's buy-in. Sonnichsen (2000) noted that it is the team leader's responsibility to cultivate trust, market the value of the evaluation to key stakeholders, and locate and cultivate champions for the evaluation and its findings. When making its oral or written proposal to upper management, the team should present all of the important characteristics of the plan and provide a budget with timelines. The team might find it useful to put their plan in tabular form to facilitate organization and to lessen the likelihood that important details have not yet been considered. Table 2.3 is a variation of the form that many teams at the U.S. Government Accountability Office use to plan their program evaluations. This scheme, as well as others, allows a large amount of information to be organized and displayed with a minimum of words so that stakeholders can focus on the crucial details of the evaluation design.

Provide an Overview of the Program Evaluation Plan

Although the team should be prepared to answer questions about all characteristics of the plan, brevity in the presentation is the key for both briefings and written proposals. The team should identify and concentrate on the most important, costly, and controversial issues in their plan. Two other issues that should be covered are pledges of anonymity/confidentiality and who (for example, all organizational members or just upper management) will be briefed on the findings once the program evaluation has been completed. Both of these issues can lead to unmet expectations if top management is not told about these constraints before they approve the program evaluation plan.

Other issues that must be included in the proposal are a cursory overview of the methods that will be used to collect the data and what types of information will be obtained from the methods. If there will be uncertainty or limitations that result from using the methods, stakeholders should be warned of those concerns and told about how the HR program evaluation team intends to mitigate the potential problems. Phillips (1997) provided a checklist that an evaluation team can use in preparing to present its proposed plan. The checklist includes reminders to develop an audience profile, use visual aids that are tailored to the audience, and anticipate the questions that are likely to arise.

Prepare to Defend the Budget

The team must be prepared to show that the resources (including time) required to evaluate the program are warranted given the strength of the evaluation plan. Earlier in this chapter, we introduced major components of the budget so that planning could be performed efficiently.

A multi-version budget and evaluation plan provides top management, and to a lesser extent other stakeholders, with an opportunity to decide what limitations and uncertainty they are willing to encounter at the end of the program evaluation. If key stakeholders are able to live with more uncertainty and limitations, a less expensive alternative can be adopted. If, on the other hand, there is a desire to minimize uncertainty and limitations, a more thorough and expensive program evaluation would be warranted.

In finalizing a budget and evaluation plan, it is sometimes advisable to prepare two or three versions of the program evaluation plan with a different budget for each. Each progressively more thorough version would show what could be done with more resources (including time). The multiple versions also show the additional benefits that each increment in resources adds.

Table 2.3 Organizing HR Program Evaluation Plans—An Example

Program Evaluation Objective	Information Needed and Source	Program Evaluation Methods and Analyses	Evaluation Concerns	What Can Be Said
What do we want to know?	What do we need to answer the question, and where can we find it?	How will we obtain and analyze the information?	What will limit the generalizability of the findings?	What can we say?
Desirable characteristics of the researchable questions: • Categorized as descriptive, normative, or impact • Clear and specific • Fair and objective • Politically neutral • Measurable • Doable Key terms defined in terms of • Scope • Time frame • Population	• External documents (for example, legal/regulatory, literature, and best practices) • Internal documents (for example, strategic plans, policies/procedures, budget, staffing, and program reports/briefings) • Data from electronic or paper personnel records • Reviews of processes (for example, from job analyses, and work diaries) • Perceptual data (for example, opin-	• Review of internal documents, literature, and environment • Content analysis (for example, categorize narrative survey responses) • Observations (for example, obtained in person, electronically, or mechanically) • Interviews (for example, in-person versus telephonic, structured versus unstructured, and individual versus group) • Contrast of perceptions and hard data	• Time • Money • Staffing of evaluation team (for example, number, internal/external, expertise, and organizational level) • Access to records and top management • Data limitations • Organizational politics	• Population values or population estimates (from samples) with specified precision levels • Cost and participant use of program • Prioritized list of potential areas of program improvement • Impact of the program or program changes • Relative advantages and disadvantage of various program options (keep program as is, modify, or replace) • Anecdotal informa-

tion to supplement harder data

from different stake-
holder groups
- Secondary analysis of previously col-
lected data
- Other types of data collection instruments (for example, surveys and data extraction forms for files)
- Quasi-experiments (comparison groups, pre-post test)
- Expert panels
- Simulations

ions and intents)
- Information on pro-
gram staff (number of staff, training, and experience)
- Other methods and sources such as those identified in our book

Note: This table is adapted from the U.S. Government Accountability Office's design matrix.

Better buy-in is obtained when stakeholders have a chance to help shape the evaluation by selecting the version that best fits the organization's needs. Also, the multiple versions present another benefit. The team has elevated the decision about accepting uncertainty and limitations to the key stakeholders who will be judging the quality of the HR program evaluation once the project is done. This precaution minimizes the potential end-of-evaluation second-guessing of why more was not done to minimize the uncertainty and limitations.

Conclusions

Effective planning is a necessary, but not sufficient condition for successful HR program evaluation. By developing a roadmap to their ultimate destination, the evaluation team can anticipate potential problems, minimize rework and other inefficiencies that can sidetrack the evaluation, and eliminate ambiguity about the roles that various team members will play. Furthermore, tasks, personnel, and other resources tied to a timeline let the team know immediately when slippage in the schedule is occurring so that corrective actions can be taken. Thoughtful planning brings the added benefit of convincing key stakeholders that the evaluation is in good hands and will, therefore, one hopes, lead to greater stakeholder buy-in to the entire evaluation process.

Suggested Resources

Edwards, J.E., Thomas, M.D., Rosenfeld, P., & Booth-Kewley, S.B. (1997). *How to conduct organizational surveys: A step-by-step guide*. Thousand Oaks, CA: Sage.

Prosavac, E.J., & Carey, R.G. (2003). *Program evaluation: Methods and case studies* (6th ed.). Englewood Cliffs, NJ: Prentice Hall.

Rossi, P.H., & Freeman, H.E. (1993). *Evaluation: A systematic approach* (5th ed.). Thousand Oaks, CA: Sage.

Phase 3

COLLECT DATA

"Errors using inadequate data are much less than
those using no data at all."

—*Charles Babbage*

Chapter Objectives

- Remind evaluators of the many data sources and data collection methods that are available so that they can make informed choices
- Provide a basic understanding of research design principles that will provide the evaluation team with a basis for balancing rigor and practical organizational considerations
- Describe steps that should be taken to enhance the quality of the collected information

For most HR program evaluations, data collection will require more time than any other phase in our six-phase approach. At the same time, data collection can be one of the most rewarding parts of the program evaluation. Evaluators have opportunities to interact with members located throughout the organization and develop a better appreciation of how the various parts of the organization fit together. Developing content knowledge of the HR program will also increase the evaluator's credibility. Assuming that these interactions go well, the evaluators can learn more about the HR program, understand the interdependency of various organizational units, and begin professional and personal relationships that will help them with future endeavors in the organization.

Our advice regarding tasks performed for this phase can be viewed as parts of four interrelated steps, with the activities in some steps occurring at the same time as the activities in other steps. The four steps are (a) selecting the appropriate data collection methods and data sources for evaluating an HR program, (b) using evaluation research designs that make sense in the context of practical organizational constraints, (c) enhancing data quality, and (d) avoiding sidetracks during data collection.

Select Optimum Data Collection Methods and Data Sources

As we mentioned in the planning phase, HR program evaluation teams are fortunate because many data collection methods and data sources are available to them. While some methods (for example, interviews) and sources (for example, extracts from personnel and payroll databases) may be used in almost every program evaluation, teams need to consider carefully *all* of their data options, rather than merely using only those methods and sources that were of value in prior data collection efforts. Different HR programs and different reasons for conducting an evaluation might mean that different methods and sources are needed to acquire the most relevant data possible, relative to time, money, and other organizational constraints.

When we were asked to develop and provide an HR program evaluation workshop for a professional society, we generated and distributed a list of HR-relevant data collection methods and data sources that participants found very useful. Table 3.1 expands on that list and classifies each method or source into five general categories. This list can be used to remind an experienced as well as inexperienced HR program evaluation team of both common and less common methods/sources. A sample application for each method/source is also provided in the table. This list might be made even more meaningful to

Table 3.1 Data Collection Methods and Data Sources
Used in HR Program Evaluation

Category and Type Data	Example Source or Use
1. Internal Documents and Files	
a. Program results and related data	Outcome of, time required to resolve, and demographic breakout for each discrimination complaint
b. Prior evaluation, accreditation, and licensure reports	Previously conducted selection system evaluation or study devoted partially/wholly to the program
c. Program policies, criteria, and procedures	HR policy manual with an outline of the steps and timeframes used to file a labor grievance
d. Program funding/ budgets	Five years of budget and expenditure data for 360-degree feedback (in case the two types of data disagree)
e. Cost information	Three alternative levels of investment (and resulting benefits) to upgrade the HR information system
f. Inventory records	Location, size, condition, and so forth of each chemical/biological suit available to incident responders
g. Staff positions (that is, spaces): Actual and planned	Filled and vacant positions on organizational charts during a re-alignment of functions after a merger
h. Qualifications of current program staff (that is, faces)	Resumes of training department staff to determine types of formal training, experience, and certification system
i. Archival data on organizational personnel system	Expatriate demographics extracted from paper personnel files or an electronic HR information
j. Lists of program participants	Roster of people who received a one-week managerial training course
k. Strategic and tactical plans (organization-wide and HR-specific)	Statement that the organization wants to be the industry leader in employee safety

Table 3.1   continued

Category and Type Data	Example Source or Use
2. Internal and External Perceptual Data	
a. Individual interviews (structured or unstructured)	Former participants' identification of strengths and weakness in the executive development program
b. Group interviews (focus, Delphi, or nominal)	Focus groups to determine ways to get more people to use the 401(k) program
c. Expert panels (internal or external)	Information gained from a multidisciplinary team so that the diversity profile can be improved
d. Organizational surveys (paper, fax, or web)	Annual organizational climate assessments and exit surveys to learn more about retention problems
3. Internal Processes and Procedural Information	
a. Job analysis data	Job-relevant person characteristics used to design a test battery for selecting first-line managers
b. Time-motion studies	Determination of staffing needs to "right-size" the Sales Department
c. Process analysis information	Examination of activities performed in a typical day to see whether team orientation has been implemented
d. Observations (in-person, video, or electronic)	Quality of customer support: sample, record, and rate service calls
e. Work diaries or logs	Overlap of functions when re-engineering the management succession program
f. Needs assessment findings	Training documents identifying course topics to close gaps between desired and existing skill levels
g. Equipment and training manuals	Determination of whether organizational members are following prescribed safety procedures
h. Communication diagrams	Pictorial representation of whom staff contact during a typical week—used to redesign the workplace
4. External Documents and Environmental Scans	
a. Legal and regulatory materials	International, federal, state, and local compensation laws applicable to a multinational corporation

Category and Type Data	Example Source or Use
b. External literature on the subject HR programs	Meta-analysis or a narrative review on pay equity—obtained from journal articles, books, and the web
c. Best practices	Association and consortia ethical guidelines for ensuring survey confidentiality

5. Other Types of Evaluation Data

a. Tests of job knowledge, skills, and performance	Certification/license (for example, CPA or realtor) and job-sample tests (for example, for welding, typing, or driving)
b. Simulations of job knowledge, skills, and aptitudes	Assessment centers for fast tracking managers, or proficiency testing on a flight simulator
c. Models, scenarios, and forecasts	Projections and assumptions for the organization's future healthcare costs as the workforce ages
d. Recommendation systems	Recommended changes to realign work centers—made through quality circles or suggestion boxes

Adapted from Scott, Edwards, & Raju (2002).

and generate even more discussion from an evaluation team if the more experienced evaluators on the team (a) provide organization-specific examples about how the methods and sources apply to the specific HR program being evaluated and (b) add additional methods and sources that are relevant to that organization.

The rest of this section introduces readers to general aspects of the five categories of data collection methods and data sources. Entire books have been written on the methods and sources that we are covering, and we would encourage evaluators to consult such sources when applying any methods that may be unfamiliar or have not been used for some time by the evaluation team. Such independent study would prepare evaluators to (a) begin the process of acquiring more program evaluation skills and (b) interact more effectively with other team members who are using the described data collection methods and accessing the cited data sources.

Use Internal Documents and Files—Current and Historical

An organization has a wide variety of internal documents and files that tell how the HR program fits into the organization as a whole. The team will need time to assemble these materials and determine their relevance to the evaluation. While it is not uncommon for some of the materials to be out-of-date, the evaluation team—probably with the help of the HR program staff—will often find it easier to update information than to create such documentation from scratch. Two common reasons for the materials being out-of-date are (a) inattention to evolutionary changes in the HR program and (b) competing pressures that limit the time that program staff have available for updating documents and files.

Although a review of internal documents and files can be time-consuming, an initial review of these materials is essential in order to gain sufficient context or background on the HR program before proceeding with other data collection steps. In addition to making the evaluation team better informed about the HR program, this review can increase the team's efficiency when using more intrusive data collection methods (for example, interviews and surveys). The evaluators still must confirm what appears to be true in order to avoid making erroneous assumptions, but they can do this review more quickly than they can gather other types of data from scratch. Also, using existing documents and files to learn about the basics of a program will aid the data collectors in establishing their credibility with the stakeholders when they are later asked to provide data.

The types of current and historical files and materials that may be accessed include technical documentation outlining the program's original development and implementation, data or documentation outlining program results for one or more periods in the past, prior evaluation and accreditation reports, program policies and procedures, program funding/budgets, qualifications of the program staff, archival data on organizational personnel, lists of program participants, and strategic and tactical plans for the program and the organization.

While much of this information does not require specialized skills to collect or interpret it, it is nonetheless extremely useful in the evaluation. Among other things, the information provides an evaluation team with baseline knowledge about the HR program. In addition, it can be used to determine the factors that influence the effectiveness and efficiency of an HR program or an entire organizational function such as safety.

Gather Internal and External Perceptual Data

Organization members' and external program users' perceptions can help an evaluation team identify and understand an HR program's strengths, weaknesses, and other key attributes. It then becomes a responsibilty for evaluators to determine whether those perceptions have merit. Often, a perception (for example, of racial discrimination or favoritism)—regardless of its veracity—is a compelling force within and outside an organization. The program evaluation team therefore needs to determine, through the use of appropriate research methods and empirical data, the prevalence and accuracy of these perceptions, possible reasons for any misperceptions (perhaps as a first step in correcting the misperceptions), and the impact of the perceptions on the HR program as well as on the organization. Looking for the convergence of perceptions with other types of data such as those available from personnel records (for example, performance data that reveal significantly higher ratings for males) can help the evaluation team to confirm or refute the perceptions and thereby strengthen the quality of their evaluation's findings, conclusions, and recommendations.

Most, if not all, of the perceptual data will be collected specifically for the current program evaluation, but useful perceptions may also be available from prior data collection efforts. The gathering of new data will permit an up-to-date snapshot of the current situation, whereas the data from prior surveys and other methods can let the evaluation team see how perceptions have changed over time. In addition, the current snapshot of perceptions can be more comprehensive than the information from the past efforts because it can be tailored to the specific researchable questions or objectives being investigated in the current HR program evaluation. As a cautionary note, HR program evaluation teams must realize that even small changes in the wording of interview and survey questions can cause results to appear to be different, regardless of whether the situation itself has changed. Therefore, teams must consider which is most important: using the previous wording to get clean comparisons to findings from the past or altering questions to obtain the best, most-focused answer to issues at hand.

Table 3.1 lists four general types of methods for gathering perceptual data: individual interviews, group interviews, expert panels, and surveys. Individual interviews seem to be a part of every HR program evaluation. When the same issues will be discussed with multiple individual interviewees, evaluators would be well-served by using at least a semi-structured protocol so that (a) all interviewers ask the same core set of questions in the same general manner and (b) the answers can be tallied later to add a degree of quantification to this typically qualitative data collection method. Likewise, the facilitator of a group interview—be it a discussion, focus, expert panel, nominal, Delphi, or other type of group—should use a core set of questions and probes to gain advantages similar to those for the individual interviews. While group interview methods can be used to capture both the information from several participants simultaneously and the synergistic effect of the participants' interactions, evaluation teams might want to refrain from using these methods in situations in which sensitive information is to be discussed. Participants will probably be especially reticent to reveal sensitive information about themselves or others in group settings. Expert panels, a different type of group interview, are particularly useful in identifying perceptions that would be needed to answer process questions (for example, subject-matter experts in job analysis).

Organizational surveys offer a method for collecting information from a large number of people, quantifying perceptions and other data, and determining how perceptions are related to other self-reported information gathered with the survey. While a survey of a population or representative sample might readily come to mind, surveys may also be useful when administered at the beginning of a group interview composed of participants picked with purposeful sampling. Using surveys with focus groups allows evaluators to obtain both qualitative and quantitative data in a single data collection session. Books (for example, Edwards and his co-authors, 1997) tailored to conducting HR surveys offer HR evaluators better insights into the situations that they will face than will literature devoted to survey methods used in marketing and political polling. Similarly, if the team contracts for external survey development, administration, or analysis, we suggest they use consultants specializing in HR-related surveys.

Assess Internal Processes and Procedural Information

The data collection methods and data sources in this category are of eight general but overlapping types: job analyses, time-motion studies, process analysis information, observations, work diaries or logs, needs assessment findings, equipment and training manuals, and communication diagrams. Individuals trained or experienced in job analysis may have used all of these methods and sources while gathering data on the processes and procedures that job incumbents use to carry out their work-related activities.

This set of methods and sources is particularly important in answering evaluation questions that require information about the steps that (a) users take when accessing and using the program and (b) program staff perform to administer, monitor, and improve an HR program. For example, program staff may have a flowchart of the general steps—as well as the range or maximum amount of time required to perform each step—that users and program staff should take when adding new dependents to the organization's health plan. This set of methods and sources can also provide information about worker characteristics (for example, knowledge, skills, and abilities), environmental conditions (for example, extreme cold or noise), physical demands (for example, strength or particular activities such as climb-ing), training and time required to acquire knowledge, decision-making responsibilities, and other job-relevant characteristics. Some of these types of information can be useful for other program evalua-tion tasks such as assessing the qualifications of the staff administering the program, quality of staff recruitment, or compensation equity.

Out-of-date or incomplete information about processes and the time required for different job tasks can greatly slow the progress of a program evaluation designed to look at staffing, organizational re-engineering, or related HR issues. A related problem is occasionally found in decentralized organizations when the processes documented in the HR files at the headquarters may not reflect how an HR pro-gram is actually used or administered in the field.

In still other situations, general guidelines may be provided, but wide discretion in program processes and procedures would be al-lowed in different functional areas of the organization. For example, the general parameters for administering a compensation program may be documented for the organization in a central HR file, but in-dividual divisions may be allowed to determine their specific com-pensation criteria and otherwise administer their merit-based salary increases and bonuses. This possibility of differences in processes then requires an assessment to determine whether and how the HR program varies within the organization, as well as a comparison of the strengths and weaknesses of the various types of implementation. Sometimes, the information that results from comparisons of these implementation processes and procedures can be used as the bases for developing best practices for an organization-wide HR program.

Overviews for using these methods to describe processes and in-terpreting the resulting data are available from books on job analy-ses (for example, see Chen, Carsten, & Krauss, [2003] for suggested sources). Many of the skills that are necessary for gathering new, in-depth information on internal processes are specialized. Therefore, the evaluation team might need to supplement its membership with individuals who have expertise with these specialized methods.

Utilize External Documents and Environmental Scans

The review and inclusion of external documents such as legal and regulatory materials, external literature, and best practices from other organizations provide valuable sources of independent criteria and performance standards against which the HR program can be evaluated. External data are important for placing the HR program in context. In addition, they can help the team to identify or develop the criteria, which will be used in its own evaluation. Comparisons to external data and standards lend credibility to the evaluation, and they pique the interest and buy-in of stakeholders, who generally want to know how their program stacks up against the programs for other organizations in the industry. If external statistics (for example, nationwide or industry-wide average compensation for top managers) or standards (for example, minimum qualifications for licensure) for the criteria are available, top management will be in a position to decide whether the HR program will be an industry leader, on par with the industry, or a program with deficiencies relative to the same program in other organizations.

In Phase 1, we mentioned the need for assessments against legal standards when we urged the HR program evaluation team to include an organization's legal representative as a stakeholder. The attorney's review and interpretation of relevant legal or regulatory issues are essential to ensure that the HR program conforms to all applicable laws and regulations. Overlapping local, state, national, and international laws and regulations establish a minimum set of HR-related conditions that an organization must meet to avoid adverse legal consequences. Legal minimum standards exist for such HR concerns as safety standards, compensation, hours of work, equal employment opportunities, job security for military reservists, and protection of retirement accounts. While organizations may wish to offer more than the minimum, HR evaluation teams need to ensure that the program at least meets the minimum prescribed levels.

If the evaluation identifies and eliminates sources of potential legal challenges, it will almost surely have paid for itself—even for those challenges that the organization could have won—through the avoidance of legal fees and settlement costs.

Additional guidance for understanding the HR-related legal considerations can be found in books (for example, Landy, 2005) devoted specifically to those issues.

Another valuable source of external information is HR literature: books, professional publications (journals and pamphlets), conference presentations, materials distributed by professional consortium and trade associations, web searches, and other readily available materials. With due caution, a team can identify empirically based external HR literature that will be useful in selecting and defining criteria, picking expert panels, and performing the other tasks necessary to conduct an HR program evaluation. An evaluation team will be particularly well-served if it can find a meta-analysis addressing aspects of the HR program being evaluated. A meta-analysis is a literature review technique that statistically combines findings from many studies. Meta-analytic findings have the advantages of both quantification and the avoidance of over-reliance on findings from a single study.

Best practices provide data for interpreting the quality of the organization's HR program relative to that found in other organizations. Organizations such as the Conference Board and the Saratoga Institute regularly conduct best-practices reviews that can be used as a component of an HR program evaluation. In a recent evaluation conducted to assess the effectiveness of an organizational structure within a large pharmaceutical organization, a best-practices review that had been conducted by the Conference Board served as an effective starting point for the evaluation. In a similar vein, magazines (for example, *Fortune*) and books appearing in the popular press regularly pick organizations that are top ranked overall or for selected programs. An evaluation team should guard against inappropriately generalizing from overall rankings by assuming that the practices of the highly ranked organizations are likewise among the best for the HR program of interest. If an evaluation team chooses to use best practices as the standard against which to judge an organization's HR program, it is imperative that due consideration be given to potential differences between the evaluated organization and the organizations identified for best practices. Contextual differences outside the control of the HR program itself may have contributed to why other organizations are judged as having best practices. These contextual factors might include the organizations' size, profitability, philosophy, industry, and geographic location.

Don't Forget Other Types of Evaluation Data

A variety of other evaluation methods can be used to assess the functioning of HR programs. Foremost among these are tests, simulations, models/scenarios/forecasts, and recommendation systems.

Tests can play important roles when evaluating recruitment and selection, workforce quality, succession planning, and training-acquisition programs. Following the popular dictum that "You can't manage what you don't measure," an organization that utilizes tests for its staffing and development programs will be better positioned to evaluate the quality of its programs, relative to organizations that use less quantifiable methods. Data from tests can be used to evaluate applicant trends, including the effectiveness of recruitment programs, the quality of new hires, and the effects of training or other interventions, to name a few. Tests provide objective criteria against which to measure HR programs. Some common types of tests that evaluators may find useful in their review include:

- *Job knowledge tests.* These types of tests can be particularly useful in evaluating the impact of technical training and recruitment programs and are designed to tap the critical knowledge areas needed to be successful upon entry into a particular job. Generally, these tests are developed and applied to more technically oriented jobs. For example, an electrical knowledge test that assesses the fundamentals of electricity, basic circuitry, electrical code, and equipment might be used for hiring network technicians for a telecommunications company.

- *Skills tests.* These tests are particularly useful in evaluating training interventions geared toward the development of basic skills for incumbents. Unlike aptitude tests that are generally considered stable over time, the results of skills tests can be expected to change based on interventions or experience. They are designed to tap skills needed to be successful in a variety of positions. For example, a word processing test may be applied to secretarial candidates, or a writing test may be administered to applicants for corporate communications jobs. Basic skills tests that measure minimum levels of reading and math may also be useful gauges of workforce quality.

- *Aptitude tests.* These tests can be developed to cover a range of capabilites needed for a variety of jobs within an organization, from mechanical and clerical occupations through executive-level positions. They are particularly useful in evaluating recruitment, selection, and succession-planning programs. Examples of the sorts of aptitudes measured by these tests include problem solving, detail orientation, business reasoning, mechanical comprehension, troubleshooting, and critical thinking.

- *Performance simulations.* These tests are useful in evaluating selection and training programs for hourly through executive positions. Tests that measure abilities by simulating a key element of the job are very effective means of screening candidates for complex or physically demanding or dangerous jobs. For example, the airlines and military use simulations to train and test their pilots' skills at handling a wide variety of dangerous conditions that might seldom be encountered in real life. In other types of simulation tests, executive candidates may be placed in an assessment center situation with a group of other candidates and evaluated on their abilities to interact and lead. In contrast, line-worker candidates for a utility company may be asked to climb a pole and do some electrical work on an elevated platform as part of their assessment.

Models, scenarios, and forecasts (with explicit assumptions) fill important niches for such issues as large-scale organizational expansion, downsizing, or mergers. These types of infrequent changes present situations in which top management must consider different scenarios about how the restructuring will influence the size and shape of the workforce. By modeling different sets of assumptions, top management (a) is able to make better-informed decisions and (b) has a basis for reacting quickly if the chosen decision does not meet the assumptions. Love (1991), however, cautioned that "forecasting is difficult under the best of circumstances" because of four endemic problems: inadequate skills of evaluators making the forecasts, inaccurate historical data, incorrect assumptions, and biased data.

Information from recommendation programs (for example, a suggestion box) and other organizational feedback mechanisms may be additional sources of data for identifying deficiencies in the current HR program and alternatives for improving the program. These types of data can provide insights into problems previously encountered with the HR program, program staff interactions with users, and steps taken to resolve problems and emphasize the strengths of the program.

Use Evaluation Research Designs That Address Practical Constraints

The complex environments found in applied organizations rarely afford opportunities to use true experiments, since experiments require random assignment of organizational members to experimental/treatment and control groups. Instead, evaluators often use quasi-experimental designs to ameliorate the effects of these real-life constraints (see Shadish, Cook, & Campbell, 2002). Quasi-experimental designs compare characteristics of existing organizational subgroups (a) to one another and/or (b) at different points in time. For example, attitude survey results obtained before and after implementing a downsizing program in one organizational division could provide valuable information to management. In this example, employees would not have been assigned at random to the division experiencing downsizing or to a comparison division that did not go through downsizing.

A disadvantage of using a quasi-experimental design, rather than a true experiment with a randomized design, is that evaluators are often faced with uncertainty about what caused an outcome. They must determine which factors besides the program or intervention might have influenced the observed levels of the criterion measures used to assess program effectiveness. In the downsizing example, changes in employee attitudes such as increased dissatisfaction with management from last year to this year could be due to the downsizing or other factors such as the organization's overall economic health. After identifying the possible influences, the evaluation team must attempt to assess whether the program or external influences were largely responsible for any subsequent changes in the efficiency and effectiveness of the HR program. By understanding prior and recent situations along with potential alternative explanations for any differences or even similarities, the HR program evaluation team may be able to work toward at least tenuous cause-and-effect conclusions. The attribution of cause and effect is somewhat tenuous because the evaluation team typically cannot perform an evaluation with the laboratory-like experimental precision needed for definitive cause-and-effect conclusions.

HR program evaluation often involves using one of four types of quasi-experimental designs: subgroup comparisons, before-and-after comparisons, time-series designs, and case studies. They are briefly described below, and Table 3.2 offers an overview of the first three designs.

Table 3.2 Examples of Quasi-Experimental Designs

Name of Design	Notation			Comments
Subgroup comparison				Only the experimental group will be the subject of the intended intervention/HR program, but both groups will be assessed before and after the intervention. The time period between observations depends on the type of intervention involved. The difference between the post- and pre-intervention measures can be compared across the two groups to assess the effectiveness of the intervention. One might also use the pre-intervention measure as a covariate in assessing the post-intervention measures between the two groups.
Experimental group	O	X	O	
Comparison group	O		O	
Before-and-after comparison				Only the experimental group will be assessed before and after the intervention, and it will serve as its own "control" group, that is, there is no comparison group. The difference between the post- and pre-intervention measures would be used to assess the effect of a given intervention.
Experimental group	O	X	O	
Comparison group (none)				
Time-series design				This is an expanded version of the before-and-after comparison design. For example, assessments can be conducted annually or semi-annually. Again, the experimental group will serve as its own "control" group.
Experimental group	O O O X O O O			
Comparison group (none)				

Note: O = observation or assessment and X = intervention

Subgroup Comparisons

A subgroup comparison generally involves using pre-existing groups of non-randomly assigned employees in experimental and comparison conditions. The performance of the experimental group after it has received an intervention (such as a training seminar for new managers that the organization is pilot-testing) is compared with the performance of another group that has not received the intervention. This design is also referred to as the nonequivalent control group design.

While the assignment of employees to subgroups is not random in this design, it is important that the employees belonging to the two groups have similar characteristics, such as tenure and job duties, to minimize the possibly that such extraneous characteristics will influence the findings in subsequent analyses. Again using the example of training for new managers, employees in both the change and comparison groups must be new managers in order for the analysis of the post-training performance levels for the two groups to be meaningful. It should be noted, however, that any significant performance difference between the two groups may not be entirely due to the intervention (that is, training). Other factors such as the mere inclusion of employees in a group that participates in a special program can result in changes in outcome measures. Such changes, regardless of whether the intervention has any true effect, have long been documented with organizational studies and are often referred to as Hawthorne effects.

Before-and-After Comparisons

Another quasi-experimental design commonly used in HR program evaluation is sometimes referred to as either a before-and-after design or a pretest-posttest design. It is given this name because criterion measures (for example, attitudes or performance) for the same group are compared before and after an intervention. In a design of this type, the same group serves as its own comparison group. For example, an assessment of employees' satisfaction with their benefit program before and after the introduction of a new health benefits package falls into this category. Again, by not having random assignment and a separate control group, an HR evaluation team would not be able to attribute all changes in attitudes to the introduction of a new health benefits package. Among other things, changes in the outcome measures could have resulted from other factors that changed during the period between the first and second data collections.

Another problem that can result when using this type of design—as well as with the time-series designs that are presented next—is the addition and loss of personnel during the time periods of interest. Anyone who is subsequently added to the unit that received the intervention will not have the pretest measure, and anyone who leaves before the second data collection occurs will not have the requisite posttest scores. The numbers of usable people who have both types of data will probably continue to decrease as time goes by, until the sample size is not sufficient to draw any useful conclusions. Even if there is a sufficient number of employees with both the pretest and posttest data, attrition should still be examined to determine whether it offers alternative explanations for the findings. The interpretation of the findings may be different if individuals left the study for positive reasons such as a promotion versus negative reasons such as turnover from the organization and demotion because of performance-related problems.

HR program evaluation teams also sometimes use a more problematic variation of the pretest-posttest design. They collect data only once, asking employees to report their perceptions or opinions about issues of interest for both current and past periods. Although this type of data collection has the advantage of obtaining both types of data from everyone who has been there for the specified period, it really is not a true pretest-posttest design and leads to more tenuous conclusions than does the actual pretest-posttest design. While some employees may be able to indicate accurately whether they experienced a major event such as a work-related injury two years ago, they may not be able to provide reliable assessments of their attitudes or other information for periods even six months earlier. Also, the attrition that occurred between the prior and current periods can result in a biased view about the issues of interest because the evaluators will have little or no information on those who left before the data were gathered.

Time-Series Designs

Another variation of the before-and-after quasi-experimental design is the time-series design. For the time-series design, data for the same criterion measures are gathered at several (equally spaced) time periods before and after the HR intervention. Because of the many time periods (sometimes spanning years) involved in such a design, the employees making up a subgroup may not remain the same from one time period to the next. That is, this year's employees at an organization will probably not be the same as last year's employees at the organization. Thus, the change in organizational or subgroup membership makes it more difficult to attribute all changes in levels of the criterion measures to a given HR intervention. On the other hand, since measurements are available for several time periods before and after the HR intervention, the time-series design may offer a more accurate assessment than the before-and-after design.

Compared to the before-and-after design, the time-series design has an important benefit—the ability to make statements about trends. A relatively higher or lower value at a single subsequent point could be due to the characteristics of the sample being studied, a temporary change that will revert to the prior level, or any number of other influences. Including additional later time-based data points allows the evaluation team to determine whether an earlier increase or decrease was an artifact or a real change that showed consistency over multiple time periods.

Because a time-series design involves multiple observations before and after an organizational intervention, it may take longer to complete an HR evaluation. The longer length is unlikely to be an option if historical data cannot be used to develop the database for earlier intervals or if the time interval between observations is substantial. The time interval may depend on the nature and content of the evaluation. If the time interval between observations is long and the evaluation itself necessitates multiple observations, the evaluation team may want to issue interim reports so that top management can be kept abreast of the evaluation team's progress on a regular basis. These procedural and timeline details must be addressed and planned for as part of the initial planning for the HR evaluation.

Case Studies

The use of case studies in HR program evaluation typically involves a more in-depth, narrower focus than that which might be used for other types of program evaluation. For example, to limit the scope of their assessment to a doable project, an evaluation team might determine that it would be more useful to look at all aspects of management succession planning in a single division rather than fewer issues across the entire organization. Case studies are useful when studying a program that is differentially effective across the organization. They are very useful when evaluating infrequently occurring behaviors (for example, violence in the workplace) and HR programs that are limited to certain units. Often, an HR evaluation team uses purposeful sampling to pick examples of good and/or poorly functioning organizational units or parts of an HR program. For example, an evaluation team might contrast the selection system as it is implemented in an eastern regional office to that implemented in its southern region if the eastern and southern regions had the best and worst rates of career progression.

According to evaluation experts (see Patton, 1990), a case study typically involves three major steps. In the first step, the evaluator collects as much relevant information as possible about a program or person. Both qualitative and quantitative data are part of this step. In step two, the collected raw data are edited, organized, and classified.

In the final step, the evaluation team prepares a readable and holistic narrative of a program or person under consideration.

Although there are many manifestations of the case study, one common case study method is preparing lessons-learned reports. The U.S. military makes extensive use of this type of case study after large-scale training exercises, war games, and actual military interventions. A lessons-learned report is also relevant to HR program evaluation. A lessons-learned report might address several aspects of the program: the environment, actions taken, the effects and effectiveness of the actions, and potential actions to be considered if a similar situation were to occur in the future. A downsizing program can be used to illustrate the types of data that such an HR report would contain. The report might note environmental and organizational factors that led to the downsizing, the alternative actions considered and why those actions were used or not used, effects (for example, lawsuits by dismissed and demoted employees as well as the morale of survivors), and additional factors to be considered if the organization were faced with the same problem again. Regardless of the type of program being studied, a potentially serious drawback from using case studies is that there can be great uncertainty about external validity, that is, how well the results from one portion of the organization—sometimes chosen for study because it *is* different—generalize to the remainder of the organization.

"It is essential that quality control procedures be introduced for all facets of data collection: sampling, measurement, data entry, and the like. . . . And, before diving into a fancy statistical analysis, it is essential to carefully inspect the data for errors and missing information that will almost certainly be present. Addressing these data quality concerns requires more than merely searching for isolated outliers; it also necessitates internal consistency checks for anomalous relationships among key variables" (Berk & Rossi, 1990, p. 99).

Enhance Data Quality During Data Collection

Although Berk and Rossi wrote this passage about conducting research on the effects of social policies (for example, air pollution regulations and sentencing of criminals), their sentiments are equally true for HR program evaluation. Using data without adequate concern for the quality of the information can lead to the proverbial case of "trash in, trash out." Without taking steps to maximize data quality, the evaluation team will be left with much uncertainty regarding the faith that can be put in their findings, conclusions, and recommendations.

Evaluation teams can take multiple actions to enhance data quality. All the actions share three requirements: (a) a solid alignment with the evaluation plan, (b) ability to follow standardized data collection procedures, and (c) focused attention on all details of the data collection. Feeling time pressures and an eagerness to start on the data collection are factors that can work against good data collection. Solid planning before the actual data collection minimizes rework and the need for additional data collection. Figure 3.1 summarizes seven key quality control actions than can enhance data collection efforts. Each of the activities will be covered separately in this section.

Check for Potential Vested Interests or Biases

Evaluators may bring vested interests or biases to their data collection tasks. As we showed in Phase 1 (see Table 2.1), some types of evaluators may be more susceptible to certain kinds of vested interests or biases than are other types of evaluators. For instance, it may be unwise to use regular program staff as interviewers when assessing satisfaction with an HR program. The understandable desire to show how well the HR program is functioning could result in an unconscious or even a conscious coloring of findings. In his discussion of internal evaluator integrity, Sonnichsen (2000) noted that it is important for evaluators to be viewed as being honest and fair, balancing positive and negative points, and providing information in accurate and non-inflammatory

Figure 3.1 Quality Control Actions to Enhance Data Collection

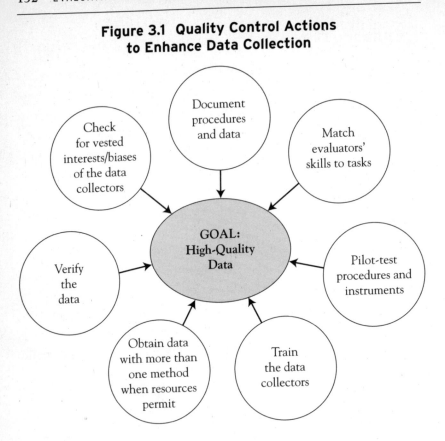

language. Conversely, external consultants could have a vested interest in showing that a program was not functioning optimally if they had a particular bias for a certain approach that they are more familiar with or one that they have implemented in other settings.

Other potential vested interests/biases may be less easy to anticipate or detect, but no less harmful to the quality of the evaluation. Therefore, vigilance by the evaluation team leader and team members is key. The vigilance should start by having a discussion of potential vested interests/biases in one of the early meetings of the evaluation team. In general, team members should feel neutral about whether a particular aspect of the evaluation will show the program in a positive or negative light. While this may not always be possible, the team should focus on how their assumptions, decisions, methods, and other aspects of their evaluation can be adequately defended to partisan stakeholders. Often, there will be at least one key stakeholder or subgroup that likes a particular finding and others that dislike the same finding.

Document Procedures and Data

A hallmark of good research is documentation. Documentation throughout the program evaluation—rather than once when the evaluation has been completed—is essential. Details are easily forgotten as time passes, but those details can yield important clues to resolving contradictory and unexpected findings. For example, an evaluator may read the documentation for one type of procedure and recognize that someone else used a different procedure or asked a question in a slightly, but meaningfully, different way. Bourque and Clark (1992) outlined a checklist of nine key points that should be documented: sample design, data collection instrument, data collection training and procedures, coding of data, data entry for computerized files, data processing that precedes analysis, frequency distributions for all study variables, archives of data files, and after data processing and analysis are finished.

Documentation is also important for future program evaluators because the program will likely be evaluated again. If so, the documentation can provide the future team with a head start for completing the next evaluation. Also, it is not uncommon for stakeholders to raise questions about the program long after the evaluation has been completed. Frequently, documentation and data from the earlier evaluation can be used to answer such questions without requiring added data collection.

Part of the documentation will consist of little more than collecting paper or electronic copies of materials such as surveys, structured interview protocols, data extraction forms, materials used to train data collectors and coders, and databases with the statistics programs used to analyze them. Other documentation could include lessons-learned notes from some of the data collection and analyses that did not progress as expected and were not part of the findings presented to stakeholders. Care needs to be exercised when documenting the data. If confidentiality has been promised to data providers, steps may need to be taken to destroy original documents and to keep the electronic versions stored with password protection and separately from other types of documentation.

Match Evaluators' Skill Sets to Types of Assignments

The lists of previously reviewed data collection methods and data sources as well as design considerations should suggest why it is important for an evaluation team to have members with diverse skills. Moreover, there is little likelihood that any one evaluator will be proficient with all the data collection methods and data sources. Therefore, during the first and second stages of our approach, the team leader, possibly in consultation with an HR staff member and/or an outside consultant, should have reviewed the major tasks and assignments for the evaluation team and determined whether the team had the requisite skills. Such planning could have examined to whom each task was assigned and grouped the tasks into major categories such as clerical tasks, personal interviewing and survey administration, observing and recording observations, and other assignments.

Determine Whether Clerical Assistance Should Be Obtained Outside the Evaluation Team.   Many data collection activities involve clerical tasks. These tasks include making copies (for example, of interview protocols or records), entering information (for example, from a paper-and-pencil survey) into a newly created electronic database, abstracting simple information verbatim from existing records or databases, filing, managing program evaluation materials according to a scheme developed by the evaluation team, and making some follow-up appeals when information is not submitted in a timely manner.

The evaluation team may rely on various types of personnel to complete clerical tasks. Although many organizations have greatly reduced the size of their clerical workforce, organizations with clerical or similar types of administrative support might be able to supply staff to supplement the evaluation team's efforts occasionally. This step can limit some costs of the evaluation by using lower-paid employees who may also have the specialized skills to perform the clerical task more efficiently. Contracted staff who are hired through temporary agencies are another potential source of relevant skills when a task involves doing the same clerical action (for example, entering survey responses) a large number of times or performing intensive typing (for example, transcribing audiotapes). In other situations, the HR program evaluation team may determine that its own members should perform the tasks for reasons that include efficiency (for example, contracting for the services would not be timely or efficient) and confidentiality (for example, the information that would be handled contains proprietary or sensitive data that should not be shared outside the organization).

Inventory All Interviewing, Survey, and Observation Tasks as Part of the Assignment Process. Many HR evaluations include conducting some combination of interviews, surveys, and focus groups. Some of these tasks may require specialized skills and others may not. Whatever the level of expertise needed, it is important that the evaluation team carefully identify and itemize all data collection tasks that require specialized skills.

Evaluation team members who meet with top management stakeholders or facilitate focus groups will need to have well-developed communication and relationship-building skills as well as a solid understanding of organizational dynamics. Poorly conducted interviews and focus group sessions can result in inappropriate or insufficient data for evaluating the HR program and might later result in questions about the credibility of the findings, conclusions, and recommendations. If surveys are to be developed and administered, it will be necessary to include someone on the evaluation team who has experience constructing survey items and who is versed in sampling techniques and data analysis. Most of us have probably had co-workers tell us that they are survey experts. Further discussion of the basis for their self-assessment might have revealed that they had previously thrown a few questions onto a piece of paper and had people answer the questions. Survey development and administration are much more complicated than that and require specialized skills if they are to yield meaningful, defensible findings. Finally, accurate observation skills and possibly well-constructed checklists are particularly needed when addressing research questions that require updating or developing new information on the processes used in an HR program. Most team members should be able to acquire the relevant observational skills if they are provided sufficient training.

In addition to assigning specific evaluation team members to these tasks, it is important that the team assign a quality control role to one or more members to check the content of all materials (for example, interview protocols and surveys) and ensure that the procedures used to collect the data are likely to produce reliable and accurate results. All materials used for the evaluation should be of high professional quality, and their content should optimally reflect the goals of the evaluation. Also, this team member can help monitor the materials developed by team members for needless duplication in the data collection efforts and nuanced differences in question phrasing that could lead to contradictory findings (caused by the phrasing rather than real differences).

Identify Other Skills Required in the Data Collection.   Other skills needed to ensure efficient data collection will vary depending on the nature of the evaluation and the particular questions to be answered. Some typical skills required for collecting HR program evaluation data include library research skills for literature reviews, proficiency in identifying best practices, ability to organize diverse sets of documentation, experience in designing coding schemes to help quantify data that are in narrative form, project management skills to ensure that the data are collected using appropriate methods and according to an established timeline, familiarity with web-based data collection technologies, and ability to build networks within the organization to support the collection of data (especially when the data collection might be considered intrusive or burdensome).

If the evaluation team leader finds that evaluation team members do not possess the requisite skills at the desired levels, alternative actions can be explored. These actions include adding other staff to the team on a full- or part-time basis, delaying certain data collection to give someone on the team time to develop the needed skill, changing the roles of team members so that someone with the needed skills can be moved from another data collection task, or replacing the data collection method with a different method for acquiring the same information.

Pilot-Test Procedures and Instruments

When the evaluators are satisfied that the procedures and instruments are ready to use, but before they start the actual data collection, procedures and instruments should be pilot-tested to see whether they work as designed. Some evaluators may think of pilot-testing as something that is done with surveys only, but it is a useful process for other types of data collection instruments such as data extraction forms, structured interviews, and work diaries. A pilot-test can reveal whether or not (a) instructions are understood and can be followed as intended, (b) people supplying or extracting data understand the questions and have a full range of response alternatives from which to choose, (c) the questions adequately capture the information sought by the evaluator, and (d) the wording or language is not offensive to members of ethnic, racial, gender, and other subgroups.

Up-front efforts to pilot-test instruments can save enormous amounts of time later, as well as minimize the chances of ambiguous findings. Pilot-testing the instruments is not a luxury, but instead an essential component of any successful data collection strategy. Therefore, this step should not be skipped, even if time demands would seem to warrant it.

The sample for pilot-testing can be small, as long as it represents the intended users. Members of the evaluation team can be part of the pilot-testing sample provided the pilot-test is not limited to the evaluation team and the members are not the developers of the procedures and instruments being tested. Also, subject-matter experts such as program administrators might be used as an expert panel to review the materials to see whether they accurately address the HR program and its procedures.

Train the Data Collectors

Sufficient time must be allocated to train the evaluators who will be interviewing, coding data, and using other data collection methods. For example, interviewer training might include sharpening interviewing skills by incorporating activities such as practicing appropriate speech patterns, avoiding certain types of behaviors (for example, nods) that can unconsciously reinforce or discourage participants from giving honest information, learning probing skills and feedback-seeking strategies, and reducing potential interview-related errors (for example, recording primarily the positive or negative points in an interview) through better self-monitoring. Regardless of how simple or obvious a data collection task seems, it is advisable to train data collectors. Because evaluators bring different experiences and talents to the various data collection tasks, it is to be expected that they might put different emphases and interpretations on the situations and information.

For large-scale program evaluations, the evaluation team should ideally have at least two appropriately trained members involved in each data collection task. This increases the likelihood that the findings can be replicated, irrespective of who is using the data collection technique. This approach reduces concerns that a single member of the team (possibly with a subconscious idea of what the data are going to show) will sway the findings for a major portion of the evaluation.

To achieve the maximum benefits from the training, the training sessions should include performing the actual data tasks. For example, if the data collection task involves extracting data from person-nel files, the training should include:

- Reviewing the instructions that tell how to code each piece of extracted information,

- Walking trainees through a file to show where to find the data and how to code the information,

- Having trainees code a sample of practice files that have already been coded by experts,

- Reviewing the coding for the practice files and providing corrective feedback to the coders, and

- Continuing the coding and feedback on additional practice files until the data extractors/coders attain a high level of accuracy and consistency.

As part of a recent evaluation designed to determine whether the performance-appraisal comments written by managers were biased against females, five trainee data collectors were asked to read ten cases and evaluate the bias in each case with a pre-established coding scheme. After the trainees evaluated the first two appraisals, the facilitator and trainees identified and discussed differences in how the trainees coded these cases. They then reached consensus on the evaluation codes that should be applied to each case. The facil-itator and trainees followed this process for the remaining eight cases until the facilitator felt that the coders were making the same cod-ing judgments about the comments.

Once the trainees have reached a high level of inter-rater consis-tency, they are ready to begin coding the files themselves. If the activ-ity is going to occur over an extended period, the trainer may want to reconvene the data extractors/coders again later and assess the inter-rater consistency to make sure that their interpretation of the stan-dards did not change. If the inter-rater consistency decreased below an acceptable level, then the team would be faced with possibly recoding many of the previously coded files. Some might suggest that every case needs to be independently coded by two coders and that a third coder would then be brought in to reconcile any discrepancies. While this 100 percent verification is the ultimate in ensuring coding consistency, it may be too expensive and time-consuming to use for some data collection efforts in an HR program evaluation. This concern about the amount of effort required for 100 percent verification is particularly relevant if the coded data do not address one of the central issues of the evaluation or if corroborating data are also being obtained from other sources or with other methods. It is up to the team to balance accuracy, cost, and time considerations.

Obtain the Same Data with More Than One Method When Resources Permit

By gathering data on *key* issues from multiple sources or with multiple methods, an evaluation team is able to maximize the possibility that the most important findings will be sufficiently robust to accurately address the research questions. Fink and Kosecoff (1978, p. 25) noted that the use of different methods might also be useful when assessing hard-to-measure variables such as attitudes, values, and beliefs, but they also warned that evaluators' overuse of multiple sources and methods can result in a "mass of unmanageable data that are extremely costly to read, interpret, and analyze." Conversely, it might be significantly more expensive for an organization in the long run to make a major change in a program based on weak data. Using data from multiple methods or sources to triangulate in on an accurate answer to a key evaluation question can pay for itself if the evaluation team is judicious in its use.

One common way in which multiple methods can be efficiently used is by conducting a short survey in the first few minutes before the first focus group question is asked. Obtaining the survey answers before the discussion begins avoids the "group-think" responses that can occur during the actual focus group. Even though the same group of respondents is providing the answers, they may answer differently on anonymous or confidential surveys versus through verbal comments that others in the group can hear. This pairing of methods is particularly useful when gathering sensitive information such as alcohol or drug use in the workplace. Individuals might be more revealing if they did not have to be identified with their answers. That is where the short survey becomes useful. During the discussion portion of the session, the participants could be told to describe a situation—not necessarily their own—about which they have heard in order to avoid the stigma of admitting a problem behavior. The focus group's comments can provide important qualitative insights to supplement the quantitative findings from the surveys.

Asking the questions in more than one way can provide important insights to a program evaluation team. For example, Rynes, Gerhart, and Minette (2004) noted that people might rank compensation as a relatively unimportant thing for themselves, but they typically rate it as being very important to others. They also emphasized this point with a quote from Nunnally and Bernstein (1994, p. 383), who said, "It is easy to overestimate the frequency with which adults actually go to the opera and underestimate the frequency with which they watch TV cartoons on Saturday mornings, based on their self-reports." In other words, a grain of salt needs to be applied to what we have to say about ourselves and others. We may be more alike than what initially appears to be so, especially if we can identify and control some of the face-saving views of how people perceive themselves versus others.

Having data from multiple methods for a single issue or type of information is not only more time-consuming and costly, but may also result in conflicting or non-conclusive findings. For example, asking part of the respondents to provide information in written form (for example, a structured interview questionnaire or a survey) and asking others to provide the data in person-to-person data collection can result in findings that differ by the method used to collect the data. In such cases, it may be difficult to tell which data better reflect the true situation. Despite this potential for making data interpretation more difficult at times, the use of multiple methods typically results in more comprehensive and sound HR evaluations.

Verify the Data

Data verification has to be one of the least glamorous tasks in program evaluation. Still, accurate findings cannot be obtained without clean data.

In the past, data verification typically meant finding someone to compare source documents such as responses on paper-and-pencil surveys to the data found in an electronic database. More recently, source documents are sometimes unavailable because organizations are relying more and more on electronic methods of capturing source data, and thereby eliminating the paper documentation that once could be used to authenticate that the information in an electronic database was what had actually been submitted. Computerized surveys, personnel files with passwords issued to employees, and other electronic processes now have employees entering their responses directly into the databases. In such cases, the data verification might include reviewing the computer programs that are used to capture and store the information. The procedures for preventing unwanted tampering or data peeking might also be part of verifying information in databases that have eliminated source documents. The next chapter will cover another aspect of data verification—verifying information that is entered into a database that the evaluation team generates.

Beware of Becoming Sidetracked During Data Collection

As we said earlier, the data collection phase will probably take longer than any other phase of HR program evaluation, and some of the extra time may not be value-added if the team becomes sidetracked from the essentials and timeframes in its project plan. Attention to two cautions can, however, speed the data collection to its shortest possible conclusion. These cautions entail avoiding excessive data collection and monitoring the data collection schedules closely.

Avoid Excessive Data Collection

This simple admonition is, however, easier said than done. Sometimes, evaluators will not know until much later that some of the collected data will help only tangentially in developing the message and recommendations.

Some people suggest that you cannot have too much data for a program evaluation. This outcome

> Our bottom-line advice in data collection: "Decide whether the data are must-have versus nice-to-have. And collect only the information you are going to use!"

can occur when the evaluation plan is not carefully thought out prior to its implementation. Conversely, careful planning can result in a more sound and efficient HR program evaluation, which minimizes unneeded data collection. There are at least two practical reasons for careful planning and data collection. First, collecting data that is not centrally related to the program evaluation slows the team's progress toward completing its program evaluation. The team members gathering the data of secondary interest could have been used to complete other program evaluation steps earlier had their efforts been focused on central issues. Second, collecting data of peripheral interest leaves a larger-than-necessary disruption or footprint in the organization. As we mentioned in our planning phase, program evaluation resource requirements often involve much more than the salary and benefits costs of the evaluators. It additionally includes the time-based costs of the organizational members—interviewees, survey respondents, HR staff, and others—who provide the information. Each of these types of stakeholders must be taken away from their normal work activities to provide the evaluation information.

Effective planning minimizes collecting data of peripheral interest. This is not to say that the team should put blinders on and stick strictly to its original data collection plan. Instead, it is a warning to consider seriously whether or not the team really needs such things as fifteen additional "nice-to-know" survey items, a census (instead of a sample) of data extracted from paper personnel files, or identification of best practices. The key to effective data collection is balancing the evaluation footprint against time, cost, and the organization's ability to tolerate some uncertainty in its program evaluation findings and conclusions. Many of those competing concerns should have been addressed during the planning phase by (a) explaining the costs and benefits of the various data collection efforts to key stakeholders and (b) gaining their buy-in on data collection before the actual collection efforts ever began.

Monitor Data Collection Schedules Closely

The HR program evaluation team leader should be monitoring work schedules on at least a weekly basis to determine whether the team is meeting its deadlines. While some missed milestones may have been due to poor planning or performance, scheduling problems and other obstacles can be outside the control of the evaluation team. We have been involved with teams that have faced difficulties meeting their data gathering milestones for a wide variety of unanticipated, uncontrollable events such as:

- Team members leaving the organization or being reassigned to other tasks,
- Short- or long-term illnesses of team members or their families, and
- Mail-related problems for survey returns caused by fears of anthrax contamination.

Regardless of the reason, the team leader must recognize a milestone problem quickly and develop a get-well plan as soon as possible. Quick recognition of the schedule slippage has the advantage of providing the team with the widest array of options and the most possible time for overcoming the challenge. Delayed recognition will seriously limit the use of some of the get-well options.

Conclusions

The success of data collection depends on having an effective HR program evaluation plan and implementing the plan efficiently. This chapter described several common data collection considerations, including data collection methods and data sources and research designs. These steps would, however, be for naught if the team ignored the important, but under-appreciated steps required to ensure that the data are of high quality. Because data collection typically requires more time than any other phase of an HR evaluation, careful and detailed plans for its implementation that can be adjusted for emerging issues are essential for ensuring the availability of the types and quality of data needed to successfully evaluate the HR program under consideration.

Suggested Resources

Edwards, J.E., Scott, J.C., & Raju, N.S. (Eds.). (2003). *The human resources program-evaluation handbook*. Thousand Oaks, CA: Sage.

Edwards, J.E., Thomas, M.D., Rosenfeld, P., & Booth-Kewley, S.B. (1997). *How to conduct organizational surveys: A step-by-step guide*. Thousand Oaks, CA: Sage.

Fink, A., & Kosecoff, J. (1978). *An evaluation primer*. Thousand Oaks, CA: Sage.

Shadish, W.R., Cook, T.D., & Campbell, D.T. (2002). *Experimental and quasi-experimental designs for generalized causal inference*. Boston, MA: Houghton Mifflin.

Phase 4

ANALYZE AND INTERPRET DATA

"... a difference is a difference only if
it makes a difference."
—*Huff (1954, p. 58)*

Chapter Objectives

- Provide evaluators with an appreciation of the advantages that can come from effectively creating and modifying an electronic database

- Encourage the team to use descriptive statistics, rather than more complex statistics, in many common situations

- Alert team members to some of the basic issues that can affect whether they should use inferential statistics in their HR program evaluation

Statistical data analyses and interpretations of the resulting findings are an integral part of most HR evaluation programs. Yet, members of the evaluation team may not be capable of or want to deal directly with these aspects of the evaluation, often because of their limited knowledge of statistics. Therefore, some evaluation teams may need to rely on the data analytic expertise of someone who has not been part of the day-to-day evaluation team. Irrespective of whether the needed expertise resides inside the team or is sought from an external source, there are several important tasks that must be carefully attended to during this phase of HR program evaluations. These tasks include creating and modifying the database, making full use of descriptive statistics, addressing issues that might affect the use of inferential statistics, and determining the extent to which support is available for findings that are key to answering the program evaluation questions.

Create and Modify a Database

Although some types of data needed for a program evaluation will already be stored electronically in the organization's HR information system or various stand-alone databases, other information may need to be captured in an electronic database before formal analyses can begin. This section examines the primary steps needed when an evaluation team must create a database or modify information extracted from one or more databases for its analyses. In many ways, these steps are a continuation of actions that teams should take to enhance quality during the data collection phase (for example, see Figure 3.1 in the prior chapter). Without a continued emphasis on data quality, the rigor applied during data collection may have been for naught, and the team could end up analyzing inaccurate information, which would likely lead to faulty findings and inappropriate recommendations.

Many of the Phase 4 database creation and modification steps should have been started or anticipated in the planning and data collection phases. We have, however, chosen to include all the creation and modification steps in this section to give evaluators an integrated view of the required tasks for moving various types of information into an electronic database. Also, it highlights the fact that the team members who perform database and data analysis tasks may be different from those who collect the data because different skills are required in the two phases. If different members of the evaluation team are in charge of the collection and analysis/interpretation phases, it is important that close communication occur among the team members. For example, understanding the full context in which the data were gathered often provides important insights for interpreting unexpected findings.

The three types of tasks required to create and modify a database are designing data codes, designing the database, and deciding how to handle missing data. These three tasks are carried out in an iterative, rather than sequential, fashion with the HR program evaluation team honing in on the finalized database throughout the data cleaning and analysis process.

Design Data Codes

Data coding will occur during most phases of our HR program evaluation approach. More specifically, data codes are likely to be designed when planning the evaluation, collecting the data, analyzing and interpreting the data, and communicating the findings and insights.

Code Data During the Planning Phase.   Before data collection began, the evaluation team should have determined whether it would seek the same data from multiple sources. Gathering information from multiple sources could involve activities such as surveying or interviewing organizational members, extracting data from paper personnel files, or reviewing other internal documents. If it looks as if there will be at least ten people, files, or other units of analysis providing the same type of data, the team should consider establishing codes for capturing the data. Using a data collection or coding instrument with pre-specified options for at least some of the items of interest has several advantages when a team will later determine whether there is a difference, similarity, or relationship present in the data. The following are five important advantages to data coding:

- Coding ensures consistency across team members who transcribe the data provided from interview respondents, reviews of paper files, and other sources to the electronic database.
- The codes shorten the time required to capture and enter information into the computer because the data collector can often check a box instead of writing narrative for at least part of the answer.

- Codes result in less lost data caused by illegible handwriting and cryptic note taking.
- Because every variable has a spot reserved for it on the instrument, data coders can enter special codes that distinguish when the data are missing for various reasons.
- The items and codes serve as a checklist to make sure that the team has addressed all of the relevant researchable issues that can be obtained from every person, file, or unit of analysis.

The data collection and coding instruments can still include "other [specify]" response options for information that does not fit the pre-coded choices.

When the evaluation team designs its codes, each variable should typically be coded in its smallest meaningful categories. By initially coding data in its smallest categories, it will be possible to create other variables at a more aggregated level later. The converse is not true. That is, if the evaluation team initially gathered the data at the aggregate level, the team cannot later use the aggregate variable to create another variable with finer distinctions. For example, it might be advisable to code *location* as headquarters and each of the regional offices instead of as two aggregated categories: headquarters versus any regional office.

Often when data are being gathered, it is impossible to anticipate all of the ways in which subgroups will need to be examined. Using codes that capture the finest meaningful distinctions gives evaluators maximum flexibility to regroup the cases by aggregating the codes. As with any guideline, there are, however, exceptions where capturing data in its smallest categories may not be preferred. For instance, evaluators might want to use somewhat broader/more-aggregated categories of response options on some surveys so that respondents will perceive they are truly being provided promised anonymity or confidentiality.

Code Data During the Data Collection Phase. Implicit in our encouragement for HR program evaluation teams to design much of their data coding during the planning stage is the assumption that the team should minimize designing data codes during data collection. There will, however, have to be at least some new data coding schemes designed during the data collection stage. For example, the team will need to code the "other [specify]" response options for information that does not match the pre-coded choices. The evaluation team should have only minor last-minute coding during the data collection, if team members follow Bourque and Clark's (1992) twelve rules for developing response categories for closed-ended questions. Those rules include making sure that the pre-code choices are exhaustive of possible answers and mutually exclusive.

With myriad other tasks being performed during data collection, the team might be tempted to delay coding and entering the information into an electronic database. While delaying the coding may allow the team to complete data collection more rapidly, it may also have negative outcomes. Delaying data coding can result in (a) no data being entered into electronic databases until the beginning of the data analysis phase or (b) rework when a database must be modified to add codes for the items that were not previously coded. Data initially entered into the database can be used by the data analyst to test the programs that are being written to perform the statistical analyses. Conversely, delays in coding and entering the data postpone testing and debugging the programs that will be used to analyze the data. Thus, fully accomplishing data collection tasks before moving to the overlapping tasks in the data analysis phase can speed the completion of one phase of our approach but slow the HR program evaluation team's overall progress toward project completion.

Code Data During the Data Analysis and Interpretation Phase. During the data analyses, an HR program evaluation team will almost surely want to create additional variables from existing variables (for example, creating a "metropolitan" and "rural" location variable when evaluating a recruitment program). This type of data creation and coding is usually easy and quick because it can be accomplished using statements in statistical analysis programs, rather than using labor-intensive hand-coding for each variable on each data collection instrument and then entering the many codes for each record into the electronic database. Moreover, computer programs can be used to document the original variables and response options, as well as any newly created ones. In addition, comments written into the programs can document the rationale for the original and created variables, so that future users of the database will have a precise understanding of the information contained therein. Two common reasons for creating and coding new variables from the variables already in the database are to collapse many pieces of data into a composite variable or re-categorizing a variable into a smaller number of subgroups.

Collapsing Many Variables into a Composite Variable. Analyzing responses from a survey is probably the situation in which data analysts are most likely to perform this task of collapsing multiple variables into a single variable, but it can also be used for data collected with other procedures or instruments. Surveys typically consist of several items, which are further classified into clusters of items that share a common theme. For example, a survey may contain seven items dealing with aspects of job satisfaction such as satisfaction with the work itself, with co-workers, and with pay. The average score for each item can reveal important differences about which aspects of the job are rated relatively more positive and negative by the employees when the average scores are compared. In addition to analyzing individual items for differences across subgroups, the evaluation team may opt to calculate the average satisfaction score for the combined seven items to determine subgroup differences. That is, the units of analyses are scores for each of the seven facets of satisfaction and a composite score that represents the respondents' average satisfaction for all seven items combined. There are advantages in using the mean score for the cluster of items as the unit of analysis: (a) a mean score will be much more reliable than the measure from an individual item and (b) examining the mean helps the evaluator to concentrate on the forest/big picture instead of concentrating on each tree or item. This is not to say that the HR program evaluation should not be done at the item level. Both levels of analyses provide useful information, but which level of analysis is used should reflect the purpose of the evaluation.

Re-Categorizing Existing Variables. New variables might be created by collapsing multiple categories of a variable into a fewer number of categories, or the new variables might be created to highlight even finer distinctions. For example, evaluators might have originally coded organizational members with five categories of professions (managers, technical/professional workers, skilled tradespersons, clerical workers, and others) and two categories of location (central versus regional facility). In some analyses, the evaluators might reclassify members more broadly as either office workers (the first three categories) or blue-collar workers. In other analyses, evaluators might reclassify members into finer groups. They may want to classify members by simultaneously grouping them by their profession and location.

Code Data During the Communication of Results Phase or Even Later. Invariably, questions about the characteristics of certain subgroups will arise during the briefings of the HR program evaluation results. The evaluation team may have already anticipated such questions and can provide the results quickly to stakeholders with the coded options already in the database or with newly constructed variables created from the existing codes.

Also, subsequent HR program evaluations and routine requests for information may benefit from information in a database from an earlier evaluation. As we saw in Phase 3, existing databases might contain data that help an organization determine where it has been or where it is currently. In some situations, the creation of new variables and codes might require the merging of new information into an existing database to answer questions that could not have been anticipated when an evaluation was performed years earlier.

Design the Database

Designing a sound database is an important and integral aspect of any statistical data analysis. An initial step in designing a database is deciding what types of statistical analyses will be performed on the data and which computer programs are likely to be used in such analyses. These decisions will probably dictate how to format the data for entry into the computer so that the planned statistical analyses can be performed with relative ease. Once the data are entered into the computer and prior to any data analysis, the evaluation team must satisfy itself that the data are accurate in the sense that the survey responses, archival information, or other information from data collection instruments are correctly extracted, coded, and entered into the computer. The importance of this aspect of the database development—optimizing the database to the software, identifying fields and formats, and entering and cleaning the data—cannot be over-emphasized.

Optimize the Database to the Software. The database should be designed with an eye toward the software that will be used to analyze it. HR program evaluation teams have a wide range of software that can be used to analyze data. These choices include general database programs (for example, Excel and Lotus) that come with desktop software packages, general purpose statistical packages (for example, SPSS and SAS), specialized statistical packages (for example, SUDAAN and STATA) for procedures such as analyzing weighted data, and query types of software (for example, Oracle or Access).

The choice of software will depend on a variety of factors, such as the analyst's preference and training, types of analyses to be performed, whether the analysis programs and database will be used in the future or just for the current evaluation, and what software is already available in the organization. Even if the data were prepared for use with one type of software, conversion of a database for use with other data analysis software is usually simple. There is, however, a need for careful planning and attention to detail during any database conversion because idiosyncrasies of the programs can result in data not being fully and accurately transformed from one type of database to another. For example, when one of the authors needed to convert a very large database from one specialized statistical software package to another, over one thousand lines of code had to be written. The software for the converted data could not distinguish among the various types of codes for missing data in the original software. If this problem had not been detected during initial data-quality checks of the converted database, very wrong conclusions would have been made because the newer database—among other things—treated "does not apply" responses the same as truly missing data, that is, when respondents had actually left items unanswered. Our advice: Verify instead of blindly assuming that a conversion program has captured the data exactly as it was coded in the original database.

Identify Fields and Formats. Another important database-design concern pertains to identifying the fields and formats of the data. It is important to decide up-front how many fields or columns would be needed for recording information for a given variable. It is also important to know whether the information was gathered and entered into the computer using alphabetic characters or numbers. If it is alphabetic characters for a given variable, the evaluator needs to determine the maximum number of characters allowed for that variable. For example, if the variable under consideration is gender, one character ("F" for female, "M" for male, and "U" for unspecified) may be sufficient. If it is racial/ethnic identity, more than one character may be needed to record that information.

When information for a variable is expressed in numbers, the data coders and analyst need to know whether the information is expressed as whole numbers or numbers with decimals. In either case, the evaluator must plan for the appropriate number of columns needed for collecting and later recording such information. For example, if it is age, two columns might suffice for most evaluations; if it is the date of birth, more columns will be needed, along with specific instructions on how that formation is to be recorded. If job levels are expressed in decimals (for example, 65.3), the HR program evaluation team should plan for that level of information in the survey or other data collection instrument, as well as the resulting database. In summary, the better an evaluation team plans for the fields and formats, the easier the analytic tasks are to perform later during the data cleaning and analyses.

Enter and Clean Data. Once paper-and-pencil surveys, written documentation of interview answers, coding sheets filled with information extracted from personnel files, or other types of information are received, the data will probably need to be transferred into an electronic database for the analyses. For some data collection methods such as a computer-administered survey, the data-entry step would not be needed, but the data cleaning will still be necessary to ensure that the collected data have not been corrupted between when information was obtained and when analyses were started.

Data from surveys and formalized coding sheets like those used for file extractions should be relatively simple to enter into the computer, since the codes typically can be included on the sheets. Often, data entry can be done by in-house clerical personnel who are not part of the evaluation team or by external data-entry services. This process can be facilitated further by having a team member review each data form and reconcile any coding problems before the form is provided to the data-entry personnel. While this review by a team member might seem like a needless step, it enhances data quality by lessening the odds that data-entry personnel who are less familiar with the data codes will attempt to interpret non-coded data.

Like data coders, the data-entry personnel need to be trained. After the data-entry personnel have been instructed on how to enter the data and have finished inputting their first five or ten forms, it is useful for a team member to review the quality of the data entry. This involves a 100 percent comparison of the entered data to the information in the source document. Feedback from the quality check then helps the data-entry personnel to (a) correct consistent problems that appeared on more than one record in the database and (b) obtain feedback on the overall quality of the entered data. If the overall quality is too low, the team member working with the data-entry personnel might require additional samples of ten cases from the personnel whose work was deficient until sufficient quality (for example, 95 percent, 99 percent, or 100 percent accuracy) has been achieved. Sufficient quality is in the eye of the beholder and may vary according to the type of data and how central the data are to the purpose of the evaluation. Even when double key entry (that is, one person enters the data and another person subsequently enters the same data, with any differences reconciled) is used for 100 percent of the cases, data quality cannot be assumed. Unclear instructions to data-entry personnel, among other things, can still result in inaccurate information being added to a database.

Additional data checks can be done after the database has been created. For example, the data analyst can create a frequency distribution for every variable in the database and then look at the distributions to determine whether some of the values were not included as possible codes. Impossible codes found in distributions might include having a code of "N" for gender when only "M," "F," and "U" were allowed, or having a numerical value that is likely too high or too long (for example, 22 for the number of dependents covered by the employee's health insurance policy). Similarly, other inaccurate information might be found in the database by crossing two variables. For example, if age were crossed with organizational level, it might reveal a record that needed to be reexamined because a person was identified as being twenty years old and a vice president of the company. (Nothing would be changed in the database if it were accurate information about one of the owner's children!) Whenever potentially inaccurate data entries are found, they should be checked against the original source documents. Then data-entry errors should be corrected in the database.

Decide What, If Anything, Needs to Be Done About Missing Data

Missing data are facts of life in almost any data collection effort, and they may even be more so with surveys than with other data collection methods. After reviewing the database for the extent of missing data, the evaluation team must decide how to address the concern.

At an extreme is the situation in which so much data are missing that findings from the database could cause erroneous generalizations to the population of interest.

In all probability, some data will be unavailable despite an HR program evaluation team's best efforts to gather all of the desired information. Missing data can cause major problems for evaluation teams if (a) a large amount of data is missing from a sample or population or (b) a lesser amount of data is missing, but the missing data are concentrated in certain subgroups or variables representing particular content areas. During data cleaning, the evaluation team can determine where missing data are clustered, an important first step in identifying what, if anything, extra needs to be done about the missing data. To gain a better understanding of missing data, let's look at two types of missing data and the resulting consequences.

Table 4.1 shows how part of a database might look for an evaluation of a health benefits program. It shows that (a) the external contractor received 2,207 surveys from company employees and (b) each employee's survey is represented by a separate record (also commonly called a case or line) in the database. (Other people who did not return a survey are not in this database, but they will be considered when the analyst computes overall and subgroup response rates and compares the demographic characteristics of the respondents to the demographics for the whole company.) To facilitate this discussion, we have shaded the variables for which respondents did not provide an answer despite returning a survey. Records 2 and 3 show that one or more questions were left unanswered. For Record 2,205, the respondent returned the survey but did not answer any of the questions.

In these types of situations, the data analysts are faced with the question of how to treat records with missing data. They have at least three options: deleting records on a variable-by-variable basis, deleting records on a case-wise basis, or using advanced procedures to estimate the missing data.

Delete Records on a Variable-by-Variable Basis.   Typically, data analysts will want to use all of the information available. For example,

Table 4.1 Missing Data in an Evaluation of a Health Benefits Program

Record #	Sex	Locale	Pay Grade	Years with Company	Health Plan Option	# of Persons on Policy	# Sick Leave Hrs Last Year	# Health Claims Last Year	...	Out-of-Pocket Costs Last Year	Use of Generic Drugs	Use of On-Site Health Club
1	M	HQ	5	26	High	2	10	1	...	$300	Never	Yes
2	M	HQ	4	3	Low	3	0	0	...		Some	No
3	F				High	2	136	3	...	$3,005	Some	Yes
4	F	HQ	1	1	Low	7	5	1	...	$15	Some	Yes
.												
.												
2,204	M	Central	3	2	High	3	7	0	...	$23	Always	Yes
2,205		Central			High	3			...			
2,206	F	Central	2	15	High	3	31	1	...	$55	Some	No
2,207		West	2	10	Low	1	78	2	...	$178	Some	No

Record 3 in Table 4.1 might be dropped from the analyses when examining the relationship between the number of sick leave hours used in the last year and whether the employee used the on-site health club, since information on health club use was not available for the employee documented by Record 3. In contrast, Record 3 would be included in an analysis examining the relationship between the number of persons on the employee's insurance policy and the number of sick leave hours used last year because both pieces of needed data are available.

This common decision to delete a record from a specific analysis that uses a variable whose value is missing, rather than delete the record from all analyses (even those for which the record contains other information of interest), is logical when the records have almost all of the desired data. This option for dealing with missing data has the major advantage of maximally using all of the available data.

Delete Records on a Case-Wise Basis.   This method of dealing with missing data might be used when the HR program evaluation team is unable to obtain any information or obtains only limited information from an employee. For example, the evaluation team might not have any survey data from an employee because the survey was not returned or was returned blank. Similarly, an employee may not have been available for an interview at the required time, or the employee's paper personnel file may have been unavailable at the time because a selection or termination board was using it to make its decision.

If only records with complete data are included in a statistical analysis, the effective sample size will be smaller, leading to larger standard errors for estimates of the population values (for example, means or correlations). This is generally not considered a serious concern if the percentage of records with missing data is small and the number of records with available data is large. The generalizability of the estimates, however, becomes a serious problem when the proportion of records with missing data is substantial or when a subgroup with a large amount of missing data is no longer a representative sample of all relevant members of that population or population subgroup.

Use Advanced Procedures to Estimate the Missing Data. If the reasons for missing data are known and can be (statistically) modeled, then one can use some statistical software packages that contain advanced data analysis techniques to obtain unbiased estimates of the population values of interest.

The use of these advanced statistical techniques would require some specialized professional knowledge that may not be readily available among the HR program evaluation team members. Therefore, the team should plan for outside professional help if this situation arises. Even if the HR program evaluation team gets outside statistical help to deal with its missing data problems, it is important that the team be knowledgeable about the assumptions underlying these advanced techniques. If the team cannot conceptually understand what the statistical experts did or advised, they should think seriously about whether or not to use the techniques. After all, someone from the team will later be responsible for explaining techniques, assumptions, and findings to stakeholders who are possibly less methodologically sophisticated than the team evaluation members.

> The inability to explain and defend the statistical procedures used to generate findings—particularly to those findings that might disagree with a key stakeholder's position—could lead to concerns about the accuracy of those findings, as well as the quality of the whole program evaluation.

Anticipate and Monitor the Consequences of Missing Data. Evaluation teams often assume that the missing data are distributed like the obtained data. For example, a team interpreting survey data might assume that if 7 percent of the respondents were found to be dissatisfied with supervision, that 7 percent of the non-respondents would also be dissatisfied with supervision. However, higher and higher levels of missing data make this assumption more and more tenuous. At the extreme, missing data can lead to biased findings because the analytic results do not reflect aspects of the full population. There is no set level to say that, once that point has been reached, there is too much data missing to have meaningful findings or that advanced procedures for dealing with the missing data are no longer advised.

To some extent, the availability of corroborating data from other sources can lessen the effect of missing data obtained with a different method or from a different source. Even if corroborating data are not available, the HR program evaluation team may find it necessary to use a database with more missing data than the team would like to use. Sometimes, a team will be forced to decide whether providing findings from a database with many known problems is better than saying that the information in the database was not of sufficient quality to analyze. In either situation, the team should be very explicit in warning stakeholders about the data limitations and how they could affect the findings and conclusions.

If the team elects to report it could not use a database that was needed to answer an important question, the team should recognize that the key stakeholders may still make needed decisions—possibly in the total absence of data. For example, key managers in an organization that is moving rapidly towards a merger decision may not be able to wait six months to gather more complete data, even if the wait means they could base their decision on better information about whether or not employees say they would opt for early retirement if downsizing were necessary. Even though this information on retirements would be useful in determining the future financial condition of the potential merger partner, it is unlikely that the key managers would want to wait the extra time to make their decision or possibly tip their hands and let other companies learn of the potential merger. In such a situation, some information—with appropriate limitations discussed—can be better than none. It is in everyone's best interest to figure out a workable solution to a less-than-perfect database and provide information that can be of some use for decision making.

Take Full Advantage of Descriptive Statistics

Once the data have been coded, entered into the electronic database, and cleaned for errors, the team members are poised to begin receiving the fruits of their data analyses. Data analysis is a process of summarizing information with statistical methods. This summarization provides an evaluation team with a bigger-picture view of what the data say. The downside of the bigger-picture view is that the analyses may result in some loss of the specifics for each case, subgroup, or another unit of analysis. The key for the HR program evaluation team is to determine the point at which the summary statistic conveys optimally useful information about the data being discussed. To do this, the team may determine that descriptive and possibly inferential statistics would be useful.

Descriptive statistics merely summarize information from the population or subgroup being studied, with no attempt to determine the probability with which the findings generalize beyond the groups being studied. In some cases, it is a moot issue because the data will have been gathered on the full population. In contrast to descriptive statistics, inferential statistics are concerned with determining the probability that the findings (for example, a difference between two groups or the relationship between two or more variables) are reliable or generalizable beyond the group(s) being studied. Let's explore more about descriptive statistics in the remainder of this section before addressing inferential statistics considerations and tests in the next two sections of this chapter.

Consider the Many Types of Descriptive Statistics Available to the Team

For many HR program evaluations, the team may determine that it will use nothing other than descriptive statistics. This decision may be the result of not needing to generalize the findings any further than the applicability of the findings to the group of employees from whom the data were collected. In other cases, the decision to use only descriptive statistics might be the result of (a) team members' limited expertise with the more complex inferential statistics or (b) other concerns such as some of the extra considerations and assumptions confronted when using inferential statistics. Although the context is a bit different—guidelines and explanations for statistical methods in psychology journals—than HR program evaluation, the advice offered by Wilkinson and the Task Force on Statistical Inference (1999, p. 7) is applicable here.

> "Do not choose an analytic method to impress your readers or to deflect criticism. If the assumptions and strength of a simpler method are reasonable for your data and research problem, use it."

Using only descriptive statistics still provides evaluation teams with numerous ways to summarize the data. Many of the most common descriptive statistics used in HR program evaluation are presented in Table 4.2. For each of the cited types of statistics, we have provided an example of the type of statement that an HR program evaluation team might make. The use of descriptive statistics has an important side benefit—the statistics should be easy for stakeholders to understand when the findings are briefed because the statistics are the types of indices that appear in newspapers and other mass media. The example information on twenty-five employees (see top of right-most column in Table 4.2) provides a simple data set that team members can use to see whether they can derive the statistical findings described for each type of statistic.

Evaluation teams may want to compare some organizational subgroups, even though they are using only descriptive statistics. In such cases, we suggest that program evaluators give serious attention to how much numerical difference would need to be present for that difference to be *meaningful from a practical standpoint*. For example, if the data were expressed in percentages calculated from the analysis of survey data, a team might say that it would talk about only those differences of at least 3, 5, or some other number of percentage points. One of the authors used such a rule when comparing many subgroups in

Table 4.2 Descriptive Statistics Often Cited in HR Program Evaluations

General Type or Specific Statistic	Operational Definition of the Statistic	Example Statements Derived from the Sick Leave Days Used by 25 Marketing Division Employees: 0, 0, 0, 0, 0, 1, 1, 1, 2, 2, 2, 3, 4, 5, 5, 5, 6, 6, 7, 8, 8, 8, 8, 8, and 9
Total		
Total	The sum for all scores for the group	Marketing Division employees used a total of 99 sick leave days in 2005
Measures of Frequentness		
Frequency	The number of scores for a group	• Five of the 25 employees used no sick leave in 2005 • Nine of the 25 employees used six or more days of sick leave in 2005
Proportion	The ratio of scores for a group, a value, or set of values divided by the total number of scores	• One-fifth of the employees used no sick leave in 2005 • Over one-third of the employees used at least six sick leave days in 2005
Percentage	A proportion multiplied by 100	• Twenty percent the employees used no sick leave in 2005 • Thirty-six percent of the employees used six or more days of sick leave in 2005
Measures of Central Tendency		
Mean	Arithmetic average for all values	• The 25 Marketing Division employees used an average of 3.96 days each • The Marketing Division averaged about four days of sick leave for each employee
Mode	The value or group of values that occurs most often	• The most often numbers of sick leave days used in 2005 by Marketing Division employees were 0 and 8
Median	Value at which 50 percent of the scores are below and above that point	• The median number of sick days used by Marketing Division employees was four • About 50 percent of Marketing Division employees used four or fewer days of sick leave
Measures of Variability		
Range	Number of scale values between the smallest and largest scores, plus 1	• The range of sick leave days used by Marketing employees was ten days • Marketing employees took from zero to nine days of sick leave in 2005
Standard deviation	A measure of the variability of values around the mean	• The standard deviation of the sick leave used by Marketing Division employees in 2005 was 3.2 days

hundreds of analyses. Similarly, a team might decide to establish baseline criteria for when it is meaningful to evaluate other types of group differences. For instance, in evaluating differences among groups in the average number of continuing professional education hours taken, a team may say differences are meaningful only if they exceed ten hours. As will be seen later in our discussion of statistical power and sample size considerations, adoption of these meaningfulness-based rules might also be beneficial when using inferential statistics.

Well-regarded statisticians and researchers have offered similar perspectives on the usefulness of descriptive statistics. For example, Cohen (1990) noted that the emphasis on inference in modern statistics has resulted in a loss of flexibility in data analysis. Similarly, Wilkinson and his colleagues (1999) reminded readers that tables can be improved by performing such actions as sorting rows and columns by marginal averages, rounding to a few significant digits, and avoiding decimals when possible.

Look for Opportunities to Use Descriptive Statistics with Qualitative Data

The applicability of descriptive statistics goes beyond their use with just quantitative data, and includes methods for making better use of qualitative data. Descriptive statistics also can be used once coding has been done for qualitative data such as narrative responses to survey questions, answers provided during individual and group interviews, and comments offered during focus groups. Qualitative data can put meat on the bare bones that come from the quantitative data. For example, qualitative data provided in interviews can be used to illustrate specific reasons why the organization's employee turnover rate was 22 percent last year, and those reasons can be phrased in the interviewees' own words.

Care should be used in choosing the narrative information that will be used to illustrate and clarify quantitative findings. An HR program evaluation team may be tempted to select narrative responses that agree with a point that it would like to make, even if the response is not typical of views that others offered regarding the same issue. Instead, the team should more often use their quantitative analyses of qualitative information to clarify and enrich the more prevalent points of view.

The key to developing descriptive statistics from qualitative data is to develop and refine a process for coding the narrative information. Exhibit 4.1 illustrates how one of the authors was able to quantify a large amount of narrative data and then order the information by the frequency with which particular themes were voiced. Quantification and ordering by frequency can help to identify consistent themes that occur in qualitative data. The frequency, along with the significance or importance, of a theme can be a useful index for prioritizing which problem areas should be addressed first—or at all—in the briefings and reports.

As a warning, developing descriptive statistics from qualitative data is very labor intensive. If sufficient planning was not given to how many days it would take to develop the descriptive statistics from the qualitative data, the team might lose valuable insights because of a need to curtail or abandon its coding and quantification efforts in order to keep the overall evaluation on the timeline that was promised to stakeholders. Although there are computer programs that assist teams in content-analyzing qualitative data, use of those aids can still require much time before the data are summarized into meaningful points that can be used to supplement other types of findings.

Address Additional Concerns in Deciding Whether Inferential Statistics Are Appropriate

At some point in the analyses, an HR program evaluation team may want to advance from merely describing the data in general quantitative terms to conducting statistical tests to determine whether means are *reliably* different or two or more variables are *reliably* related. While computer-based statistical programs have made it very easy for people with little statistical or computer programming knowledge to perform the procedures required to conduct such tests,

Exhibit 4.1 Quantifying Narrative Information and Developing Descriptive Statistics

How the Qualitative Data Were Gathered

We held focus groups sessions at thirteen military installations to obtain perspectives on a broad range of personal finance topics. Service members who participated in the focus groups were divided into three types of groups: junior enlisted personnel, mid-grade and senior enlisted personnel, and junior officers. At some installations, we also held separate focus groups with spouses of service members. Typically, focus groups consisted of six to twelve participants.

The moderator led the focus group sessions with a standard protocol that contained seven central questions and several follow-up questions. During each focus group session, the moderator posed questions to participants who, in turn, provided their perspectives on the topics presented. An observer recorded the participants' comments using paper and pencil.

How the Data Were Coded

The write-up for each session was broken into separate statements for each qualitatively different issue or position discussed in a focus group. Evaluation team members read through the comments and developed themes for grouping the statements. The team then content analyzed the 2,090 statements obtained from the sixty focus groups. Specifically, two staff members independently assigned the statements to the previously identified themes. A third staff member resolved any discrepancies.

How the Qualitative Data Were Described Statistically

A theme and the number of installations at which the theme was mentioned are provided below in a partial example of the comments generated for the first question. In the full analysis, the team provided two examples of the statements categorized for each of the reported themes.

Question 1. How has deployment affected military families' financial conditions in your unit?

Theme 1.a. Other reason deployment affects families financially (N=13 installations).

Example: Financial problems stem from relationship problems. Many Marines file for divorce when they return from a deployment.

Example: Another sailor said they have to buy a lot of supplies, such as stocks of deodorant and other toiletries, to take on the deployment. The government does not pay for those supplies.

Only those themes cited at a minimum of three installations were presented in the report. The number of installations—rather than the number of statements—is provided because (a) the focus of the engagement was on Department of Defense-wide issues, rather than installation-specific concerns and (b) a

lengthy discussion in a single focus group may have generated numerous comments. The number of installations where a theme was cited could then also be
used to rank-order the themes so that stakeholders could determine how widespread a theme was, regardless of whether the perception was true or not.

Adapted from U.S. Government Accountability Office. (2005). *Military personnel:
More DOD actions needed to address service members' personal financial management issues*
(GAO-05–348). Washington, DC: Author. Additional details are available by down-
loading the full report from www.gao.gov.

obtaining a printout with an answer is much different from understanding whether or not a particular statistical test is appropriate and
what the findings on the printout really mean.

Statisticians and others have offered even stronger cautions
about the use of inferential statistics. Cohen (1990, p. 1,310) stated,
"I believe, together with such luminaries . . . that hypothesis testing
has been greatly overemphasized in psychology and in other disciplines that use it. It has diverted our attention from crucial issues.
Mesmerized by a single all-purpose, mechanized, 'objective' ritual
in which we convert numbers into other numbers and get a yes-no
answer, we have come to neglect close scrutiny of where the numbers came from." Some researchers have even questioned whether
significance testing should be abandoned. While it is beyond the
scope of this book to settle this debate or to provide the team with
a thorough coverage of statistical considerations, we are reviewing
some basic concepts to help teams understand that many factors
can influence whether they should advance from descriptive statistics to inferential statistics and will test whether a finding is statistically significant.

Prior to, during, and after the data analysis phase, the evaluation
team must address and document its decisions regarding major statistical considerations that can affect the meaning and interpretation
of its findings. In interpreting both statistically significant (that is,
concluding that the results are not due to chance alone) and non-
significant findings, the evaluation team should pay careful attention
to Type I and II error rates and statistical power, which, among other
things, depend on sample sizes. Finally, the evaluation team should

be concerned about the practical significance of the statistically significant findings.

Balance the Concerns for Type I vs. Type II Error Rates When Using Statistical Tests

An HR program evaluation team uses a statistical test to help it arrive at a conclusion about when a real difference or relationship is present in the data, but there is always a possibility of error any time that a team concludes that a finding is or is not statistically significant. For example, when evaluating a performance appraisal process, an analysis of mean differences in performance ratings between subgroups (for example, males versus females) is frequently conducted to assess the program's fairness. Tests of significance are run to determine whether reliable differences exist between the groups of interest. Findings of significant differences may lead to a conclusion that the performance appraisal is biased and that sensitivity training or some other intervention is warranted. The key for the evaluation team is to balance the probability that it will make a Type I or Type II error. A Type I error occurs when a null hypothesis (for example, a belief that the mean scores for males and females are not different on the performance rating scale, or that the performance appraisal is fair) is rejected, but the assumption of no difference or no relationship is actually true. A Type II error occurs when a null hypothesis is retained as being true, but it is actually not true. Figure 4.1 illustrates these points with a concrete example of the four situations that might occur if a statistical test were performed to determine whether training improved performance.

When conducting a statistical analysis, the likelihood that a Type I versus a Type II error will occur can be manipulated by adjusting the probability or alpha level for the statistical test. The most typical value for alpha is .05. With a .05 alpha level, our rate of committing a Type I error is five times per one hundred independent samples that we might draw from the population and compare. If the team chooses a smaller value for alpha (for example, .01), the team has decreased

Figure 4.1 Type I and Type II Errors in an Evaluation of a Training Program

		What Is the *Actual Effect* of the Training Program?	
		Training Program Improved Performance	Training Program Did Not Improve Performance
What Is the *Evaluation Team's Conclusion* About the Training Program?	Training Program Is Useful	Correct Decision ($p = 1 - \beta$)	Type I Error ($p = \alpha$)
	Training Program Is Not Useful	Type II Error ($p = \beta$)	Correct Decision ($p = 1 - \alpha$)

Note: The letter p stands for the probability of a correct decision, a Type I error, or a Type 2 error. This probability depends on either α (Type I error) or β (Type II error).

its likelihood of committing a Type I error but has increased the likelihood that a Type II error will occur. Interestingly, probabilities are based on assumptions about findings from infinite numbers of independent samples and tests. Therefore, an evaluation team can never be sure which of its specific statistically based conclusions are correct.

Other alpha levels may be considered for adoption if deemed appropriate. For example, if an organization wanted to look at whether a new safety procedure would be worth implementing, it might adopt a .10 or a .15 alpha level to increase the likelihood that the new procedure would be adopted if there were even a small

There is nothing really unique about the commonly used .05 and .01 alpha levels. In fact, it has been said that the great statistician R.A. Fisher decided on these two levels for his 1932 book on statistical methods because he could not get the data for all probability levels from Karl Pearson, and Fisher did not want to compute them himself.

chance that some deaths or injuries could be prevented. Conversely, an organization might adopt a .001 alpha level if it were considering replacing its current selection program with only a slightly more valid program that would cost much more to administer. In both cases, the practical consequences (deaths, injuries, and monetary costs) of being right or wrong about a conclusion would be important considerations when choosing an alpha level. An evaluation team should also take into account anticipated effect sizes (discussed later) in choosing alpha levels. Thus, blindly adopting an alpha of .05 or .01 may not be in the HR program evaluation team's or the organization's best interests.

Determine Whether You Are Really Using the Alpha Level That You Said You Would Use

Often, data analysts violate the alpha level that they stated they would adopt when they analyze a large number of variables, with each analysis at the stated alpha level. For example, teams commonly compare two or more subgroups for every item from the data collection instrument. When this happens, the alpha level (Type I error rate) set at .05 or .01 is expected to inflate. For example, when two groups are compared on each of ten items with an alpha of .05 for each item, the overall (family-wise) alpha for all ten statistical tests could be as high as .50 (Winer, Brown, & Michels, 1991). That is, the probability of finding a statistically significant difference in the ten comparisons is almost 50 percent—not 5 percent as would be assumed from adopting a .05 alpha level.

There are advanced statistical techniques (for example, Bonferroni adjustments) that an evaluation team could use to retain its overall adopted alpha level when multiple comparisons are being made. For example, if the evaluation team wants the overall alpha level to be .05 for ten comparisons, it might use an alpha level of .005 (.05/10) for each individual comparison. This would ensure that the overall or family-wise alpha is not greater than .05. One negative consequence of such advanced statistical techniques is that they make it very unlikely that any analyses will reach the adopted alpha level. In other words, a program evaluation team using these types of adjustments might incorrectly conclude that a difference (or relationship) is not statistically significant, even though it can be reliably found. Again, evaluation teams must be aware of the tradeoffs that they make when using one statistical procedure to lessen a problem experienced with another statistical procedure. Even when the team has an example that shows that someone else used the procedure in a similar situation, caution is warranted because all of the details for why the procedure was appropriate may not have been conveyed in the other example.

Be Clear in Understanding What Statistical Significance Is and Is Not

In addition to the Type I and II error rates and inflated alpha level problems mentioned above, there are other important issues that an HR program evaluation team has to consider when evaluating or interpreting findings obtained with inferential statistics. Some of these issues: practical versus statistical significance, small samples and statistical power, and differences in populations versus samples, are addressed below.

Distinguish Between Practical and Statistical Significance. Pedhazur and Schmelkin (1991, pp. 202–203) said, "The point we wish to stress is that tests of statistical significance have become a blind ritual. . . . The idea that findings be examined in light of their substantive importance and meaningfulness is so self-evident that one cannot help but wonder why various authors find it necessary to remind researchers of it. What may be even more puzzling is that most researchers do not heed exhortations to be concerned primarily with magnitudes of effects or relations, and they instead persist in relying almost exclusively on significance testing."

When is a statistically significant mean difference not practically significant? This is an age-old question in data analysis. One of the popularly cited recommendations for partially answering the question is to look at the effect size rather than the simple mean difference. An effect size is a standardized mean difference, which is expressed in the z-score metric. There are designations that an HR program evaluation team can use to classify an effect size as small, medium, or large (see Cohen, 1988). The effect sizes and their designations can be helpful to practitioners in assessing the practical utility of statistically significant mean differences as well as relationships, especially when large samples are involved.

While Cohen's guidelines help to characterize the quantitative size of a statistical effect, they still may not fully address the practical significance of a difference or relationship—a much more subjective issue, but one of importance. Moreover, differences or relationships that are judged to be statistically significant may not be judged to be of practical significance, and vice versa. Using the examples of reductions in deaths, injuries, and costs that we provided earlier could provide critical contexts for judging whether the size of an effect is of practical importance. It may be the case that an effect size labeled small using Cohen's guidelines would be judged to be of large practical significance if a change in a safety training program were predicted to cost two fewer lives during a major construction project. Conversely, an effect size labeled large using Cohen's guidelines might be judged as having little practical significance if, for example, a group participating in a before-and-after study of the effects of exercise during the work day showed that amount of sick leave decreased by ten days from last year, but the employees were away from their work for around an hour each day (around 250 hours or about thirty days each work year) for the exercise program. While other positive effects may result from the workplace exercise program, even a large effect size for decreased days absent could not be judged to be of practical significance if the number of days absent were the only criterion measure used to judge the success of the exercise program.

In conclusion, data analysts should be able to help the evaluation team define when things are statistically significant. The more subjective determination of practical significance will require reflection on the situational context and the importance of increasing or decreasing values of the criteria. Subject-matter experts for the HR programs being evaluated can often help the evaluation team to understand the practical impact of findings.

Recognize When Statistical Findings Merely Reflect Sample Size and Statistical Power. Statistical power refers to the probability of rejecting a false null hypothesis (for example, no difference in means) at a given Type I error rate, effect size, and sample size. Because we have already discussed the Type I error rate and briefly mentioned effect size, let's look at how sample size affects whether an evaluation team concludes something is or is not statistically significant.

Other things being equal, small samples have lower statistical power than do larger samples for detecting a statistically significant mean difference or relationship. That is, if the sample size is small, the statistical test may not be able to detect a true (non-zero) difference or relationship when one exists. This situation is particularly easy to discern when looking at tables of critical values for statistical tests such as t tests. In general, as the sample size gets larger, the critical value gets smaller until it finally levels off at the point at which there are about two hundred cases. To illustrate, if a company's East and West divisions had mean job satisfaction scores of 3.5 and 3.8, respectively, on a 5-point scale, a statistical test comparing the scores would probably not result in a statistically significant finding if only twenty of the five hundred people in each division were included in the samples. The same difference of 0.3 would, however, probably be found statistically significant if each division's mean score were based on information from samples of 250 people.

A basic understanding of the relationship between statistical power and sample size is especially useful in applied research such as HR program evaluation. When the groups being compared have few observations or members, very large differences may need to be present before the obtained statistical test values equal or exceed the critical values required to conclude that the differences (or relationships) are statistically significant. Very large organizations may face the opposite situation—almost any comparison might result in a conclusion of statistical significance because thousands of cases are being compared, even for subgroup analyses. The point is that the program evaluation team should interpret findings from inferential statistics with due consideration to the statistical power it has for detecting statistically significant findings.

Differentiate Between Analyses That Use Populations Versus Samples. Strictly speaking, there is no need to perform statistical tests when data are available on all cases in the population (for example, everyone in the organization was surveyed, or the HR information system was used to derive values on all employees). All observed differences in population values (sometimes called population parameters) are real, and there is no sampling error involved in identifying the population value overall or for subgroups of the population for which all cases in that subgroup are used to derive the values for populations. The population values may, however, have other types of error (covered earlier in Table 2.2) associated with them.

In contrast, inferential statistics are used with samples when it is important to know whether we could expect similar results if we obtained other samples from the population. Conceptually, it is a little like playing the children's game of twenty questions. If we get to gather data/ask a question from only one person, we probably do not have a very good idea of what we want to know. If we ask twenty-five people the question, we stand a much better chance of having a true picture of what we want to know. And if we can ask hundreds of people, we can be fairly confident that we have a true picture of a particular subgroup or the population, even if the overall or subgroup population has tens of thousands of people in it.

Use Inferential Analyses If Warranted and Underlying Assumptions Can Be Met

Our discussion of the aforementioned considerations should not be taken as a blanket recommendation to avoid using inferential statistical tests. Rather, the considerations are merely reminders that there are many factors that influence the decision about whether to use such tests. Like any other research method, each type of inferential statistical test has situations for which it is ideally suited and other situations for which it should not be used.

The specialized skills and years of experience to really understand what the findings from the tests mean cannot be taught in a portion of this chapter. This conclusion is based on our years of having taught graduate-level statistics and using a wide range of inferential statistics in our HR program evaluations and academic research. Any coverage here would not be adequate to teach team members how to be effective users of the tests and interpreters of the results. Therefore, we strongly urge HR program evaluation teams contemplating the use of such statistics to have a person with in-depth knowledge and experience with the statistical tests. We do not want to sound like a bad television commercial warning an audience, "You should not try this at home without sufficient training because great harm can result." At the same time, it is important to emphasize that if inferential statistics are used, the analyst will have to help the team to develop effective methods for presenting the complex statistics in meaningful ways to possibly statistically unsophisticated stakeholders.

Look for Areas in Which Findings Support and Conflict with Other Findings

Regardless of the types of statistics used in the analyses, the team must begin to organize the descriptive and possibly inferential statistical findings to determine where the findings support and conflict with one another. The data collection and analysis plans are one source for looking for overlapping findings. Other overlapping findings will become apparent as the team sifts through the results from other data sources such as narrative comments from surveys, interviews, and focus groups. This organization of findings will suggest additional data analyses that are needed but could not have been anticipated when the analysis plan was developed earlier. By this point in the program evaluation, the team will have a greater understanding of how the various pieces of the program fit together, where its strengths and weaknesses lie, and unexpected but important issues that require extra exploration with available data.

One way for the HR program evaluation team to organize the findings is to construct a findings-confirmation matrix (Silverstein & Sharp, 1997). Table 4.3 shows how a portion of a confirmation matrix might look when organizing findings from an evaluation of a recruiting program. Although it would be too complex for presentation to most stakeholders, this type of matrix serves as a nice summary for the team to show how the evaluation questions aligned with the project goals, what techniques were used to answer these questions, and what resulted from the data collection effort. While our example uses only a few findings, an evaluation team might find it advantageous to use an even more elaborate process for determining how its various findings support or conflict with one another. In addition to leading to more analyses that could not have been anticipated in the planning phase, this step in the analysis phase begins the interpretation and feedback of findings that are the topics covered in our next chapter.

Conclusions

Data analysis is an integral part of HR program evaluations but can be intimidating to team members who have limited statistical skills. This chapter described some of the major steps involved in analyzing and interpreting the data collected during the evaluation process. It is only with the effort that comes from sometimes laborious data coding, entry, and cleaning that the team will be able to generate meaningful findings. Although descriptive statistics offer the advantage of being easily calculated and understood by stakeholders, inferential statistics may provide additional insights into the findings if the evaluation team (a) determines that the latter type of tests are warranted and (b) has someone skilled in using such advanced statistics. Regardless of the types of statistics used, organization of the

Table 4.3 Findings-Confirmation Matrix

Project Goals	Issues or Sub-Questions	Data Collection Methods (see codes below)				Results
		a	b	c	d	
Increase the success of the overall minority recruiting program	Did the recruiters who received individualized coaching change their recruiting practices?		X	X	X	85 percent of recruiters added at least two nontraditional recruitment sources, 10 percent added one nontraditional, and 5 percent added no nontraditional sources
	Why did recruits who rejected the company's job offers say that they did not want to work for the company?	X		X		Recruiters who did not implement changes claimed that recruitment efforts were met with resistance due to company reputation, urban location of the office, and compensation that was too low
Increase minority candidates for professional and supervisory jobs organization-wide	Was there an increase in minority applicants compared to last year?	X	X			Minority recruits increased by 35 percent compared to last year's data
	What percentage of these new applicants met the qualifications for the job?	X	X	X		40 percent of the new minority recruits met the minimum requirements for the targeted positions
	How does this year's minority selection rate compare to last year's selection rate?	X				Minority selection rate increased by 10 percentage points to 25 percent, relative to the selection rate for last year.

This table follows the general format advocated by Silverstein & Sharp (1997).

a = review of archival recruitment data from personnel office
b = self-report checklist completed by recruiters after each recruiting trip
c = in-house individual interviews with recruiters
d = anonymous surveys of recruiters by consulting firm offering the coaching

findings into content areas can provide insights into how much support is present for drawing conclusions about the strengths and weaknesses of key portions of an HR program.

Suggested Resources

Bourque, L.B., & Clark, V.A. (1992). *Processing data: The survey example*. Thousand Oaks, CA: Sage.

Cohen, J. (1988). *Statistical power analysis for the behavioral sciences* (2nd ed.). Mahwah, NJ: Lawrence Erlbaum Associates.

Dollinger, S.J., & DiLalla, D.L. (1996). Cleaning up data and running preliminary analyses. In F.T.L. Leong & J.T. Austin (Eds.), *The psychology research handbook: A guide for graduate students and research assistants* (pp. 167–176). Thousand Oaks, CA: Sage.

Pedhazur, E.J., & Schmelkin, L.P. (1991). *Measurement, design, and analysis: An integrated approach*. Mahwah, NJ: Lawrence Erlbaum Associates.

Phase 5

COMMUNICATE FINDINGS AND INSIGHTS

"Don't cram fifteen minutes of findings and recommendations into an hour-long briefing."
—*Adage from an otherwise forgotten briefing*

Chapter Objectives

- Demonstrate how to craft communications to target stakeholder issues and address bottom-line concerns
- Present how to visually depict findings that will facilitate stakeholder interpretation of statistics and complex concepts
- Assist evaluation team in leveraging their oral and written communication of results to promote stakeholder action

Each stakeholder group involved in an HR program evaluation will likely have its own set of questions and criteria for judging program effectiveness. As such, it will be necessary to engage these groups in discussions about how and when to best communicate the progress and findings of the evaluation. Gaining a commitment to ongoing dialog with stakeholders will increase ownership of and motivation to act on what is learned. Nurturing this relationship through the project will also help the evaluation team in making timely and appropriate refinements to the evaluation design, questions, methods, and data interpretations. This communication must, however, occur within the parameters that top management approved early in the program evaluation.

Communicating findings and insights should not be treated as a one-time event occurring at the culmination of the evaluation. Rather, information should be exchanged throughout the evaluation process so that there are no surprises when the final presentation and report are delivered. The extent and nature of this information exchange should be established during the planning phase of the evaluation, and an agreed-on communication plan with timelines and milestones should be followed throughout the evaluation.

While information must flow to stakeholders throughout an evaluation, it is also important to manage this process carefully and to avoid communication of results that have not been properly vetted. For example, it is not uncommon for stakeholders to periodically approach evaluation team members with requests for preliminary findings, particularly when high-exposure programs are being evaluated. While this sort of informal request is to be expected, a hurried response, often motivated by a desire to promote goodwill between the evaluation team and stakeholders, can do more harm than good if it turns out that the information provided was incorrect or prematurely released. If such an unfortunate event were to occur, it could lead to a loss of credibility and jeopardize the overall impact of the evaluation. Therefore, it is important that the communication plan developed during Phase 2 include ground rules that specify not only how and when information should be delivered, but the roles and responsibilities of various team members in the delivery of the information. Moreover, the team leader will probably want to coordinate and approve the release of any information by team members.

This chapter will present a number of established techniques and practical strategies for ensuring the successful communication of HR program evaluation results. These techniques should be adapted as necessary to address the unique perspectives and concerns of the various stakeholder groups. In the first section, we will review the basics of separating the wheat from the chaff by delivering evaluation findings that address bottom-line concerns and target key stakeholder questions. Next, we will present approaches for visually depicting findings and facilitating stakeholders' interpretation of statistics and complex concepts. In the final section, we provide practical guidelines for the delivery of both oral and written presentations that facilitate stakeholder action.

Stick to the Basics Found in Any Good Communication Strategy

Whether the effort invested in an HR program evaluation bears the fruit of corresponding actions is heavily dependent on how effectively the evaluation team communicates its findings and insights to the program's primary stakeholders. Program stakeholders will expect evaluation results to be communicated in a timely, logical, and interpretable manner so that decisions about the program are appropriately informed. While the nature and medium of this communication will vary based on the evaluation's focus and stakeholder requirements, the overarching goal is always the same: well-timed and targeted dissemination of evaluation results, conclusions, and recommendations. The key challenge for the evaluation team is to distinguish between what is essential to communicate and what is nice to know. As Chelimski (1987, p. 15) noted, "To its author all of the evaluation's findings seem important. It is painfully difficult to trim surgically what is not relevant, to condense, to rank, to decide not only which finding is most important, but which is most important that is also manipulable by policy." The evaluation team's success at accomplishing this task may literally mean the difference between results that are acted on versus those that are placed on a shelf.

Before proceeding with a discussion of effective communication strategies, it is necessary to review an important and sometimes challenging issue—keeping confidentiality promises in HR program evaluations. After which, we will cover a variety of communication strategies: adapting communications to the audience, getting to the bottom line, determining what to do with findings that do not fit, and tying everything together.

Maintain Confidentiality When It Was Promised

During the planning in Phase 2, the evaluation team was cautioned that it had to resolve whether or not interviewees and survey responders would be promised confidentiality. At that time, the team may have obtained buy-in from top management and other key stakeholders that the greater honesty from confidential responses would be a worthwhile tradeoff for a decrease in information about who said what.

Despite this buy-in, an HR program evaluation team is occasionally faced with a dilemma—some stakeholders in positions of power want access to the interviewee- or respondent-identified information that was collected with a pledge of confidentiality. In such cases, the decision-makers may be truly interested in taking steps to correct a serious or egregious situation (for example, people who said that they had observed drug use at work or were sexually harassed). In other cases, decision-makers may want to know who said something so that they can take action against the person supplying the information. Exhibit 5.1 provides a brief case example of an HR program evaluation team that was pressured to break a promise of confidentiality. Notably, the exhibit highlights that the situation does not necessarily have to be an all-or-nothing conclusion. Instead, an alternative source of data provided some empirical insights to address the stakeholders' concerns. This case brings home the point that concerns raised about confidentially promises and the desire for more information need not escalate into an us-versus-them situation. It should be approached as a cooperative exploration of what more can be offered without real or perceived compromises of confidentiality.

The reason for wanting access to the confidential information should not influence the decision about whether or not the pledge will be violated. The team leader might short-circuit the request for confidential information by informing the requestor of the long-term consequences of violating the pledge. Specifically, the leader may note that once the pledge is broken—regardless of good or bad intentions—(a) important information-collection strategies like con-

Exhibit 5.1 A Case of Confidentiality

In a recent evaluation of a succession management process, several claims surfaced that the organization's leadership team was biased against women. Specifically, some employees alleged that all of the "plum" developmental assignments were given to men and that women were relegated to less distinctive, low exposure assignments. As part of the data collection phase, explanations were offered for why this may be the case, most centering on a perceived paternalistic culture that had been established by the owner. During an early briefing in which these preliminary findings were being presented, it became very clear that the organization's leadership wanted to know specifically who was making these statements. The evaluation team pushed back by stating that participants in the evaluation had been informed that their responses to both a survey and an interview would be aggregated and not reported out at an individual level. This did not satisfy the leadership, despite the reminder that they had agreed to the confidentiality provision before the evaluation began. To head off this escalating situation, the evaluation team convinced the stakeholders that, before breaching the promised confidentiality, they should first determine whether there was any merit to the claim. As it turned out, differences were found between the assignments provided to men and women, but not as dramatic as originally suggested. This finding was presented in the next briefing, along with recommendations for addressing the situation. This seemed to satisfy the stakeholders, and they no longer called for the identification of those who had raised the issue.

While this outcome could have been different, the point here was that the evaluation team stood its ground while seeking a solution that would keep the confidentiality provision in place. Assuming that the leadership team had pushed for disclosure of individual names, the next likely path would have been to pursue the issue with the organization's legal counsel and gain their support and advice on how to appropriately address the situation.

fidential surveys and interviews may be rendered useless in the future and (b) the short-term gain of additional information in the current HR program evaluation can deepen suspicion of management and its intentions. These effects are too great a price to pay for violating the pledge.

That being said, there may be occasions (hopefully rare) in which confidential evaluation findings surface legal, ethical, or safety issues that could put the organization or its employees at risk. In these instances, the findings may have to be brought to the attention of the organization's internal or as-needed external legal counsel so that a decision can be made about how to appropriately handle them. While

the collective judgment of the evaluation team could supply alternative strategies for balancing confidentiality against potentially larger
concerns, when in doubt, it is best to begin formulating a strategy to
address the information sooner rather than later. The legal counsel
may want the information restricted until it can further investigate the
situation and determine how best to proceed. If the program evaluation team already includes legal counsel, that attorney would likely be
able to advise on the appropriate approach in these situations.

Adapt Communications to the Audience's Skills and Needs

The key to effective oral or written communication of findings,
conclusions, and recommendations is knowing your audience and
adjusting the dissemination of information to their skills and needs.
As we have implied before, communicating findings to audiences
with limited methodological and statistical skills is not a time for an
evaluation team to try to impress others with their ability to use
complex statistics and methods. Instead, the briefings and reports
(except perhaps for a technical appendix) should be prepared at a
level that is understandable to all or almost all stakeholders who
have a need to know the evaluation team's findings, conclusions,
and recommendations.

   Much of the oral or written communication will likely involve
basic statistics such as means and percentages, even if the findings
were derived from advanced inferential statistics. In general, discussion of the methods should arise only when it is necessary to establish
the credibility of the findings, set the context for other information,
or cite important limitations to the data and findings. Professional jar-
gon such as "quasi-experimental design," "hypothetical constructs,"
and "factor loadings" rarely have a place in communications to stakeholders in applied settings, even if they were central to the research
design and analyses that the HR program evaluation team actually
used. These terms should be reserved for discussions with professional

colleagues and in technical documentation that could later be important for a legal challenge to the HR program.

This does not mean that the evaluation team should not have used optimum evaluation design or complex statistics in gathering and analyzing the data. Rather, it suggests that the team must translate those complexities into readily understood information. For example, an HR program evaluation team still has to compute the very complex statistics used to assess personnel selection and compensation systems for potential racial and gender bias, but the team must translate their procedures and findings into something that the stakeholders can use. Effectively translating the complex statistics into more understandable concepts and findings will help stakeholders to perceive that (a) the HR program evaluation was thorough and (b) the conclusions and recommendations were based on sound findings. The team should have the more complex information available if someone in the audience (such as engineers or quantitatively oriented personnel in the marketing or financial departments) suggests that other statistics or methods would have been more appropriate. In general, we prefer to err on the simple side during our communication preparations. All of this is not to imply that the stakeholders are "too dumb to understand." Rather, it merely acknowledges that their professional experiences and education have centered on other issues, and that the members of the evaluation team are to use their professional experiences and education to find ways to translate their findings into information that can be readily grasped.

Get to the Bottom Line Early

Key stakeholders for the HR program evaluation will want to know the primary findings and recommendations very early in the team's oral or written presentation. This is one of the reasons that many reports start with an executive summary or other type of synopsis, so that executives as well as other key stakeholders have a general framework upon which they can organize their thoughts about the subsequent specifics that led to the bottom line message. This orientation often stands in stark contrast to an academic publication or presentation that may emphasize an in-depth literature review and description of methods before even beginning to cover the findings and recommendations. That is not to say that applied stakeholders do not care about what others have found in prior HR research, what methods were used, and the contextual factors that influenced the findings. Getting to the bottom line early emphasizes business constraints placed on key stakeholders who have myriad issues competing for their time and their need to delegate methodological responsibilities and duties to those most qualified to evaluate them—the HR program evaluation team. Royse and his colleagues (2001, p. 382) described the tendency and possible reason why evaluators often overwhelm their audience with too much information: "Wanting the sponsor to feel that the contract amount was truly earned, evaluators may compile such an awesome assemblage of tables, charts, and dry, boring paragraphs that only the boldest of academics would attempt to wade through that portion of the report."

Determine What to Do with Findings That Do Not Fit

Regardless of how vigilant a team is with regard to staying on course and answering the assigned evaluation questions, the team will almost always identify important or provocative findings that are only tangentially related to the evaluation questions. Decisions about whether or not these issues are communicated to key stakeholders are influenced by a variety of factors, two of which are described in more detail below.

Consider the Amount of Information Substantiating the Issue. The HR program evaluation team may have only one or two instances when the provocative issue surfaced. These may have been identified in off-handed remarks made by participants during interviews, or the team may have inadvertently discovered something in its review of documents or other archival materials related to the program. More preparatory information might have to be gathered before the organization would choose to devote resources to checking on the prevalence of the issue. The decision to raise an issue that has not been fully checked out should be driven by its perceived importance to the evaluation at hand and couched with the need to investigate further. The risks are that the issue may not turn out to be that prevalent and its discussion could divert the stakeholders from those findings that are central to answering the evaluation questions and have been fully researched. HR program evaluation teams must remember during their preparation and presentation that their time with key stakeholders is limited and that presentation of the additional issues could limit the thoroughness of the case that they can make for their primary findings, conclusions, and recommendations.

Take into Account the Relevance of the Issue to the Stakeholder Groups. The stakeholder groups may not contain the correct people to address the tangentially related issue, even if the issue merits further discussion. For example, interviews conducted during an evaluation of training for administrative personnel could have contained allegations that some administrative staff did not have the credentials claimed when they were hired. The allegations surfaced when two interviewees discussed the wide variation of performance among clerical personnel (one of the HR program evaluation's outcome measures). The training evaluation team might not brief the issue in-depth because background checks were tangentially related to the training evaluation, were not a core responsibility for any of the key stakeholders, and were mentioned by only two interviewees late in the evaluation. In this case, valuable briefing time would be lost raising an issue with people who could not take the actions necessarily to address the issue appropriately. The evaluation team will need to judge how relevant and important an "outlying" issue is in this context.

Provocative but tangentially related findings can be raised with key stakeholders in one-on-one or small group meetings that are held independent of the dissemination of the program evaluation findings, conclusions, and recommendations. With the limited time available to cover what are often months of work to answer the evaluation questions, HR program evaluation teams cannot afford the possibility of being sidetracked and using valuable time on important, but extraneous issues that stakeholders cannot or will not chose to address.

Tie It All Together:
Findings ➤ Conclusions ➤ Recommendations

Stakeholders will expect evaluation briefings and reports to provide a direct link between their questions and the evaluation's findings, conclusions, and recommendations. Each conclusion and recommendation that makes it into the briefing or report should be tied to an original evaluation question and findings. This can be organized relatively easily by presenting each question or issue, followed by the relevant key findings, conclusions, and resulting recommendation(s) (Morris, Fitz-Gibbon, & Freeman, 1987).

The foundation and justification for the conclusions reached from an evaluation should also be clearly presented. This step to tie together the various parts of the communications will ensure that stakeholders can independently assess the correctness of each conclusion and trace the evaluation team's logic and procedures for reaching these conclusions. Conclusions that are based on hard data should be distinguished from those that are more speculative. In addition, alternative conclusions that are plausible but have been rejected might also deserve presentation after an appropriate explanation.

The credibility of the conclusions and recommendations will also be enhanced to the extent that the context (for example, organizational culture, competing program demands, staff, and politics) within which the HR program was evaluated has been taken into account and described. This step will (a) assist stakeholders in interpreting the findings, (b) increase the likelihood that the conclusions are realistic, and (c) produce recommendations that can be implemented in the conditions surrounding the HR program. The Joint Committee's (1994, p. 49) professional standard on report clarity stated, "Evaluation reports should clearly describe the program being evaluated, including its context, and the purposes, procedures, and findings of the evaluation, so that essential information is provided and easily understood."

Depict Findings and Recommendations Visually

Visual depiction of findings, conclusions, and recommendations can help the team distill months of work into the hour or less allotted for conveying all of the key information. As part of determining the evaluation team's composition during the planning phase of the evaluation, due consideration should have been given to ensuring that someone on the team had the requisite skills needed to develop visual aids. Alternatively, a team in a large organization may have arranged to obtain assistance from other organizational personnel such as graphic artists or marketing specialists.

As Royse and his co-authors (2001, p. 174) stated, "many agency directors and advisory board members' eyes will glaze over when you start talking about *t*-tests and chi-squares in the analysis of evaluation data, but they will quickly perk up at the sight of a crisp, clean graph showing things clearly going up or down." In this section, we explore four of the more common types of visual aids that might supplement the bullet-filled and other word-intensive slides or pages appearing in project presentations and reports. These supplemental visual aids include pictures to document a situation, schematics to show processes that are followed in an HR program, graphs to depict numerical findings from the evaluation, and tables or arrays of findings.

Excusing the cliché, often a picture *is* worth a thousand words. And the greater speed and ease with which visual aids can be developed, the more options an evaluation team has to construct alternative pictures of the same information so that members can determine which version contributes best to the story that is to be told.

Picture the Situation to Let Stakeholders See How It Really Is or Might Be

Just a few years ago, we rarely used pictures for our HR program-evaluation reports or presentations. Pictures printed in our reports could be expensive and were often of poor quality. Our oral presentations with pictures from a camera or graphic arts professional sometimes necessitated either capturing the entire presentation on slides or switching back and forth between overhead and slide projectors. Moreover, the pictures sometimes limited us to black-and-white representations.

Digital cameras and computers have greatly enhanced the ability of program evaluators to document their findings with pictures and discuss their points concretely with their audiences. Digital cameras provide for a quick and easy process of visually capturing a situation and transferring it to a paper or electronic image. The ability to see immediately whether or not the situation was captured in a desired way allows the picture-taker to continue taking pictures until a satisfactory visual aid has been produced. Similarly, the capabilities and ease-of-use of computers, image scanners, and graphic arts programs offer many possibilities to HR program evaluation teams wanting to add other types of pictures.

Pictures can be useful to document the situations found in a wide range of HR programs. For example, Figure 5.1 shows a mildly humorous picture appropriate for the beginning of a presentation detailing the evaluation of a performance appraisal program. The subsequent presentation could then be organized around the positive effects derived from a web-based system for eliminating much of the displayed paperwork. Additionally, the mound of paperwork and the winsome smile of a well-known and well-liked employee could subtly show that each stakeholder needs to find ways to achieve greater efficiency in managing and coaching their employees.

Other types of pictures that might be found in HR program evaluation briefings and reports might include an organizational chart depicting positions and reporting relationships for the staff of the program being evaluated, proposed physical security measures to

Figure 5.1 An Example of an Electronic Picture

limit access to the organization, past and recommended changes to increase safety in the manufacturing plant, potential barriers to or implemented enhancements for physically challenged staff, physical layout of a work team (for example, a customer-service call center), and pictures of computer screens to show employees how to use on-line training aids or communications technologies. Such pictures can be enhanced with software to include pointers to and annotations for special points of interest depicted in an image. Moreover, the use of before pictures contrasted with the proposed ways that the situation might be changed are particularly useful in providing concrete information to stakeholders who may not be familiar with specific situations relevant to the HR program or able to visualize the current and proposed future conditions mentally.

Show Stakeholders a Path Through the Process

Many HR programs use multi-step processes that are difficult to explain in words alone. Conveying this type of information can be particularly difficult if there are many steps within the larger or longer stages of the process. The explanation often becomes much easier when the audience can be referred to a schematic that allows the reader or listener to think about the current step while seeing the prior steps and anticipating the steps that are yet to be explained. Nearly ten years ago, one of the authors saw a particularly memorable schematic depicting the retention of U.S. military officers. The schematic used an oil pipeline as an analogy for how the officer pipeline refines the person (through a military academy, ROTC, or officer candidate school) and then brings all commissioned officers through each hierarchical level, with no lateral hiring. The leaks in the pipeline showed the percentage of officers lost at each step in the officers' generalized career cycle.

An evaluation team might also use schematics to show timelines. For example, organizations generally have a set of escalating steps that are followed to resolve labor grievances or equal employment opportunity complaints, with each step tied to a deadline and the entity that would work with the parties to the grievance or complaint. Figure 5.2 shows a four-stage appeals process, with each stage having three or four steps. The process shows the order in which the stages and steps occur, the prescribed actions within each stage, the employees involved in the steps, and time limits if certain types of actions are taken. Also, the bottom portion of the schematic provides a caution about a prohibited action that might otherwise be violated by employees who have never or infrequently used this process.

The purpose of this schematic is to describe a formal appeals process for handling all employee objections related to the performance management process in a fair, objective, and consistent manner. This process applies to all salaried employees who participate in the performance management process.

Figure 5.2 An Example of a Schematic Showing a Process

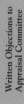

Discuss Objections with Manager

1. An employee begins the appeals process by verbally discussing objections with his/her immediate manager.

2. This discussion must occur within one (1) week after the final appraisal discussion.

3. If the objections are unresolved through this discussion, the employee clearly documents disagreements in writing and forwards this within two (2) weeks from this discussion to his/her immediate manager.

4. The management team must meet with the team member to review this issue within two (2) weeks of receipt of the employee's correspondence.

Objections Unresolved OR Rating Change Considered

1. If the objections are unresolved by management OR if management decides that a rating change should be considered, the original written communication is forwarded to HR.

2. HR facilitates a meeting with the employee's immediate manager, second-level manager, and general manager to determine if a rating change is warranted based on the employee's written objections. This meeting will occur within two (2) weeks of the management team meeting.

3. The employee's immediate and general manager will communicate the results of this meeting to the employee at the conclusion of this meeting.

Written Objections to Appraisal Committee

1. If the employee is dissatisfied with the outcome of the meeting facilitated by HR, the employee may submit the written objections to the Appraisal Appeals Committee.

2. Written objections must be submitted to the committee within five (5) working days of the meeting facilitated by HR.

3. The appeals committee will be comprised of three department general managers: the department general manager involved(if not the immediate or second-level manager involved), one department general manager selected from a list by the grieving employee, and one general manager selected by Human Resources.

4. The Appraisal Appeals Committee shall determine what persons, if any will appear before them.

Review by Appraisal Committee

1. The Appraisal Appeals Committee will review all written documentation provided by the employee and management to make a final determination concerning the appraisal.

2. This determination will be based on the facts presented.

3. The appraisal appeals committee will complete this process within 30 days if practicable.

Rating Changes

Please note that rating changes may ONLY be made through consultation with HR. No manager is permitted to change a rating without involving HR.

Clarify Numerical Findings with Graphs

Graphs are visual depictions commonly used to convey quantitative HR program evaluation findings. They can communicate complex ideas and summarized information from large databases effectively. While a graph can help the audience to grasp many individual findings at once, it is important to recognize when graphs either may be misleading or display the wrong types of data. Even though there are exceptions to almost every graphing guideline, we will offer some general guidelines that we have used successfully in our work.

Ask, "Is That Graph Misleading?" A graphing problem nearly made one of the authors late for his briefing on the evaluation of a developmental program for new professionals. The author's assistant graphed numerous employee survey findings for the briefing but failed to recognize the perceptual problems that resulted when the software automatically adjusted the percent depicted on each graph's Y axis. The author had to quickly re-work all of the graphs and then print new copies of the report, just in time for the briefing. The key takeaway from this experience was to remind staff that they should not unconsciously allow a computer program to decide how best to convey the information from an HR program evaluation.

Figure 5.3 illustrates five ways that a single set of data might be displayed. Figure 5.3.a is the graph that we would typically use to present percentage-based findings. The graph's Y or vertical axis is about three-fourths as high as its X or horizontal axis is long, a scaling proportion that some statisticians have long advocated. Although it would be nice if software programs kept the ratio constant except when the evaluation team consciously chose to modify the ratio, many programs vary the ratio from graph to graph. This seemingly innocuous change in the ratio of X-axis to Y-axis is another situation that can inadvertently lead to over- or under-emphasis of differences. This situation is especially evident when looking at a series of graphs that depict related findings (for example, for three separately graphed items showing subgroup differences in satisfaction with pay, supervision, and working conditions) using perhaps one inch to display ten percentage points on the Y axis for one chart and one inch to display twenty-five percentage points on another chart. In such graphs, the software is attempting to emphasize just the portion of the 100-point percentage scale that is "relevant" to each graph.

In contrast to Figure 5.3.a, Figure 5.3.b depicts the same data using an X-to-Y-axis ratio that far exceeds the three-quarters high rule. Elongating the X-axis without also changing the Y-axis can easily mislead readers. If most of the graphs in a briefing or report are done with a smaller X-to-Y-axis ratio, the audience could misperceive that the differences are less than they actually are. In a visual comparison of the two graphs at the top of Figure 5.3, the five percentage-point differences between the bars in Figure 5.3.b look half as large as the same differences shown in Figure 5.3.a. Hopefully, a decision to change the ratio is not a conscious effort to mislead readers into believing that a difference was smaller than it actually was (such as for a selection ratio that shows equal employment opportunity concerns).

Figure 5.3.c depicts the opposite problem of that shown in Figure 5.3.b. This opposite effect was obtained by magnifying the differences in Figure 5.3.c so that they appear to be larger than those in Figure 5.3.a. This type of change to the ratio could mislead the audience into believing that a difference in, say, before- versus after-training scores was larger than it actually was.

Figure 5.3.d magnifies the group differences much more than even Figure 5.3.c, but it does so by graphing only a small range of the possible values on the Y axis. In contrast, the graph in Figure 5.3.a uses the full range of the 0 to 100 percent scale—something we *typically* do in graphing percentages. If a difference is so small that it can be seen only when a small portion of the scale is graphed, it may not be identifying a sufficiently meaningful difference to warrant discussion. Our advice is to make a conscious determination about whether a portion of the full scale (for example, 100 percent or a 1-to-5-point scale) provides a more meaningful depiction than the full scale. Letting a graphics program determine the best way to display data can result in confusion for stakeholders when the findings are presented and

Figure 5.3 An Example of Contrasting Numerical Graphs

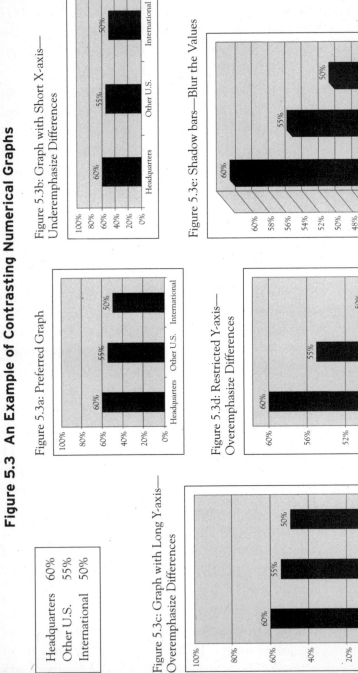

Figure 5.3a: Preferred Graph

Figure 5.3b: Graph with Short X-axis—
Underemphasize Differences

Figure 5.3c: Graph with Long Y-axis—
Overemphasize Differences

Figure 5.3d: Restricted Y-axis—
Overemphasize Differences

Figure 5.3e: Shadow bars—Blur the Values

possibly the loss of both credibility and valuable briefing time if such confusion occurs and the briefer must take the additional time to explain findings that could have been graphed more clearly.

Finally, we heartily agree with Wilkinson and his colleagues' (1999, p. 12) advice to "Avoid complex figures when simpler ones will do." Some evaluation teams add more visually complex features such as using shadow boxes in their bar charts. Although some members of the audience may find the shadow boxes and 3-D look shown in Figure 5.3.e more aesthetically pleasing than the graph in Figure 5.3.a, we are proponents of keeping the message as simple as possible by avoiding ornate graphs with "enhancements" that can be difficult to read and understand. For example, it is difficult to tell whether the reader should be paying attention to the front or the back of the bars in Figure 5.3.e. The first priority for an evaluation team should be to advance an understanding of the findings, where the design features of the graph seamlessly facilitate this objective.

Ask, "What Types of Graphs Can I Use to Display My Findings?" Among other things, the choice of design for displaying quantitative results will be based on the nature of the findings, amount of data to be presented, and labeling requirements. Since the number of pieces of information can be a major determinant of the types of graphs that will be appropriate for displaying the information, we will explore that issue further by discussing some of the graphs that we have used most often.

Single Variable Findings. Evaluation findings that involve single categorical variables are often presented as bar charts because these graphs are particularly easy to interpret. Means, percentages, or other data can be presented above each bar to increase the precision depicted in the graph. While pie charts are also used to facilitate interpretation of single variable data involving percentages or proportions, there is some question as to how useful pie charts actually are in the interpretation of findings. One graphics display author (Tufte, 2001, p. 178) exclaimed, "the only worse design than a pie chart is several of them." He stated, along with others (Bertin, 1981), that pie charts are confusing and should never be used due to their (a) low "data-density" (number of entries in data matrix/area of the graph) and (b) failure to order data along a coherent visual dimension.

Two Variable Charts. A stacked, or the more common side-by-side, bar graph is a useful way to show two or more categories of results at once. The length of the bar graph represents one hundred percentage points, which is subdivided to allow comparison of individual category percents. Figure 5.4 presents an example of a stacked bar graph, showing the percent of survey participants who reported being very dissatisfied/dissatisfied, neither satisfied nor dissatisfied, or very satisfied/satisfied with the complaint process. More specifically, respondents who reported one or more situations of racial/ethnic harassment or discrimination by civilian(s) or military personnel in a 1996 survey were asked to answer six items for only the situation that they considered most bothersome. This type of graph might be particularly useful when presenting two years of statistics—survey findings, budgets, staffing, or other variables—side by side. Also, the graph displays another way to enhance communication when constructing a graph or table. Here, the evaluation team ordered the findings within the graph to allow the audience to easily see which aspects of the complaint process were rated most favorably by the largest percentage of respondents and which were rated least favorably. Finally, collapsing the five survey response alternatives into three graphed categories of responses gives the stakeholders a clearer view of the big picture about satisfaction versus dissatisfaction.

Trends and Patterns. Line graphs are particularly useful for comparing two or more groups across time. The amount of the effect, funding, or some other aspect of the HR program evaluation is plotted on the vertical axis and time periods are plotted on the horizontal axis. Tufte (2001) suggested that line graphs should be greater in length than height (by about 50 percent), in contradiction to the

Figure 5.4 An Example of a Stacked Bar Chart

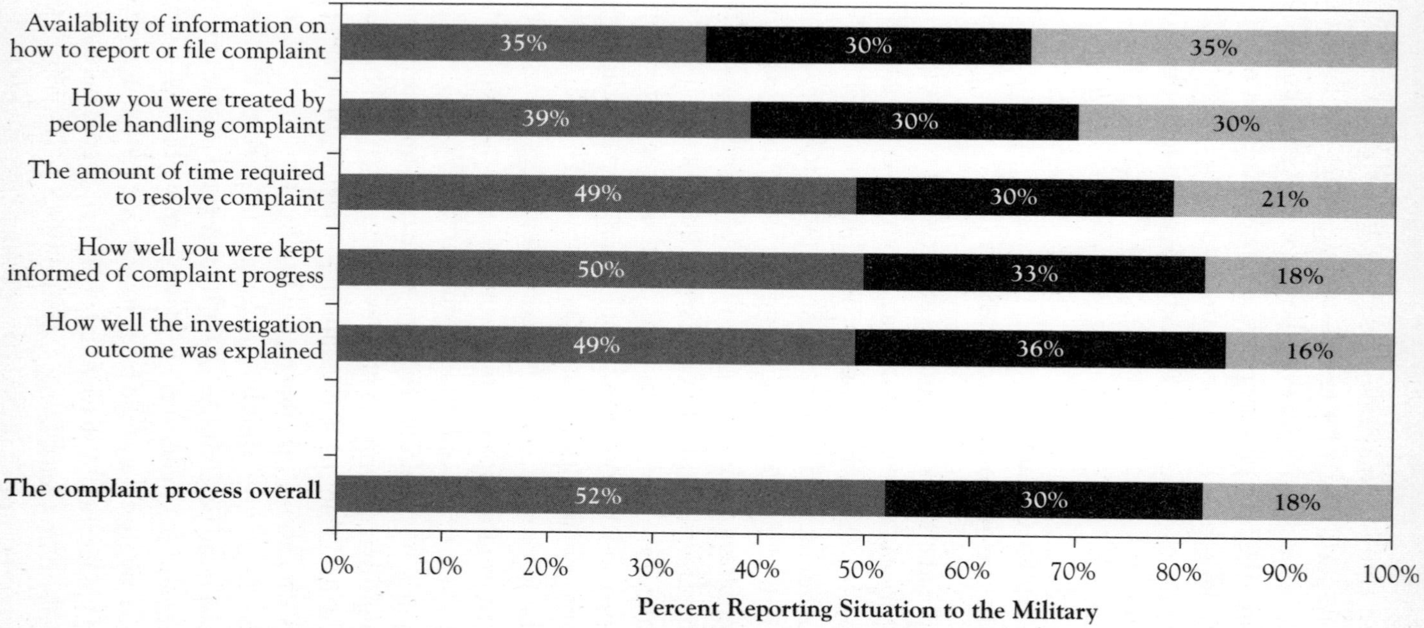
Availablity of information on how to report or file complaint
35%
30%
35%
How you were treated by people handling complaint
39%
30%
30%
The amount of time required to resolve complaint
49%
30%
21%
How well you were kept informed of complaint progress
50%
33%
18%
How well the investigation outcome was explained
49%
36%
16%
The complaint process overall
52%
30%
18%
0%
10%
20%
30%
40%
50%
60%
70%
80%
90%
100%
Percent Reporting Situation to the Military
Very dissatisfied/Dissatisfied
Neither satisfied nor dissatisfied
Very satisfied/Satisfied

Graph taken from J. Scarville, S.B. Button, J.E. Edwards, A.R. Lancaster, & T.W. Elig. (1999, August). *Armed forces equal opportunity survey* (DMDC Report No. 97-027). Arlington, VA: Defense Manpower Data Center.

earlier cited three-fourths rule advocated by others. It is his contention that, particularly for trends or time-series displays, a wider base is more accessible to the eye, allows for easier reading of labels, and facilitates the interpretation of the causes. Another result of increasing the length is that changes from year to year do not appear to be so abrupt because there is more space between units on the horizontal axis.

Use a Table to Convey
Easily Misunderstood Information

Many people first think of columns and rows of numbers when tables are mentioned as a way to display information in evaluation reports. As we have shown in numerous exhibits in this book, tables are also a useful method for organizing narrative information. A primary strength of both numerical and narrative tables is that they allow stakeholders to view the most salient HR program evaluation factors in an organized manner and with the least amount of irrelevant information. The stakeholders are then free to compare and contrast one row to another or to focus on multiple findings such as cost or employee attitudes in a single column. The focus on a particular column or row occurs, for example, when the information carries more weight with top management stakeholders or it indicates a situation that needs immediate attention.

Tables may be preferable to graphs when discussion of the findings will highlight differences of more than one type. The information shown in Table 5.1 shows findings that might benefit from separate points about (a) the overall finding that more than two-thirds of the employees said they took pride in working for the organization, (b) large percentages of both males and females expressed this feeling, and (c) males were somewhat more likely—than were females—to say that they take pride in working for the organization.

Tabled values should be rounded off so that there is a balance between precision and readability. Cohen (1990, p. 1,305) noted that findings are sometimes reported to unjustifiable numbers of decimal places. He also stated, "These superfluous decimal places are no better than random numbers. They are actually worse than useless because the clutter they create, particularly in tables, serves to distract the eye and mind from the necessary comparisons among the meaningful leading digits. Less is indeed more here." In our HR program evaluations and academic research, we rarely present survey-derived percentages with decimal places because the decimals suggest a level of precision that does not exist or is irrelevant (see Table 5.1). For instance, getting a few more people to respond to a survey might change a finding from, say, 72.6 percent to 72.8 percent, but any recommendation made about 72.6 percent would be the same as that made about 72.8 percent. Similarly, other HR program data such as dollars in budgets can be rounded to much larger units such as thousands or tens of thousands to make it easier for stakeholders to see the bigger picture. Keys to providing successful HR program evaluation briefings and reports are knowing the stakeholder audience and presenting the level of precision needed for that audience.

Tables also present a way to display several important qualitative characteristics that include multiple conditions, settings, or alternative actions. We have most commonly used tabular presentations of qualitative information to display advantages, benefits, or strengths versus disadvantages, costs, or weaknesses. For example, Table 1.1

Table 5.1 An Example of Numerical Information Displayed in a Table

Survey item: "I take pride in working for this organization."

	Employee Gender		
Response to Item	**Males**	**Females**	**All Employees**
Strongly Agree/Agree	72%	65%	69%
Neutral	18%	24%	20%
Strongly Disagree/Disagree	10%	11%	10%
Total	100%	100%	99%

Note: Columns may not total to 100 percent because of rounding.

shows the relative advantages and disadvantages of using three types of evaluators against each of eight criteria. And Table 2.2 shows six types of error that might be present as well as an example, the cause, and a method for lessening the error. HR program evaluation teams should find it particularly useful to create tables when they are

- Comparing alternatives (for example, an alternative health insurance plan versus the current plan),
- Showing how different units have instituted a program (for example, the performance appraisal system for the parent company versus the one in a company that has just been acquired), and
- Contrasting characteristics of the organization undergoing the HR program evaluation and characteristics for similar bench-marked organizations (for example, the organization's executive compensation system versus that of industry leaders).

Deliver the Product Orally and in Writing

In most cases, the HR program evaluation team should have planned to provide one or more briefings and a written report of the full evaluation. While the two types of products may be delivered at the same time, some organizations may desire briefings on the findings, conclusions, and recommendations as soon as the information becomes available. Such organizations may view the written product as something for the archives, which will not be needed until the program is evaluated again. At any rate, the timing of the products is but one of many differences that we cover in this section that first outlines the requirements for briefings and then outlines those for a report.

Share Findings When the Promise Has Been Made

During the planning in Phase 2, the program evaluation team should have held discussions with top management to determine the types of information that would be fed back to organizational members after the program evaluation was over. This decision should have been made before interviews, focus groups, and surveys started because the individuals providing the requested information will have inevitably asked questions about whether or not they would be able to see the findings. Typically, decision-makers would have told the HR program evaluation team that the findings would be shared with organizational members.

Use Briefings to Put the Word Out Quickly and Answer Questions

The evaluation team should negotiate a realistic timeline for disseminating briefings to meet the information and decision-making needs of the program's stakeholders. Briefings can serve as a powerful tool for ensuring ongoing stakeholder engagement and support for the evaluation and its findings, conclusions, and recommendations. The briefings may be used as both interim and end-of-evaluation communication tools. As with any other successful communication strategy, the evaluation team should prepare their briefings to take into account the composition of its stakeholder audiences, the audiences' priorities, and what findings or issues are most likely to spark debate or resistance. Regardless of the medium

Once the earlier phases of the evaluation have been completed and top management has been briefed, management may want the HR program evaluation team/contractor to renege on the promise of feedback. The reasons or excuses given for this change of heart might be due to the perception that the results (a) are too negative, (b) could open the organization up to lawsuits, (c) could provide competitors with too much information, or (d) are too politically sensitive. As with the confidentiality pledge, serious harm can be done if the promise of feedback is broken. Moreover, all but the most closely held information seems to have a way of leaking out, and rumors about what the findings revealed are often wrong and possibly worse than the actual findings.

(including verbal, written, or multi-media) used for disseminating the information, the briefing should be succinct and easy for the audience to understand.

Adapt the Presentation to Different Audiences.   There are a number of factors to consider when preparing for a briefing, from the specific preferences of the audience to the physical layout of the room. In part, the success of a briefing will depend on how thoroughly the evaluation team considered the format and context of its communication (Joint Committee, 1994).

Perspective of the Audience.   Representatives of a stakeholder group might be consulted prior to the briefing to ensure that the presentation is tailored to their informational needs and preferred style of communication. For example, a briefing provided to top management will almost surely be different from the briefing that is given to other stakeholder groups. Executives will more than likely expect a briefing to get to the bottom line early and quickly surface any critical issues for discussion. Other stakeholder groups such as the HR program staff may wish to focus more narrowly on a specific set of issues or to drill into the data when attempting to discredit findings and recommendations that might disadvantage their group.

Separate the "Have to Know" from the "Nice to Know."   It will be important to assign priorities to information that is to be communicated so that the briefing meets the audience's needs and can be modified "on-the-fly." This level of preparation allows the briefer to skip over results if, or when, the initial discussion unexpectedly uses a disproportionate amount of the allotted presentation time on a few initial issues. The briefer must get the presentation back on track without the audience feeling that the presentation has been very uneven. Back-up information on the HR program evaluation should be available just in case an issue arises that requires presenting information from a more in-depth analysis. A clear understanding of the audience's priorities—before the briefing—will help the evaluation team determine which issues are likely to require a "deep dive" into the bases for findings and conclusions during the presentation.

Use a Murder Board—Anticipate the Worst. Murder boards are often used when advocates of a person or position want to do their utmost to prepare for those who would like to kill a high-stakes HR program, idea, or recommendation. The members of the murder board attempt to antici-pate and ask the tough questions that stakeholders might later raise during the briefings.

This process can be a particu-larly useful preparation technique when the HR program findings, conclusions, and recommendations (a) are controversial, (b) are not supported by all key stakeholders, or (c) will likely result in expensive or disruptive changes. The idea is to grow used to the questions and pressure, develop a logical presen-tation of the facts, and make sure that the message does not become diluted. Preparation is a key ele-ment in minimizing the chance that others will later be able to gain the momentum and take the pre-sentation in a way that would not reflect favorably on all of the work that led to the findings, conclusions, and recommendations.

Practicing answers aloud and in front of a murder board allows the presenter to gain feedback from multiple perspectives re-garding what was good and bad about the organi-zation of the presenta-tion, answers to expected and unexpected ques-tions, and the presenter's communication style. In some cases, the presenter might want to videotape the practice sessions and watch the sessions to gain additional insights.

In situations in which the stakes are not so high and the findings, conclusions, and recommendations are likely to be acceptable, a murder board may not be needed. It is, however, still a good practice to try to anticipate the questions, verbalize the answers, and seek feedback from other evaluation team members on how to improve the presentation.

Select Feedback Mechanisms. There are a variety of media through which information can be communicated, and a mix of two or more of these media may be needed to deliver an effective message. The choice of media should be based on the target audience and timed according to their information requirements. Some common formats for conveying HR program evaluation information include PowerPoint presentations, informational question-and-answer sessions, an intranet-based presentation or document containing answers to frequently asked questions, summary reports, articles in the organization's newsletter, and videoconference or videotape.

Determine Who Will Disseminate Information to Which Stakeholder Groups. The evaluation team will have to designate who will brief evaluation results to which stakeholder groups. As previously mentioned, a set of ground rules should be established early in the evaluation and integrated into the overall communication plan. Among other things, it should outline team members' roles. The choice of which team members will be the primary briefers should be based on their role on the team, influence within specific stakeholder groups and the organization as a whole, and interpersonal and communication skills. The organizational level of the stakeholder audience is another key concern when deciding who will brief evaluation results.

Top Management. When it is time to review the findings, conclusions, and recommendations with these stakeholders, the team leader is often the logical choice for presenter. Her experiences in earlier meetings with top management, gaining their buy-in and giving updates, should provide insights into this stakeholder group's priorities, biases, and other potentially sensitive concerns. While it might be tempting to allow several members of the team to present portions of the briefing, we suggest that no more than two team members provide the briefing. In the short time that will be allotted for the briefing, more than two presenters would inhibit the flow of the presentation as well as the answers to any questions that might arise. The team leader can acknowledge the other key team members' contributions in a brief opening remark.

Other Key Stakeholder Groups and the Organization as a Whole. During the briefing to top management, certain executives may convey their desire to communicate evaluation findings to other stakeholder groups within the organization. Top leaders may decide that they are in the best position to provide evaluation results to other groups, particularly their own departments. If this is the case, the evaluation team will almost surely still be asked to prepare each leader's script and accompanying slides, and to be on hand should assistance be needed answering questions during the briefings. As was the case in preparing the briefing for top management, the evaluation team members will want to make sure that they clearly understand the perspective and informational requirements of the target audience, since most groups will be asking slightly different questions, even for the same general issues. If, on the other hand, the evaluation team is responsible for presenting the information to the other types of stakeholders, team members other than the leader could share the responsibility of providing feedback and answering questions.

While organizational realities will at times dictate how certain information is shared, the integrity of the evaluation team must not be compromised. The use of common sense and negotiation will generally result in a middle ground that allows the team to present the controversial finding(s) if they are central to the HR program evaluation's findings, conclusions, and recommendations.

Be Ready to Deal with Possible Hurdles. It is not unusual for an evaluation team to be faced with ethical or professional dilemmas during the communication phase of an HR program evaluation. This is particularly true when program evaluation findings are unexpected, are negative or do not support a key stakeholder's specific point of view. The dilemma about what the team should do in such situations has been addressed by others. According to an inscription on the National Academy building in the U.S. capital, Albert Einstein said, "The right to search for truth implies also a duty; one must not conceal any part of what one has recognized to be true."

Write a Report to Preserve Information and Organize Documentation for Storage

In addition to providing briefings, most evaluations will involve writing a formal report and organizing and storing supporting documentation that does not appear in the report. This report should document the purpose of the study, describe the methods, present results and conclusions that are tied to each evaluation question, and finally, provide recommendations. The report should also describe the context within which the study was conducted, explain the study's limitations, offer appropriate caveats for interpreting the results, and provide insights to a future program evaluation team.

Organize the Report for the Quick Location of Information. A report can be organized into any number of components. We tend to prefer seven components—executive summary, background (the program's objectives and activities), evaluation questions, methods for data collection and analyses, findings, conclusions and recommendations, and appendices—for such things as supporting materials and expanded analyses. While one or more of the outlined actions within the seven components are probably missing from every research project report that we have prepared, we work within the constraints of doing research in dynamic, real-world settings and strive toward these ideals. (Readers are referred to the American Psychological Association [2001] and Morris and his associates [1987] for more detailed instructions on writing a program evaluation technical report.)

Executive Summary. The executive summary is probably the most crucial component of the report because it is likely to be the one section of the written report—if any—that key stakeholders read, due to their hectic schedules. This section should provide a concise (often one-to-four pages) summary of the full report. It should address why the evaluation was conducted, highlight the methodology and findings, and present the recommendations. The executive summary is typically written last, after the full report has been assembled (Morris & colleagues, 1987).

Background. The background section should provide an overview of the program's key objectives and activities, including such information as why and when the program was started, how it was implemented, what its stated goals are, who participates in the program, who manages the program, and any other relevant descriptive information. Internal documents that describe the program, such as the program proposal, prior evaluations or studies, program policies, criteria and procedures, strategic plans, or staffing charts, can be referenced in this section and either included as appendices or in other supporting documentation that is otherwise stored with the report.

Purpose. This section outlines the objectives of the evaluation and describes considerations that may have influenced the decision to conduct the HR program evaluation. The stakeholders who requested the evaluation should be identified, along with the evaluation concerns that led to the HR program evaluation. It is also important to include the procedures used for generating the evaluation questions and to indicate whether all key questions were addressed and, if not, why (for example, limited resources or outside of the research scope). This section should provide an indication of the extent to which stakeholders agreed with the relevance and importance of the final set of evaluation questions.

Methods. This section describes the procedures used for answering the evaluation questions. It should detail the overall evaluation design, data collection methods, instruments (including surveys and interview protocols), criterion measures, sampling design and characteristics, steps taken for ensuring measurement accuracy (including measurement qualities or psychometric characteristics of the data collection instruments), and factors that could limit how much the findings can be generalized. It is very important that this section provide full details regarding how the study was conducted and how the particular evaluation design was executed. The credibility of the findings and recommendations will rest on sound methods and full descriptions of those methods. All instruments and materials (such as interview and focus group protocols, surveys, training materials) created for the HR program evaluation should be included in an appendix to this report. Also, as we mentioned in Phase 3 on data collection, this type of information can be extremely important to a future HR program evaluation team. It can save the future team time and money and can provide insights into potential reasons why results were different in a subsequent program evaluation.

Findings. This section provides the answers to each of the evaluation questions. An attempt should be made here to organize the statistics into simple-to-interpret tables and graphs and organize the qualitative information into meaningful categories. The goal is to translate complex statistics and potentially voluminous qualitative data into understandable findings. When both qualitative and quantitative data have been collected, it is important to synthesize these two types of data into an integrated picture. The rich qualitative data can bring the numbers to life and answer evaluation questions with greater impact than can either type of data on its own. The tables and graphs that were produced for the briefings can typically serve as the foundation for organizing the findings in the final report. There should also be a clear link established between each evaluation question and its corresponding findings. Each question can be presented as a header in this section of the report and the relevant findings presented below each header. To the extent possible, we attempt to incorporate table and graph exhibits into the text, rather than placing them in the appendices or at the end of the section. This integration makes it much easier for the reader to absorb the results and tie the findings to the evaluation questions. If the text is separate from the tables and graphs, many busy readers may be tempted to review only the former or latter. Inconsistent or contradictory findings should be presented and interpreted within the context of the study and further dealt with in the next section.

Conclusions and Recommendations. Prior to writing this section, it is necessary to consider what the findings mean in relation to the evaluation questions and the organization as a whole. It is essential to determine whether the data are credible and able to withstand alternative explanations. The readers will not be at a loss to offer up alternatives, particularly if a result deviates from their point of view. Inconsistent or contradictory findings have to be considered and explanations presented as to whether, and how, they impact the general results. The credibility of the conclusions will be driven, in large part, by the extent to which the report presents a balanced accounting of the strengths and limitations of the entire HR program evaluation. The recommendations will generally focus on improving various aspects of the program, but may also suggest additional research that should be conducted. A word of caution is needed here about recommending additional research because that is likely to be the last thing that key stakeholders will want to hear!

Appendices. Appendices may contain supporting materials and documents, along with expanded findings from the analyses. Documents used to support each phase of the evaluation can be included in a separate appendix.

Store Documentation Supporting the Briefings and Report. Some of the documents and analyses from the evaluation may be better preserved and accessed using storage that is separate from that for the report and the most relevant supporting materials. Initial general decisions about the storage of the technical documentation, as well as a copy of the briefings and report, should have been made at the beginning of the evaluation. Changes to the methods and other unexpected events may, however, result in a need to revisit those initial decisions.

The following questions should be posed to the evaluation sponsor(s) and/or the legal counsel so that the evaluation team and stakeholders have a common set of expectations when it comes time to store the documentation: (a) Who owns the documentation, particularly if the evaluation was performed partially or wholly by external contractors? (b) What should be kept and by whom? (c) How long should it be kept? (d) What types of storage will be used (especially when confidential information is stored)? and (e) Should a "lessons learned" be performed and documented for the program evaluation?

Conclusions

The overall success of an HR program evaluation may well hinge on how effectively the communication plan is designed and executed. We have discussed a number of practical strategies for ensuring that evaluation results are meaningfully communicated. These strategies, which are common to all good communications, are most influential and consequential when adapted to the particular needs and bottom-line concerns of the key stakeholders. Each stakeholder group will have a preferred means for receiving communications regarding the evaluation's progress and its findings. It is incumbent upon the evaluation team to disseminate information in a medium that not only targets each group's unique set of needs, but that engenders ownership of the results and motivation to act on the findings. The next chapter will further detail how the evaluation findings and insights can be converted into relevant, meaningful action.

Suggested Resources

Chelimski, E. (1987). What have we learned about the politics of program evaluation? *Evaluation Practice, 8,* 5–21.

Joint Committee on Standards for Educational Evaluation. (1994). *The program evaluation standards: How to assess evaluations of educational programs* (2nd ed.). Thousand Oaks, CA: Sage.

Morris, L.L., Fitz-Gibbon, C.T., & Freeman, M.E. (1987). *How to communicate evaluation findings.* Thousand Oaks, CA: Sage.

Royse, D., Thyer, B.A., Padgett, D.K., & Logan, T.K. (2001). *Program evaluation: An introduction.* Belmont, CA: Brooks/Cole.

Tufte, E.R. (2001). *The visual display of quantitative information.* Cheshire, CT: Graphics Press.

Phase 6

UTILIZE THE RESULTS

"Never underestimate just how much human beings
are willing to change if you only engage them the
right way."

—*Mahatma Gandhi*

Chapter Objectives

- Develop awareness of the skills and techniques needed to implement useable evaluation results
- Present the various forms and underlying causes of resistance to change
- Illustrate how to overcome resistance by leveraging organizational politics and stakeholder input
- Demonstrate proven strategies for implementing results

Any of us who have conducted program evaluations can readily provide an example when methodologically sound study findings were disregarded or recommendations failed to be implemented. In reviewing the history of program evaluation, the chief criticism that emerges is that evaluation reports frequently go unread and findings are rarely used (see Fetterman, 2001; Torres & Preskill, 2001). This situation can be frustrating, particularly given the time and resources expended in the design and execution of an evaluation. While logic would dictate that the presentation of credible findings addressing the evaluation questions should be enough to drive action, this is rarely a sufficient condition. Being allowed to put data-driven knowledge to use is one of the most important yet intransigent challenges facing an HR program evaluator.

Resistance to change is not unique to the practice of HR program evaluation. It is a recurring dilemma for organizational change efforts that, if not properly addressed, can undermine any program recommendation. Program implementers can be blindsided by this resistance, which can take many forms and originate from varied sources. Michael Beer and Russell Eisenstat (2000) identified six "silent killers" that they believe exist in most organizations and that serve to block organizational change and strategy implementation. These killers of change are depicted as silent because they are rarely discussed openly, much less addressed, despite being known to everyone in the organization. Anyone attempting to effect organizational change will likely be challenged by one or more of these six barriers: (1) a top-down or hands-off senior management style, (2) unclear organizational strategy and priorities, (3) an ineffective top management team, (4) poor vertical communication, (5) poor coordination across functions and businesses, and/or (6) inadequate down-the-line leadership skills and development (p. 31). It is not particularly surprising that the silent killers are not openly addressed, as they primarily emanate from the top managers themselves. This raises the stakes for the implementer of the HR program changes, who will need to ensure that she is positioned to effectively interact with top management throughout the evaluation to appropriately diagnose and address these barriers and navigate through the accompanying politics.

Since the results of program evaluations are likely to impact the interests of one or more parties, it is natural to assume that resistance and politics will play roles and have to be addressed when attempting to act on evaluation results. Smith (2001, p. 287) characterized the politics of evaluation as inevitable and not necessarily negative. He stated, "The push and pull between the needs of stakeholders and the 'flush' of political adversaries do not make evaluation neutral but rather compels it to be more relevant to the situation under study."

The program evaluation and organizational change literatures suggest that any planned intervention or change within an organization will likely be met with opposition in one form or another. The exact nature and source of this resistance will depend on the particular program, stakeholders involved, leadership capabilities, and culture of the organization. By understanding that resistance to change is a natural state for individuals and organizations, the program evaluation team can better anticipate and address this challenge to the use of evaluation results and recommendations.

A basic premise of Phase 6 in our approach is that an HR program evaluation should produce useable results. Useable results refer to meaningful actions that directly address the stakeholders' original researchable questions and the subsequent evaluation findings. Meaningful actions in this context may refer to targeted adjustments, full-scale in-house replacement, or outsourcing of an HR program.

Much debate and research have focused on understanding what conditions are necessary for ensuring effective implementation of evaluation results. The accumulation of general program evaluation experiences, research, and theories has produced insights that bear directly on the effective implementation of HR program evaluation results. We will address some of these insights and outline specific actions for optimally implementing program evaluation results and recommendations. First, however, we will review some of the variables of concern when deciding to adjust, replace in-house, or outsource an HR program.

Adjust, Replace In-House, or Outsource the HR Program

Recommendations about whether to adjust, replace, or outsource an HR program will be driven by a variety of considerations. The nature of the stakeholder questions and resulting findings will heavily influence how recommendations are formulated. In addition, the evaluation approach (for example, formative versus summative) will influence the focus of the recommendations. Formative evaluation approaches that are designed to identify how a program can be improved on an ongoing basis will generally lead to recommendations that focus on program adjustments. Summative evaluation approaches that are designed to examine a program's overall worth may often lead to keep-or-replace (including outsourcing) recommendations. We (Scott, Edwards, & Raju, 2002) have argued that HR program evaluation should be an ongoing event and not one that occurs only at the end of a program. Furthermore, while demonstrating effectiveness and efficiency is critical, equally important is the need to focus on how to improve a program. That being said, there are situations that call for program replacement either in-house or through outsourcing.

Some decisions to replace a program or major components of a program are easy because of major program deficiencies. However, most such decisions will be more difficult because of the need to weigh multiple strengths and weaknesses of the program as well as other considerations. In addition, recommendations to replace a program are often revisited in light of resource constraints.

A primary consideration in the adjust-or-replace decision is cost. In most cases, the short-term costs will probably favor modification of the existing program, and the long-term costs will probably favor replacement. Table 6.1 illustrates this point by showing the cumulative return on investment calculations associated with replacing a paper-based selection system with a web-based process. After considerable up-front investment, the replacement system more than paid for itself in the first three years. With organizations continually facing the need to be good stewards of their financial assets, building a business case for a large financial commitment to replace a functioning—even if non-optimal—program might be a non-starter.

It should be noted that replacing an HR program is almost always more disruptive than adjusting an existing system. Program staff members as well as key stakeholders often prefer workarounds and

Table 6.1 Cumulative Return on Investment (ROI) Associated with Selection Program Replacement

Project Outcome	ROI–Years 1 & 2	ROI–Year 3	ROI–Year 5
Reduced turnover[1]	$250,000	$375,000	$625,000
Automated pre-screen[2]	$108,150	$162,225	$270,375
Elimination of second interview[3]	$200,000	$300,000	$500,000
Automatic reporting[4]	$4,988	$7,482	$12,470
Company owns selection process[5]	$90,000	$135,000	$225,000
Replacement of pre-screen phone calls with interactive voice response[6]	$47,930	$71,895	$119,825
Costs of purchasing, customizing, and maintaining web-based selection system	–$750,000	–$40,000	$40,000
Cumulative ROI	**–$48,932**	**$1,011,602**	**$1,712,670**

Key assumptions:

[1]Assumes a very conservative reduction in annualized turnover of 5 percent from the new selection system. The average cost to terminate a non-exempt employee has been calculated to be approximately equal to six months of pay and benefits. These figures are conservative, as they do not include secondary costs associated with the loss of customers and other market consequences associated with the departure of experienced employees.

[2]Reflects the estimated labor cost savings that would result from automating the pre-screening. The estimate assumes HR will review the pre-screen information of approximately 30,000 candidates a year and the review will take approximately five minutes per candidate. The median salary of employment specialists in the company is $45,000 annually or $21.63 per hour. 30,000 reviews x 5 minutes x .3605 per minute in HR salaries = savings of $54,075 annually.

[3]Assumes an annual savings of $100,000 based on company cost per hire data detailing labor costs of conducting the second interview.

[4]Assumes a company statistician would spend approximately eight hours per month to compute adverse impact analyses. The median salary of the statistician is $54,000 annually or $25.98 per hour. 8 hours x $25.98 per hour in statistician salaries x 12 months = savings of $2,494 annually.

[5]Assumes company spends $45,000 per year on test materials and scoring.

[6]Assumes that the interactive voice response pre-screen will eliminate the need for pre-screen phone calls such as those handled by outside vendor. Elimination of these phone calls will result in an annual savings of $23,965 based on company cost per hire data.

other inefficiencies associated with the current program, rather than the uncertainty that comes with replacing a program. Outsourcing an HR program or function may also be disruptive, as the HR program staff may accurately perceive that their jobs are in jeopardy. In addition, other key stakeholders—for example, users and program sponsors—may resist outsourcing due to concerns about loss of control, return on investment, quality, and vendor capabilities. These concerns are most likely present when a program such as succession planning or compensation is high exposure and linked to the stakeholders' performance accountabilities in the organization. As we have stated, change is often resisted and can result in people simply sticking with what is familiar, even though it is not ideal.

Adjust the Existing Program

When stakeholder questions center more on a program's strengths and weaknesses and how to improve the program, the focus of the evaluation is likely to be more on adjustments that can be made, rather than program replacement. The goal of this type of evaluation (for example, formative) is to improve the program, and HR program evaluation findings should support decisions and actions about how best to do so. The specific findings might be used to identify program challenges and opportunities and provide strategies for continuous improvement. Most formative evaluations seek to improve efficiency and ensure that the program is responsive to changing needs. Formative evaluation is equally applicable to either an internal or outsourced HR program or function.

Make an Effective Program Even Better. The premise for an evaluation that focuses on improving instead of replacing an HR program is that, at its core, the program is worthwhile. There is a belief that the HR program just needs to be reviewed and tweaked—sometimes quite a bit—to ensure that it is operating optimally and meeting stakeholder requirements.

As an example of this approach, consider an evaluation of a web-based selection system that is used to assess candidates for customer call center positions. Over 30,000 candidates are assessed each year and the system appears to be screening in high-performing new hires. The three-year-old system has had minimal adverse impact, but this has not been regularly monitored. The positions have recently been redesigned to accommodate newly introduced technology, and the scope of responsibility has been expanded to cover sales activities. The vice president of HR and the organization's legal counsel requested an evaluation to determine how well the existing selection program covered the new position responsibilities, the extent to which adverse impact was present, and ways to both reduce testing time and eliminate proctoring.

In reviewing the evaluation objectives, the stakeholders seemed to be satisfied with the overall selection system but wanted to ensure that it was performing both effectively and efficiently in the changing environment. The evaluation team was charged with identifying program strengths and areas of opportunity in which the program should be enhanced, while keeping in mind stakeholder, professional, and legal guidelines. Potential adjustments that were reviewed with the stakeholders and ultimately implemented included adding a test to cover sales ability, lowering the cutoff score to deal with mounting adverse impact issues, incorporating a mechanism to monitor pass rates and adverse impact, and creating an up-front screening test to reduce the volume of applicants who had to take the full selection test battery. By reducing test volume, on-site proctoring of the test-takers could remain in place and ensure quality control over the assessment process.

By adjusting rather than replacing a well-accepted system, there was less disruption to the business and staff, and the focus on continuous improvement was more widely embraced by the selection program staff.

Engage Program Staff and Users When Recommending and Implementing Program Adjustments. One of the biggest mistakes an evaluation team can make when attempting to implement program changes is to minimize the input and expertise of program staff. As Posavac and Carey (2003, p. 273) have stated, "Working at a distance without close contact with stakeholders who administer and provide the services will be an obstacle to full utilization when an evaluation is completed. When people are involved with an evaluation, utilization of recommendations to effect program improvements is more likely."

It is important to remember that program staff live with the program, understand its subtleties and why previous decisions were made, and can ultimately make or break the success of any recommended changes. It is therefore critical that the program staff and end users (for example, hiring managers) be solicited for input regarding the proposed changes and be engaged in planning, communicating, and executing the recommendations.

> Because the program staff is not necessarily the sponsor of the evaluation, there may be a tendency to overlook their opinions or ignore the impact of their resistance. This issue tends to show up more in program adjustment situations than with program replacements. This may be due, in part, to the perception that program adjustments are less intrusive and the tacit assumption that surely everyone would be on board with making "obvious" improvements.

Follow Up on the Change Effort.   A mechanism and an expectation also must be established for periodic follow-up on the change effort to ensure that the newly adjusted program is operating as desired. While this applies to adjustment, in-house replacement, and outsourcing situations, it is sometimes more difficult to convince stakeholders of the need to follow up on a program that has just been evaluated and adjusted, unless a formative evaluation design had already been integrated into the HR program. Cost and resource requirements usually make their way into the argument against adding formative evaluation, and a business case to justify the inclusion of more program evaluation may be needed at this point.

Objective data as well as qualitative reports should be gathered and interpreted against the criteria established for determining the success of the HR program. These resulting data may indicate the need for further adjustments to the program once the changes have taken effect. For example, in reference to the selection program evaluation presented above, it is possible that the cutoff score would need further adjustment after collecting sufficient applicant data on the new sales test. Or it may turn out that the new screening test is eliminating too many candidates and will have to be adjusted accordingly. It is therefore important to convince stakeholders that follow-up evaluation (that is, formative evaluation) is necessary when making adjustments to an existing program—much the way the initial evaluation was necessary—to ensure that the change had the desired effect and to build a sustained focus on continuous improvement.

Replace the Existing Program

When the evaluation questions focus on issues of accountability or the overall merits of the program, stakeholders are likely to consider decisions around continuing or replacing, rather than improving, an HR program. These assessments, usually called summative evaluations, are designed to provide data that will assist in making decisions about the program's worth (Patton, 1997). Some examples of the sorts of events that will stimulate a summative evaluation include staff transitions, new technology, and changing strategic plans. As with formative evaluation, summative evaluations are equally applicable to outsourced HR programs.

Use Staff Transitions as an Opportunity to Consider HR Program Replacement. Sometimes, a key component of the decision to replace a program is the hiring or the recent or eminent departure of key program staff. New staff with their content-matter knowledge of best practices may have been part of the impetus for conducting the program evaluation. Sometimes, it takes someone from outside the organization to recognize all of the inefficiencies of an existing program.

Similarly, the natural transition that occurs when employees depart the organization offers a chance for a clean break from the old HR program to the new one. In some cases, the departing individual was able to help a program limp along because of his knowledge about every detail of the software and other procedures used to administer the program. If the procedures, assumptions, and other keys to the software and procedures have not been well-documented, it would be easy for errors to occur in the future and for the program performance to degenerate.

Reap the Benefits of New Technology. Technology improvements are another prime reason for replacing an existing HR program. While the existing program may serve most of the organization's needs pretty well, it might limit the HR program—and even the organization as a whole—as attempts are made to move both to the next level of performance and efficiency.

Revolutions in information technology such as computer enhancements and telecommunications are two such areas that are having greater and greater influence on HR programs (for example, see Craiger, Collins, & Nicoll, 2003). Replacement of some parts of a traditional training program with computer-based training is a prime example of this change. Instead of having employees travel to a single location—possibly at an inopportune time—for training, the training can be delivered to desktops via the web, CDs, or even streaming video. Similarly, video communications offer organizations with multiple locations flexibility that they never had before. Organizations can construct virtual teams using the most appropriate people throughout the organization. In the past, team composition was sometimes limited by the ability to send faxes and emails, conduct conference calls, or occasionally take days from one's schedule to go to another location for meetings. An HR program evaluation that embraces these technological changes could also help to identify the portions of the old program that might have to be kept, contracted out, or otherwise taken into account for situations in which in-person training might be advantageous.

Rapid advancements in HR information systems (for example, see the writings of Stanton and his colleagues, 2003) suggest another type of program for which a summative evaluation might be appropriate. New HR information systems with their seamless integration of information from multiple programs can provide an organization with capabilities that allow it to function more smoothly and with lower personnel and maintenance costs, once the initial investments are made. For example, the organization could quickly search its HR database, locate all members who have a unique set of skills (for example, proficiency in a given foreign language and knowledge of a particular production line), and dispatch a team to meet a crisis or unforeseen opportunity. We have all been associated with organizations that had HR programs and program staff that could not talk to one another. The inefficiencies that come with requiring organizational members to supply and update the same information for multiple HR programs (for example, both the locator system and health care benefits program) can be eliminated, but the financial cost of replacing an existing system(s) can be significant. Still, organizations may find the resulting benefits well worth the expenses, especially over the long term.

Realign HR Programs as Strategic Plans Change. Organizations might alter their HR programs and practices as they reexamine their vision and strategic plans. Rapid changes in workforce demographics, marketplaces, and technology compel organizations to increasingly rely on their HR programs to play key roles in addressing these challenges, since their people are a primary determinant of the organization's level of success. It is not unusual in today's rapidly evolving climate for wholescale program changes to occur based on the emerging needs of the organization. As HR plays an

Although a full-scale replacement of a program is usually more disruptive to the organization than is the improvement or adjustment of an existing program, using existing HR programs could greatly hamper an organization attempting to set a new course. As such, the strategies for implementing change and ensuring that the results of the evaluation are used will take on more significance under these conditions.

increasing role in supporting the strategic direction of the organization, HR programs are increasingly called upon to demonstrate a measurable return on investment and link to the organization's bottom line. As a result of this focus on value, HR programs may be replaced, even treated as a commodity, if they are not perceived to be fulfilling the talent acquisition and management needs of the organization.

Outsource the Existing Program

The decision to outsource an HR program or function may be based on a variety of factors, not the least of which will include the capabilities of internal staff, effectiveness of the existing program, and the impact that the program has on the organization's business operations (Holincheck, 2003). While the Gartner Group estimated that HR outsourcing will be a $32 billion business by 2010 (Brown, 2006), Sullivan (2004) has cautioned that it may not be the cost-saving, business-performance-enhancing solution that organizations believe it to be. He pointed out that when an organization outsources its HR programs, HR is less likely to function as a strategic, innovative leader in the organization. He asserted that outsourcing minimizes opportunities for HR's ongoing contacts with stakeholders, which can help build and sustain a strong HR function. In addition, he noted that HR outsourcing (a) minimizes the organization's competitive advantage by handing the program to a vendor who may also be working with the organization's competitors, (b) limits the growth and capability of the HR function, (c) may result in increased costs, and (d) potentially puts company secrets and data security at risk.

There are, however, proponents of HR outsourcing who argue that outsourcing frees up the HR staff to focus on more strategic issues, while at the same time gaining access to expert knowledge from the vendor(s) running the outsourced program(s). The point here is not to debate whether it makes sense to outsource or not. Rather, this discussion highlights the need to base HR outsourcing decisions on the results of a program evaluation. In addition, if an HR program is outsourced in total or part, it should be evaluated against the same criteria that would be used for an in-house program. These criteria will depend on the nature of the program and stakeholder needs. The expectations and criteria for success should be specified before the decision is made to outsource. Once it has been determined that outsourcing makes economic and practical sense, a service level agreement should be established between the organization and the vendor. This agreement should specify the metrics and criteria of success, including performance, costs, and quality expectations.

For example, if an organization decided to outsource its online supervisory selection system, the service-level agreement should specify performance and reliability ("up-time") levels for the servers, along with consequences such as reduced per-test fees if the vendor does not meet these expectations. In addition, turnaround time of score reports, adverse impact reporting, and schedule for software upgrades would be examples of other components that should have performance expectations specified in ways that can be objectively measured and tied to consequences. The service-level agreement helps ensure that the outsourced HR program and the buyer-vendor relationship are managed appropriately and that performance metrics and service-delivery levels are clearly spelled out and understood by both parties. This sets the stage for ongoing evaluation and adjustments to the program.

Leverage Insights Relevant to Evaluation Use

Numerous insights have been offered by authors and experienced practitioners from many professional disciplines for overcoming the challenges faced when attempting to translate the evaluation results into viable recommendations for program adjustment or replacement. Most relevant to our purposes are those that address the relationship between evaluation use and the (a) evaluation team's accountability and skill set and (b) extent of stakeholder participation.

Build Team Accountability and Skill

A consistent theme running through the literature on the use of organizational evaluation (for example, program evaluation, organizational change, and balanced scorecards) is that the evaluators are more often than not held accountable for the impact of their studies. This places a significant burden on the evaluation team to ensure that they are proficient enough to meet the individual and organizational challenges faced when implementing evaluation findings. The more the evaluation team possesses the required skills and organizational knowledge, the greater likelihood that the implementation of evaluation findings will proceed as planned.

As the focus begins shifting from the assessment activities involved in the evaluation to the implementation of the recommendations and organizational change, it may be time for some members to transition off of the team and new members to be added. This decision will be based on the scope and complexity of the implementation plan, experience/expertise of the team members at implementing organizational change, and the urgency with which team members must either move to another evaluation or back to their normal job duties. For some HR program evaluations, there will be times when it makes sense to fully transition the change effort from the evaluation team to an implementation team. The skill set, content expertise, and resource availability needed to implement large scale or politically sensitive changes may be best found in organizational members outside of the original evaluation team.

McClintock (2003) believed that the ideal professional in the field of program evaluation should be a combination of evaluator, organization development scholar, and practitioner. He asserted that it would be difficult to facilitate the use of evaluation findings or meet the full range of professional practice criteria outlined in the professional standards (Joint Committee, 1994) unless the evaluator understands and is able to apply organizational theory in the context of implementing change. He indicated that this hybrid professional should possess all of the methodological skills required to produce sound evaluation findings, while being adept at communicating with all levels within the organization, establishing trusting relationships, and instituting change dynamics (which could include team-oriented interventions with the top management). Other researchers have added to this list of success factors, but what is clear is that the program evaluation team requires a high degree of expertise, both within and across disciplines, to ensure successful implementation of evaluation recommendations.

Involve Stakeholders Early and Often to Increase the Odds That Results Are Used

The relationship between stakeholder participation in the evaluation study and the likelihood of effective and efficient implementation of program evaluation recommendations has been well documented. As we and others have emphasized, increased stakeholder involvement in the earlier phases of the evaluation results in greater acceptance and use of the findings, improves decision making, and enhances the credibility of the results. All of these activities are important to the successful implementation of recommendations and ultimately to the modification, replacement, or outsourcing of an HR program.

Patton (1997) based his utilization-focused evaluation approach on this participative premise. He contended that, unless the primary users and other stakeholders of the evaluation results are fully on board and have had significant input throughout all phases, there is generally little likelihood that the results will make it off the shelf. He argued that stakeholders should be identified at the beginning of the evaluation and that they should be able and willing to use the information generated by the study. Patton advocated that during the question-generation step (Phase 1 of our approach), stakeholders should be engaged in framing how they would apply the answers to the evaluation questions and thinking through the potential barriers to action. Initial involvement sets the stage for stakeholder ownership by providing actionable, end-point alternatives for them to envision. In addition, by assessing potential barriers at the outset of the evaluation, a plan can be set in motion during our Phase 2 to attack the "silent killers" of organizational change and engage the key players who are most likely to derail the recommendations.

This participative approach uses the stakeholders' expertise and knowledge of what they need throughout all phases of the evaluation. Huberman and Cox (1990, p. 165) described this philosophy succinctly, "The evaluator is like a novice sailor working with yachtsmen who have sailed these institutional waters for years, and know every island, reef, and channel." The evaluator benefits from the stakeholders' expertise, and the stakeholders feel ownership of the results and ultimately the outcomes. Widespread use and acceptance of this and other participative models lend credibility to the involvement of stakeholders for enhancing the meaning and use of evaluation findings and recommendations.

While many professionals acknowledge that the effective implementation of recommendations requires eliciting the early and continuing involvement of stakeholders, an evaluation team must also be vigilant to perceived or actual compromises that this involvement could bring to quality and objectivity. For example, too much or disproportionate involvement from top management could result in other stakeholder groups perceiving that the evaluation team merely found what top management wanted. This situation can be challenging due to the different levels of influence that various stakeholder groups may have in the organization. Overcoming the challenge requires attention and effort on the part of evaluators to ensure that no group's input is ignored. Therefore, while stakeholder involvement is an essential component toward ensuring effective implementation of recommendations, the evaluation team must be aware of any potential compromises to the evaluation effort resulting from this involvement (or perceived disproportionate involvement), and make adjustments when necessary.

In addition to the challenges of balancing involvement and objectivity concerns of some stakeholder groups, the evaluation team may also find that requests for significant involvement throughout the evaluation may be unwelcome by other stakeholders due to interference with their day-to-day responsibilities. Sensitivity to busy schedules and awareness of when involvement is essential versus when it is simply desirable are key antecedents for optimizing stakeholder buy-in.

Incorporate Proven Strategies for Implementing Results

Regardless of the nature of the barriers to evaluation impact, a good deal of accountability rests on the evaluators to manage and deal with resistance to change. This level of responsibility requires a broad base of knowledge and skill that occurs through both ongoing training and experience. As previously mentioned, depending on the size, significance, and skill requirements of the implementation task, the responsibility for action planning may be best transitioned from the evaluation team to an implementation team.

The implementation team is usually comprised of staff and managers who are expected to institutionalize the change and deal with the operational issues that arise. Gallagher, Joseph, and Park (2002) argued that the implementation team should be provided with the latitude to decide how change is implemented in order to foster ownership. They stated that "To move forward, staff must leave behind procedures they created, roles they developed, skills they mastered, meaningful relationships, and the fit they have developed with a work group or supervisor" (p. 31). They contended that participation in the change and decision making involving implementation will help ensure a smoother transition and less resistance.

Whether it is the evaluation team or an implementation team (or some combination) that is responsible for instituting evaluation recommendations, the members of this team must understand the underlying issues that impact the ability and willingness of users to implement change and have at their disposal specific strategies and expertise for facilitating meaningful action.

Build Expertise to Engage Stakeholders

"Evaluators are credible to the extent that they exhibit the training, technical competence, substantive knowledge, experience, integrity, public relations skills, and other characteristics considered necessary by clients and other users of evaluation findings and reports" (Joint Committee, 1994, p. 31). Program evaluators must wear many hats and be versed in multiple disciplines in order to be credible to stakeholders and produce evaluation findings that are meaningful and that will be used. Ongoing training, reading (for example, staying abreast of the research), skill building, and experience are critical for evaluators as they face the many challenges inherent in producing useable results from their evaluations. Evaluators also must proactively learn from other disciplines that focus on human and organizational behavior and change. These disciplines and their literature include human resource management, industrial and organizational psychology, organizational change and development, business administration, and organizational communications.

In addition, since stakeholder engagement is so critical to the successful implementation of evaluation results, evaluators would do well to polish their communication, relationship-building, and facilitation skills. While there are specific strategies for evoking stakeholder buy-in, these strategies have to be supplemented with sound communication skills and interpersonal judgment to effectively navigate the political landscape that is so intrinsic to evaluations and organizational change efforts. Much of the evaluator's facility to engage stakeholders and sustain their buy-in through the implementation phase will be developed through experience and mentoring. Therefore, it is incumbent upon evaluators to seek ongoing feedback on these skills so that they can focus on their development and refinement.

From Beer and Eisenstat's (2000) point of view, the only real way to ensure successful, sustainable change is to engage the organization's top management in strategies for addressing the barriers to change. This step involves working with top management to surface unproductive behaviors and learn how to act in different ways. Since not all executives involved with the program under study will necessarily be motivated to change—or even see that agreed-on changes are required, this step requires skill and finesse on the part of the program implementer to create a compelling business case, not only for the change, but for top management stakeholders to engage in a set of new behaviors that support the change. The implementer of the HR program changes must therefore possess considerable business savvy and strong interpersonal skills to have the credibility needed to affect a new set of sustainable behaviors at this level of the organization.

Leverage Politics

As previously discussed, the politics of implementing change should be factored into the implementation plan as a natural part of any intervention. In attempting to understand the politics of the situation, it is useful to identify who stands to benefit from the changes and who may stand to lose ground (perceived or actual).

Once this dynamic is apparent, specific steps can be taken to structure a win-win situation in which ego-bruising can be minimized or avoided and the politics can be leveraged to facilitate successful implementation (Patton, 1997). Patton believed that a skillful evaluator can negotiate favorable solutions for all of the intended users by following certain "power rules" that he adapted from Broom and Klein's 1995 book, *Power: The Infinite*

Each situation will be different, and the politics will vary depending on the stakes involved. Higher-stakes evaluations (for example, evaluation of bias in compensation administration) will probably result in active attempts to influence the findings and recommendations. The evaluators must remain objective and empirically oriented, while at the same time managing expectations and ensuring that the recommendations meaningfully address the evaluation questions and can be supported by all stakeholders. This juggling act requires that the evaluators maintain perspective on the purpose of the evaluation, be perceptive to expressed and unexpressed stakeholder agendas, and exercise a win-win strategy with respect to recommended interventions.

Game. Some of Patton's rules include: seek to negotiate win-win scenarios; help stakeholders detach their egos from evaluation results; help
users focus on the long-term perspective of learning, improvement, and
knowledge use; and affirm over and over that the purpose of the evaluation is to seek what is best for intended beneficiaries. These rules are
designed to keep stakeholders focused on the long-term goals and to
not lose sight of the higher purpose of the evaluation. These strategies
can help keep the stakes and power games under control.

Manage Resistance

We stated earlier in this chapter that resistance is a natural reaction
to change. The HR program evaluation team can expect to experience resistance at all phases of the evaluation but none more than
during the implementation phase. It is during this phase that resources required for fixing, replacing, or outsourcing the program are
brought to light. Therefore, it is normal for those who were involved
in the original program design to worry that they may be blamed for
the resource drain brought about by the program's deficiencies and to
rely on various face-saving strategies to protect themselves. Program
evaluators who understand and proactively address this resistance will
face a much smoother transition when translating recommendations
into action.

Donaldson, Gooler, and Scriven (2002) advanced the notion
that much of the source of failed implementations may be explained
by what they termed excessive evaluation anxiety. They defined
evaluation anxiety as "the set of (primarily) affective, and also cog-
nitive and behavioral responses that accompany concern over possible negative consequences contingent upon performance in an
evaluative situation" (p. 262). While moderate amounts of anxiety
can be motivational, it is when this anxiety becomes excessive that
evaluation efforts can be sabotaged or undermined. They believed
that evaluation anxiety can result in a reduction in the reliability,
validity, and usefulness of findings, specifically deriving from the lack

of stakeholder cooperation, false reporting of data, and challenges to evaluation results, just to name a few.

One of the key strategies that these authors presented for managing evaluation anxiety is to anticipate that it is likely to occur and to prepare accordingly. The more prepared the evaluation team is to deal with this barrier to effective use of evaluation results and recommendations, the more likely they will effectively manage it. Once it is determined that excessive evaluation anxiety is present, the authors advised addressing it head on. That is, the evaluation or implementation team should attempt to understand the source of the anxiety through active listening and discussion. The team members also must remain open to the fact that there may be legitimate concerns about the evaluation findings and to be open to making necessary changes or to follow up on the concerns. Regardless, it is important to *not* rule out the notion that the resistance may be a healthy response to real problems related to the evaluation.

Interestingly, the evaluator characteristics—beyond listening and communicating—needed to manage resistance are to be nondefensive and open to the possibility that something may have been missed or overlooked in the evaluation. In a very real sense, this is an opportunity for evaluators to role model the very behaviors they desire from top management, program staff, program users, and other stakeholders. Defensiveness on the part of the evaluators to concerns that their findings were wrong must be avoided. Instead, the evaluators must provide a positive image and communicate objectively why they believe their findings, conclusions, and recommendations are on target.

Establish Follow-Up Responsibilities

The implementation of any significant change within an organization is rarely successful without one or more champions. These are individuals who have authority or power as well as respect within the organization and who can deliver results. It is often beneficial to identify those who may have the strongest initial misgivings or resistance to the evaluation and work closely with them to overcome their concerns and establish roles for them as champions. We have often found that some of these individuals subsequently become the strongest supporters of the evaluation findings and recommended actions.

For large, high-exposure, or complex evaluations, we frequently recommend that an evaluation advisory panel be formed at the beginning of the evaluation that is comprised of stakeholder representatives with policy-level decision-making power who can serve as champions of the evaluation decisions. This panel could have responsibility for overseeing the evaluation process, helping with needed resources, advocating the results, assigning implementation responsibilities, removing barriers, and assisting in maneuvering the political landscape. The advisory panel will also be in a position to recommend and assign an implementation team that can carry forth the recommendations of the evaluation team.

The advisory panel and other top management will expect updates on instituting the recommendations. Therefore, it will be important to establish reporting responsibilities lest the implementation fall through the cracks without anyone noticing.

Be Timely and Communicate

Evaluators and stakeholders should reach an agreement as to when the recommendations will be implemented and how the process will be communicated. Once target dates for the various steps in the implementation process have been established, the team can plan backward in time to ensure that the deadlines can realistically be met.

This planning should allow for unanticipated problems or resource issues and actions to mitigate potential risks, if they occur. Contingency plans should be made around the possibility of delays. It is better to establish realistic projections than over-promise and fail to meet important deadlines. The recommendations should be rolled out in concrete steps, with realistic milestone dates and clear responsibilities to ensure that the champions do not move on to other important issues.

It is also important to adequately communicate the plans for program change to all users and impacted parties. This is particularly critical to ensure that everyone understands why and how the program is changing or being replaced, what impact it will have on each person, when the change will take effect, personnel changes (if any), whether training will be involved, and specifics around how the changes or replacement program will be rolled out (for example, pilot-testing, schedules, and time commitment). Depending on the size and number of individuals impacted by a program change or replacement (including outsourcing of the program), it may make sense to involve the organization's communications department in fashioning the content and media by which the information is conveyed.

Follow Up with Hard Data

Finally, any change initiative has to be evaluated with hard data. That is, measure the results to hold the implementation team accountable and conduct ongoing evaluation. Evaluators should think of this as an evaluation of the evaluation and apply the same rigor and design elements that were applied during the HR program evaluation that had led to the organizational changes. This follows the old adage that what gets measured gets done. Figure 6.1 illustrates the ongoing feedback loops that serve to foster a continuous improvement design.

Conclusions

Resistance to change is an expected and natural consequence of any organizational intervention, and the implementation of program evaluation findings is no exception to this rule. We have discussed the various manifestations that this resistance can take and have offered some practical strategies for effectively anticipating and addressing the various challenges to the use of evaluation findings,

Figure 6.1   Phase 6 Steps in Program Evaluation–Implementation and Continuous Improvement

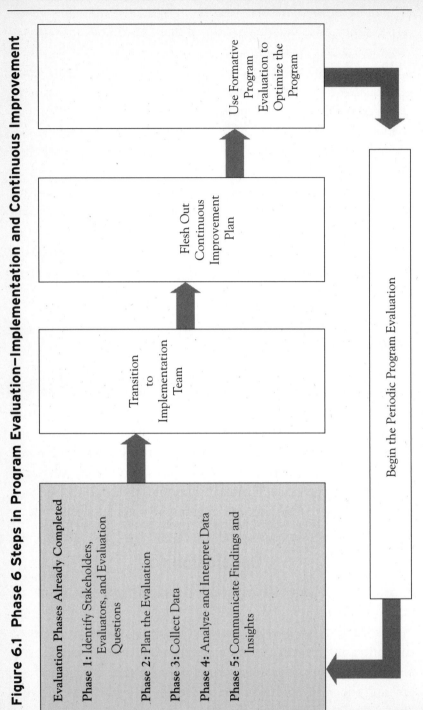

conclusions, and recommendations. Stakeholder involvement, evaluator expertise, solid planning, common sense, communication, and follow-up are some of the key components for ensuring that evaluation results will make their way off the shelf and into actionable recommendations.

Suggested Resources

Donaldson, S.I., Gooler, L.E., & Scriven, M. (2002). Strategies for managing evaluation anxiety: Toward a psychology of program evaluation. *American Journal of Evaluation, 23*, 261–273.

Hedge, J.W., & Pulakos, E.D. (2002). Grappling with implementation: Some preliminary thoughts and relevant research. In J.W. Hedge & E.D. Pulakos (Eds.), *Implementing organizational interventions* (pp. 1–11). San Francisco, CA: Jossey-Bass.

Joint Committee on Standards for Educational Evaluation. (1994). *The program evaluation standards: How to assess evaluations of educational programs* (2nd ed.). Thousand Oaks, CA: Sage.

McClintock, C. (2003). Commentary: The evaluator as scholar/practitioner/change agent. *American Journal of Evaluation, 24*, 91–96.

Patton, M.Q. (1997). *Utilization-focused evaluation: The new century text* (3rd ed.). Thousand Oaks, CA: Sage.

Torres, R.T., & Preskill, H. (2001). Evaluation and organizational learning: Past, present, and future. *American Journal of Evaluation, 22*, 387–395.

REFERENCES

Ackoff, R.L. (1953). *The design of social research*. Chicago, IL: University of Chicago Press.

Agresti, A. (1990). *Categorical data analysis*. New York: John Wiley & Sons.

Aguinis, H., & Henle, C.A. (2004). Ethics in research. In S.G. Rogelberg (Ed.), *Handbook of research methods in industrial and organizational psychology* (pp. 34–56). Malden, MA: Blackwell.

Alreck, P.L., & Settle, R.B. (1985). *The survey research handbook*. Homewood, IL: Richard D. Irwin.

American Psychological Association. (2001). *Publication manual of the American Psychological Association* (5th ed.). Washington, DC: Author.

Anastasi, A. (1988). *Psychological testing* (6th ed.). New York: Macmillan.

Bachiochi, P.D., & Weiner, S.P. (2004). Qualitative data collection and analyses. In S.G. Rogelberg (Ed.), *Handbook of research methods in industrial and organizational psychology* (pp. 161–183). Malden, MA: Blackwell.

Bailar, J.C., & Mosteller, F. (1988). Guidelines for statistical reporting in articles for medical journals: Amplifications and explanations. *Annals of Internal Medicine, 108*, 266–273.

Barnes, R.M. (1980). *Motion and time study: Design and measurement of work* (7th ed.). New York: John Wiley & Sons.

Beer, M., & Eisenstat, R.A. (2000). The silent killers of strategy implementation and learning. *Sloan Management Review, 41*(4), 29–40.

Bernhal, P., & Byham, B. (1997). Evaluation techniques for an empowered workforce. In J.J. Phillips (Ed.), *In action: Measuring return on investment* (Electronic document: SKU 71040179). Alexandria, VA: American Society for Training and Development.

Berk, R.A., & Rossi, P.H. (1990). *Thinking about program evaluation*. Thousand Oaks, CA: Sage.

Bertin, J. (1981). *Graphics and graphic information processing*. Berlin, Germany: Walter de Gruyter, Inc.

Bourque, L.B., & Clark, V.A. (1992). *Processing data: The survey example*. Thousand Oaks, CA: Sage.

Brandon, P.R. (1998). Stakeholder participation for the purpose of helping ensure evaluation validity: Bridging the gap between collaborative and non-collaborative evaluation. *American Journal of Evaluation, 19*, 325–337.

Brannick, M.T., & Levine, E.L. (2002). *Job analysis: Methods, research, and applications*. Thousand Oaks, CA: Sage.

Brinkerhoff, R.O. (2003). *The success case method: Find out quickly what's working and what's not*. San Francisco, CA: Berrett-Koehler.

Broom, M.F., & Klein, D.C. (1995). *Power: The infinite game*. Amherst, MA: HRD Press.

Brown, R.H. (2006). Dataquest insight: HR BPO market to grow to $32 billion worldwide by 2010. *Gartner Research*, IGG-09202006–20 Sept. 2006.

Cascio, W.F., & Wynn, P. (2004). Managing a downsizing process. *Human Resource Management, 43*, 425–436.

Center for Effective Teaching and Learning at the University of Texas at El Paso. (2005). *Formative and summative evaluation: The distinction between forms of evaluation that are aimed prospectively and respectively*. Retrieved Nov. 19, 2005, from http://sunconference.utep.edu/CETaL/resources/portfolios/form-sum.htm.

Chelimski, E. (1987). What have we learned about the politics of program evaluation? *Evaluation Practice, 8*, 5–21.

Chen, P.Y. (1996). Conducting telephone surveys. In F.T.L. Leong & J.T. Austin (Eds.), *The psychology research handbook: A guide for graduate students and research assistants* (pp. 139–154). Thousand Oaks, CA: Sage.

Chen, P.Y., Carsten, J.M., & Krauss, A.D. (2003). Job analysis—The basis for developing criteria for all human resources programs. In J.E. Edwards, J.C. Scott, & N.S. Raju (Eds.), *The human resources program-evaluation handbook* (pp. 27–48). Thousand Oaks, CA: Sage.

Church, A.H., & Waclawski, J. (1998). *Designing and using organizational surveys*. London, United Kingdom: Gower.

Cliff, N. (1996). *Ordinal methods for behavioral data analysis*. Mahway, NJ: Lawrence Erlbaum Associates.

Cohen, J. (1988). *Statistical power analysis for the behavioral sciences* (2nd ed.). Mahwah, NJ: Lawrence Erlbaum Associates.

Cohen, J. (1990). Things I have learned (so far). *American Psychologist, 45*, 1304–1312.

Cousins, J.B., & Earl, L.M. (1992). The case for participatory evaluation. *Educational Evaluation and Policy Analysis, 14*, 397–418.

Craiger, J.P., Collins, V., & Nicoll, A. (2003). A practical guide to evaluating computer-enabled communications. In J.E. Edwards, J.C. Scott, & N.S. Raju (Eds.), *The human resources program-evaluation handbook* (pp. 387–406). Thousand Oaks, CA: Sage.

Cronshaw, S.F., & Fine, S.A. (2003). The evaluation of job redesign processes. In J.E. Edwards, J.C. Scott, & N.S. Raju (Eds.), *The human resources program-evaluation handbook* (pp. 301–321). Thousand Oaks, CA: Sage.

Datta, L.E. (2001). Coming attractions. *American Journal of Evaluation, 22*, 403–408.

Denzin, N.K., & Lincoln, Y.S. (Eds.). (1994). *Handbook of qualitative research.* Thousand Oaks, CA: Sage.

Denzin, N.K., & Lincoln, Y.S. (Eds.). (2003). *Collecting and interpreting qualitative materials* (2nd ed.). Thousand Oaks, CA: Sage.

Denzin, N.K., & Lincoln, Y.S. (Eds.). (2005). *The SAGE handbook of qualitative research.* Thousand Oaks, CA: Sage.

DeVellis, R.F. (1991). *Scale development: Theory and applications.* Thousand Oaks, CA: Sage.

Dollinger, S.J., & DiLalla, D.L. (1996). Cleaning up data and running preliminary analyses. In F.T.L. Leong & J.T. Austin (Eds.), *The psychology research handbook: A guide for graduate students and research assistants* (pp. 167–176). Thousand Oaks, CA: Sage.

Donaldson, S.I., Gooler, L.E., & Scriven, M. (2002). Strategies for managing evaluation anxiety: Toward a psychology of program evaluation. *American Journal of Evaluation, 23*, 261–273.

Edwards, J.E., & Fisher, B.M. (2003). Evaluating organizational survey programs. In J.E. Edwards, J.C. Scott, & N.S. Raju (Eds.), *The human resources program-evaluation handbook* (pp. 365–386). Thousand Oaks, CA: Sage.

Edwards, J.E., Scott, J.C., & Raju, N.S. (Eds.). (2003). *The human resources program-evaluation handbook.* Thousand Oaks, CA: Sage.

Edwards, J.E., Thomas, M.D., Rosenfeld, P., & Booth-Kewley, S.B. (1997). *How to conduct organizational surveys: A step-by-step guide.* Thousand Oaks, CA: Sage.

European Commission. (1995, Nov. 23). European Privacy Directive (EU Directive 95/46/EC). *Official Journal of the European Communities,* No L. 28.

Federal Register. (2000, July 24). Safe harbor (issued July 21, 2000). Washington, DC: U.S. Department of Commerce. www.export.gov/safeharbor.

Fetterman, D.M. (2001). *Foundations of empowerment evaluation.* Thousand Oaks, CA: Sage.

Fine, S.A., & Cronshaw, S.F. (1999). *Functional job analysis: A foundation for human resources management.* Mahwah, NJ: Lawrence Erlbaum Associates.

Fine, A.H., Thayer, C.E., & Coghlan, A.T. (2000). Program evaluation practice in the nonprofit sector. *Nonprofit Management and Leadership, 10*, 331–339.

Fink, A., & Kosecoff, J. (1978). *An evaluation primer.* Thousand Oaks, CA: Sage.

Fisher, R.A. (1932). *Statistical methods for research workers* (4th ed.). Edinburgh, Scotland: Oliver and Boyd.

Fitz-enz, J. (2000). *The ROI of human capital: Measuring the economic value of employee performance.* New York: AMACOM.

Fitz-enz, J., & Davison, B. (2002). *How to measure human resources management* (3rd ed.). New York: McGraw-Hill.

Fleishman, E.A., & Reilly, M.E. (1992). *Handbook of human abilities: Definitions, measurements, and job task requirements*. Palo Alto, CA: Consulting Psychologists Press.

Gael, S. (Ed.). (1988). *The job analysis handbook for business, industry, and government* (Vols. I and II). New York: John Wiley & Sons.

Gallagher, C.A., Joseph, L.E., & Park, M.V. (2002). Implementing organizational change. In J.W. Hedge & E.D. Pulakos (Eds.), *Implementing organizational interventions* (pp. 12–42). San Francisco, CA: Jossey-Bass.

Ghorpade, J. (1988). *Job analysis: A handbook for the human resource director*. Englewood Cliffs, NJ: Prentice Hall.

Gigerenzer, G., & Murray, D.J. (1987). *Cognition as intuitive statistics*. Mahwah, NJ: Lawrence Erlbaum Associates.

Greene, J.C. (1987). Stakeholder participation in evaluation design: Is it worth it? *Evaluation and Program Planning, 24*, 379–394.

Gulliksen, H. (1986). The increasing importance of mathematics in psychological research (part 3). *The Score, 9*, 1–5.

Harlow, L.L., Muliak, S.A., & Steiger, J.H. (Eds.). (1997). *What if there were no significance tests?* Mahwah, NJ: Lawrence Erlbaum Associates.

Hedge, J.W., & Pulakos, E.D. (2002). Grappling with implementation: Some preliminary thoughts and relevant research. In J.W. Hedge & E.D. Pulakos (Eds.), *Implementing organizational interventions* (pp. 1–11). San Francisco, CA: Jossey-Bass.

Henry, G.T. (1990). *Practical sampling*. Thousand Oaks, CA: Sage.

Henry, G.T., & Mark, M.M. (2003). Beyond use: Understanding evaluation's influence on attitudes and actions. *American Journal of Evaluation, 24*, 293–314.

Holincheck, J. (2003). Deciding to insource or outsource human resources. *Gartner Research*, IGG-02282003–28 Feb. 2003.

Howell, D.C. (2002). *Statistical methods for psychology* (5th ed.). Pacific Grove, CA: Duxbury.

Huberman, A.M., & Cox, P. (1990). Evaluation utilization: Building links between action and reflection. *Studies in Educational Evaluation, 16*, 157–179.

Huff, D. (1954). *How to like with statistics*. New York: W.W. Norton.

Hultman, K. (1998). *Making change irresistible: Overcoming resistance to change in your organization*. Palo Alto, CA: Consulting Psychologists Press.

Joint Committee on Standards for Educational Evaluation. (1994). *The program evaluation standards: How to assess evaluations of educational programs* (2nd ed.). Thousand Oaks, CA: Sage.

Karweit, N., & Meyers, E.D., Jr. (1983). Computer in survey research. In P.H. Rossi, J.D. Wright, & A.B. Anderson (Eds.), *Handbook of survey research* (pp. 379–414). San Diego, CA: Academic Press.

Kirkhart, K.E. (2000). Reconceptualizing evaluation use: An integrated theory. In V.J. Caracelli & H. Preskill (Eds.), *The expanding scope of evaluation use:*

New directions in program evaluation (Vol. 88, pp. 5–24). San Francisco, CA: Jossey-Bass.

Kraut, A.I. (Ed.). (2006). Getting action from organizational surveys: New concepts, technologies, and applications. San Francisco, CA: Jossey-Bass.

Landy, F. (2005). *Employment litigation discrimination: Behavioral, quantitative, and legal perspectives*. San Francisco, CA: Jossey-Bass.

Leviton, L.C. (2003). Evaluation use: Advances, challenges, and applications. *American Journal of Evaluation, 24*, 525–535.

Little, R.J., & Rubin, D.B. (1987). *Statistical analysis with missing data*. New York: John Wiley & Sons.

Locke, K., & Golden-Biddle, K. (2004). An introduction to qualitative research: Its potential for industrial and organizational psychology. In S.G. Rogelberg (Ed.), *Handbook of research methods in industrial and organizational psychology* (pp. 99–118). Malden, MA: Blackwell.

London, M., Mone, E.M., & Scott, J.C. (2004). Performance management and assessment: Methods for improved rater accuracy and employee goal setting. *Human Resource Management, 43*, 319–336.

Love, A.J. (1991). *Internal evaluation: Building organizations from within*. Thousand Oaks, CA: Sage.

Love, A.J. (2001). The future of evaluation: Catching rocks with cauldrons. *American Journal of Evaluation, 22*, 437–444.

Lowman, R.L. (Ed.). (1998). *The ethical practice of psychology in organizations*. Washington, DC: American Psychological Association, and Bowling Green, OH: Society for Industrial and Organizational Psychology.

McClintock, C. (2003). Commentary: The evaluator as scholar/practitioner/change agent. *American Journal of Evaluation, 24*, 91–96.

McCready, W.C. (1996). Applying sampling procedures. In F.T.L. Leong & J.T. Austin (Eds.), *The psychology research handbook: A guide for graduate students and research assistants* (pp. 98–110). Thousand Oaks, CA: Sage.

McNamara, C. (1998). *A basic guide to program evaluation*. Minneapolis, MN: Authenticity Consulting, LLC.

Meehl, P.E. (1978). Theoretical risks and tabular asterisks: Sir Karl, Sir Ronald, and the slow progress of soft psychology. *Journal of Consulting and Clinical Psychology, 46*, 806–834.

Miles, M.B., & Huberman, A.M. (1994). *Qualitative data analysis: An expanded sourcebook* (2nd ed.). Thousand Oaks, CA: Sage.

Miller, D.C. (1991). *Handbook of research design and social measurement* (5th ed.). Thousand Oaks, CA: Sage.

Mohr, L.B. (1992). *Impact analysis for program evaluation*. Thousand Oaks, CA: Sage.

Mohr, L.B. (1995). *Impact analysis for program evaluation* (2nd ed.). Thousand Oaks, CA: Sage.

Morris, L.L., Fitz-Gibbon, C.T., & Freeman, M.E. (1987). *How to communicate evaluation findings*. Thousand Oaks, CA: Sage.

Morris, G.W., & LoVerde, M.A. (1993). Consortium surveys. In P. Rosenfeld, J.E. Edwards, & M.D. Thomas (Eds.), *Improving organizational surveys: New directions, methods, and applications* (pp. 122–142). Thousand Oaks, CA: Sage.

Murdock, J., Davis, G., & Verhagen, J. (2004, November 11). *Quotes and quips.* Retrieved from www.keypress.com/fathom/quotes.html

Murphy, K.R., & Myors, B. (1998). *Statistical power analysis.* Mahwah, NJ: Lawrence Erlbaum Associates.

Nie, N.H., Hull, C.H., Jenkins, J.G., Steinbrenner, K., & Bent, D.H. (1975). *SPSS: Statistical package for the social sciences* (2nd ed.). New York: McGraw-Hill.

Nunnally J.C., & Bernstein, I.H. (1994). *Psychometric theory* (3rd ed.). New York: McGraw-Hill.

Office of Management and Budget. (2000, March 9). *Guidance on aggregation and allocation of data on race for use in civil rights monitoring and enforcement* (OMB Bulletin No. 00–02). Retrieved from www.whitehouse.gov/omb/bulletins/b00–02.html

Office of Management and Budget. (1997, May 28). *Appendix 2: Report to the Office of Management and Budget on the review of statistical policy directive no. 15.* Retrieved from www.whitehouse.gov/omb/fedreg/directive_15.html

Owen, J.M., & Rogers, P.J. (1999). *Program evaluation: Forms and approaches.* Thousand Oaks, CA: Sage.

Patton, M.Q. (1987). *How to use qualitative methods in evaluation.* Thousand Oaks, CA: Sage.

Patton, M.Q. (1988). The evaluator's responsibility for utilization. *Evaluation Practice, 9,* 5–24.

Patton, M.Q. (1990). *Qualitative evaluation and research methods* (2nd ed.). Thousand Oaks, CA: Sage.

Patton, M.Q. (1997). *Utilization-focused evaluation: The new century text* (3rd ed.). Thousand Oaks, CA: Sage.

Patton, M.Q. (2002). *Qualitative research & evaluation methods* (3rd ed.). Thousand Oaks, CA: Sage.

Paulhus, D.L. (1991). Measurement and control of response bias. In J.P. Robinson, P.R. Shaver, & L.S. Wrightsman (Eds.), *Measures of personality and social psychological attributes* (pp. 17–59). San Diego, CA: Academic Press.

Pedhazur, E.J., & Schmelkin, L.P. (1991). *Measurement, design, and analysis: An integrated approach.* Mahwah, NJ: Lawrence Erlbaum Associates.

Phillips, J.J. (1997). *Handbook of training evaluation and measurement methods* (3rd ed.). Houston, TX: Gulf.

Prosavac, E.J., & Carey, R.G. (1989). *Program evaluation: Methods and case studies* (3rd ed.). Englewood Cliffs, NJ: Prentice Hall.

Prosavac, E.J., & Carey, R.G. (2003). *Program evaluation: Methods and case studies* (6th ed.). Englewood Cliffs, NJ: Prentice Hall.

Quintanilla, G., & Packard, T. (2002). A participatory evaluation of an inner-city science enrichment program. *Evaluation and Program Planning, 25,* 15–22.

Raju, N.S., & Burke, M.J. (1991). Utility of personnel decisions. In J.W. Jones, B.D. Steffy, & D.W. Bray (Eds.), *Applying psychology in business: The manager's handbook* (pp. 98–105). New York: Lexington Books.

Raju, N.S., Scott, J.C., & Edwards, J.E. (in press a). Confidence intervals/hypothesis testing/effect sizes. In S.G. Rogelberg (Ed.), *Encyclopedia of industrial/organizational psychology*. Thousand Oaks, CA: Sage.

Raju, N.S., Scott, J.C., & Edwards, J.E. (in press b). Statistical power. In S.G. Rogelberg (Ed.), *Encyclopedia of industrial/organizational psychology*. Thousand Oaks, CA: Sage.

Renzetti, C.M., & Lee, R.M. (1993). *Researching sensitive topics*. Thousand Oaks, CA: Sage.

Robie, C., & Raju, N.S. (2003). Glossary: Definitions of technical and statistical terms commonly used in HR program evaluations. In J.E. Edwards, J.C. Scott, & N.S. Raju (Eds.), *The human resources program-evaluation handbook* (pp. 537–550). Thousand Oaks, CA: Sage.

Roethlisberger, F.J., & Dickson, W.J. (1939). *Management and the worker*. Cambridge, MA: Harvard University Press.

Rose, D.S., & Davidson, E.J. (2003). Overview of program evaluation. In J.E. Edwards, J.C. Scott, & N.S. Raju (Eds.), *The human resources program-evaluation handbook* (pp. 3–26). Thousand Oaks, CA: Sage.

Rossi, P.H., & Freeman, H.E. (1993). *Evaluation: A systematic approach* (5th ed.). Thousand Oaks, CA: Sage.

Roth, P.L. (1994). Missing data: A conceptual review for applied psychologists. *Personnel Psychology, 47*, 537–560.

Royse, D., Thyer, B.A., Padgett, D.K., & Logan, T.K. (2001). *Program evaluation: An introduction*. Belmont, CA: Brooks/Cole.

Runyon, R.P., & Haber, A. (1972). *Fundamentals of behavioral statistics* (2nd ed.). Reading, MA: Addison-Wesley.

Ryan, K. (1998). Advantages and challenges of using inclusive evaluation approaches in evaluation practice. *American Journal of Evaluation, 19*, 101–122.

Rynes, S.L., Gerhart, B., & Minette, K.A. (2004). The importance of pay in employee motivation: Discrepancies between what people say and what they do. *Human Resource Management, 43*, 381–394.

Salant, P., & Dillman, D.A. (1994). *How to conduct your own survey*. New York: John Wiley & Sons.

Scarville, J., Button, S.B., Edwards, J.E., Lancaster, A.R., & Elig, T.W. (1999, August). *Armed forces equal opportunity survey* (Report No. 97–027). Arlington, VA: Defense Manpower Data Center. Retrieve also from www.defenselink.mil/prhome/eo96index.htm.

Schafer, L.S., & Graham, J.W. (2002). Missing data: Our view of the state of the art. *Psychological Methods, 7*, 147–177.

Schwab, D.P. (1999). *Research methods for organizational studies*. Mahwah, NJ: Lawrence Erlbaum Associates.

Scott, J.C., Edwards, J.E., & Raju, N.S. (2002, April). *Program evaluation for human resources: The art and science of measuring success.* Workshops conducted at the 17th annual convention of the Society for Industrial and Organizational Psychology, Toronto, Canada.

Scott, J.C., Raju, N.S., & Edwards, J.E. (in press). Program evaluation. In S.G. Rogelberg (Ed.), *Encyclopedia of industrial/organizational psychology.* Thousand Oaks, CA: Sage.

Scriven, M.S. (1991a). The science of valuing. In W.R. Shadish, Jr., T.D. Cook, & L.C. Leviton (Eds.), *Foundations of program evaluation: Theories of practice* (pp. 73–118). Thousand Oaks, CA: Sage.

Scriven, M. (1991b). *Evaluation thesaurus* (4th ed.). Thousand Oaks, CA: Sage.

Shadish, W.R., Cook, T.D., & Campbell, D.T. (2002). *Experimental and quasi-experimental designs for generalized causal inference.* Boston, MA: Houghton Mifflin.

Sheatsley, P.B. (1983). Questionnaire construction and item writing. In P.H. Rossi, J.D. Wright, & A.B. Anderson (Eds.), *Handbook of survey research* (pp. 195–230). San Diego, CA: Academic Press.

Silverstein, G., & Sharp, L. (1997). Reporting the results of mixed method evaluations. In J. Frechtling & L. Sharp (Eds.), *User-friendly handbook for mixed method evaluations* (NSF97–153). Arlington, VA: National Science Foundation. Retrieved February 10, 2002, from www.ehr.nsf.gov/EHR/REC/pubs/NSF97–153/CHAP_7.HTM

Smith, M.F. (2001). Evaluation: Preview of the future #2. *American Journal of Evaluation, 22,* 281–300.

Sonnichsen, R.C. (2000). *High-impact internal evaluation: A practitioner's guide to evaluating and consulting inside organizations.* Thousand Oaks, CA: Sage.

Stanton, J.M., Nolan, T.V., & Dale, J.R. (2003). Evaluation of human resource information systems. In J.E. Edwards, J.C. Scott, & N.S. Raju (Eds.), *The human resources program-evaluation handbook* (pp. 471–492). Thousand Oaks, CA: Sage.

Steinhaus, S.D., & Witt, L.A. (2003). Criteria for human resources program evaluation. In J.E. Edwards, J.C. Scott, N.S. Raju (Eds.), *The human resources program-evaluation handbook* (pp. 49–68). Thousand Oaks, CA: Sage.

Stewart, D.W., & Shamdasani, P.N. (1990). *Focus groups: Theory and practice.* Thousand Oaks, CA: Sage.

Sullivan, J. (2002). *HR metrics, the world class way: How to build the business case for human resources.* Peterborough, NH: Kennedy Information Inc.

Sullivan, J. (2004). The strategic case against HR outsourcing: Four reasons to minimize outsourcing. In K.V. Beaman (Ed.), *Out of site: An inside look at HT outsourcing* (pp. 333–340). Austin, TX: IHRIM.

Switzer, F.S., III, & Roth, P.L. (2004). Coping with missing data. In S.G. Rogelberg (Ed.), *Handbook of research methods in industrial and organizational psychology* (pp. 310–323). Malden, MA: Blackwell.

Torres, R.T., & Preskill, H. (2001). Evaluation and organizational learning: Past, present, and future. *American Journal of Evaluation, 22*, 387–395.

Tufte, E.R. (2001). *The visual display of quantitative information*. Cheshire, CT: Graphics Press.

Tukey, J.W. (1977). *Exploratory data analysis*. Reading, MA: Addison-Wesley.

U.S. Government Accountability Office. (2005). *Military personnel: More DOD actions needed to address servicemembers' personal financial management issues* (GAO-05-348). Washington, DC: Author. Available from www.gao.gov

U.S. Government Accountability Office. (2000). *Food assistance: Activities and use of nonprogram resources at six WIC agencies* (GAO/RCED-00-202). Washington, DC: Author. Available from www.gao.gov

Walker, A.J. (1993). *Handbook of human resource information systems: Reshaping the human resource function with technology*. New York: McGraw-Hill.

Weinberg, E. (1983). Data collection: Planning and management. In P.H. Rossi, J.D. Wright, & A.B. Anderson (Eds.), *Handbook of survey research* (pp. 329–357). San Diego, CA: Academic Press.

Weiss, C.H. (1988). Evaluation for decisions: Is there anybody out there? Does anybody care? *Evaluation Practice, 9*, 5–19.

Weiss, C.H. (1991). Linking evaluation to policy research. In W.R. Shadish, Jr., T.D. Cook, & L.C. Leviton (Eds.), *Foundations of program evaluation: Theories of practice* (pp. 179-224). Thousand Oaks, CA: Sage.

Weiss, R.J., & Townsend, R.J. (2005). Leading edge: Using Excel to clean and prepare data for analysis. *The Industrial-Organizational Psychologist, 42*(3), 89–97.

Wilkinson, L., & Task Force on Statistical Inference. (1999). Statistical methods in psychology journals: Guidelines and explanations. *American Psychologist, 54*, 594–604. Retrieved August 25, 1999, from www.apa.org/journals/amp/amp548594.html

Winer, B.J., Brown, D.R., & Michels, K.M. (1991). *Statistical principles in experimental design* (3rd ed.). New York: McGraw-Hill.

Wolins, L. (1962). Responsibility for raw data. *American Psychologist, 17*, 657–658.

Wood, D.J. (2005). Stakeholders. In N. Nicholson, P.G. Audia, & M.M. Pillutla (Eds.), *The Blackwell encyclopedia of management* (2nd ed., Vol. XI, pp. 375–376). Oxford, United Kingdom: Blackwell.

Worthen, B.R., Sanders, J.R., & Fitzpatrick, J.L. (1997). *Program evaluation: Alternative approaches and practical guidelines* (2nd ed.). New York: Addison Wesley/Longman.

Yin, R.K. (2002a). *Applications of case study research* (2nd ed.). Thousand Oaks, CA: Sage.

Yin, R.K. (2002b). *Case study research: Design and methods* (3rd ed.). Thousand Oaks, CA: Sage.

Zaccaro, S.J., & Marks, M. (1996). Collecting data from groups. In F.T.L. Leong & J.T. Austin (Eds.), *The psychology research handbook: A guide for graduate students and research assistants* (pp. 155–164). Thousand Oaks, CA: Sage.

Author Index

Subject Index

G

Gartner Group, 226

Goals-based evaluations: characteristics of, 6t; focusing on objectives using, 5, 7

Governmental agencies: assessing positions of, 38–39; regulations of, 39

Graphs: description and function of, 196; example of contrasting numerical, 198fig; misleading problem of, 196–199; types of, 199–202

H

HR (human resources): ever-expanding strategic role of, 1–2; research on intangibles associated with, 2–3. See also HR programs

HR program administrators, 16

HR program evaluation excuses: 1: required resources are better spent on program administration, 16–18; 2: program effectiveness is impossible to measure, 18; 3: there are too many variables to do a good study, 19–20; 4: no one is asking for an evaluation, 20–21; 5: "negative" results will hurt my program, 21–22; preparing to address, 15–16

HR program evaluation six-phase model: appropriate deviation from, 26–27; illustrations of, 23fig, 238fig; overview of, 23fig–26; phase 1: identify stakeholders, evaluators, and evaluation questions, 23–24, 30–69; phase 2: plan the evaluation, 24, 71–108, 149–150; phase 3: collect data, 24, 129–145, 150–151; phase 4: analyze and interpret data, 25, 147–180, 151–153; phase 5: communicate findings and insights, 25, 153, 181–214, 236–237; phase 6: utilize the results, 25–26. See also HR program evaluations

HR program evaluation strategies: goals-based, 5, 6t, 7; outcome-based, 6t, 9; process-based, 6t, 7–9

HR program evaluations: addressing potential excuses for not conducting, 15–22; building team accountability and skill through, 227–229; distinguishing characteristics of three strategies for, 6t; general philosophy of, 14–15; HR programs integration of ongo-

ing, 10–13; incorporated as part of strategic plans, 4; leveraging insights relevant to, 227–237; matching approach with objectives of, 5–9; stakeholder engagement in using results of, 229–231; value of, 3–4. See also HR program evaluation six-phase model

HR program staff: considering program replacement during changes in, 223–224; described, 16; engaged in program adjustments, 221–222; evaluators from among, 44–45, 46–47; expertise from stakeholders of, 34

HR programs: adjusting existing, 220–223; benefits of new technology to, 224–225; considering replacement during staff transitions, 223–224; cumulative ROI associated with replacing, 219t; evaluation recommendations on, 217–220; integrating ongoing evaluations into, 10–13; outsourcing existing, 226–227; realigning as part of strategic plan change, 225–226; replacing existing, 219, 223–226. See also HR (human resources)

HR staff evaluators: assessing against criteria, 48t–49t; described, 44–45; strengths and weaknesses of, 45, 46–47

I

Impact questions, 55–56

Implementation. See Utilizing results

Inferential statistics: issues regarding use of, 167, 169–170; underlying assumptions for use of, 176–177

Institutional review boards, 41

Interest groups, 36–37

Internal documents/files, 111t, 114–115

Internal processes/procedural information, 112t, 117–121

Internal staff evaluators: assessing against criteria, 48t–49t; described, 44–45; strengths and weaknesses of, 45, 46–47

Internal stakeholders: demographic groups more affected than other, 35–36; expertise of HR program staff, 34; five types of, 33, 32fig; identification of, 31–37; interest groups, 36–37; legal department as, 35; value of top management, 32–34

About the Authors

Jack E. Edwards, Ph.D., is an assistant director in the Defense Capabilities and Management area of the U.S. Government Accountability Office (GAO) in Washington, D.C., directing teams that evaluate human resources programs provided to U.S. military personnel. Jack has also been an assistant director in GAO's Office of Applied Research and Methods, providing methodological assistance to teams evaluating national security and international affairs programs. His other prior positions include chief of the Personnel Survey Branch at the Defense Manpower Data Center, science advisor to the Chief of Naval Personnel, personnel research psychologist at the Navy Personnel Research and Development Center, and tenured associate professor at the Illinois Institute of Technology. He has over 125 publications and presentations examining practical and theoretical human resources concerns such as program evaluation, survey methods, attitude measurement, personnel selection, performance appraisal, diversity, and utility analysis. Jack has published three books: *The Human Resources Program-Evaluation Handbook* (Sage, 2003), *How to Conduct Organizational Surveys: A Step-by-Step Guide* (Sage, 1997), and *Improving Organizational Surveys: New Directions, Methods, and Applications* (Sage, 1993). He earned his Ph.D. from Ohio University in 1981 and is a Fellow in both the Society for Industrial and Organizational Psychology and the American Psychological Association.

The opinions expressed in this book are those of the authors and do not necessarily reflect the views of the U.S. Government Accountability Office or the federal government.

John C. Scott, Ph.D., is vice president and co-founder of Applied Psychological Techniques (APT), a human resources consulting firm in Darien, Connecticut, that specializes in the design and validation of selection and assessment technologies, staffing for organizational change, performance management, and employment litigation support. He was one of the chief architects of APT's multi-source assessment and feedback system, 360 Metrics^{SM}, which won *Human Resource Executive*'s 2001 Top 10 Products of the Year Award. Prior to co-founding APT, he was a managing principal for the New York office of HRStrategies, where he directed consulting services in the areas of selection development and validation, skills assessment, survey design, performance management, and executive assessment. He was formerly a senior research psychologist for Wisconsin Electric Power Company and held an adjunct faculty position at the University of Wisconsin. Earlier, he managed the abilities test product line at the Riverside Publishing Company and directed the development and nationwide standardization of the *Stanford-Binet Intelligence Scale* (4th ed.). He has served on the program and review committees for Division 14 of the American Psychological Association, and is a member of editorial boards for the Society for Industrial and Organizational Psychology's Professional Practice book series and Blackwell Publishing's Industrial and Organizational Psychology Practice series. He is a frequent presenter in the areas of selection, assessment, and program evaluation. He is co-editor of the book, *The Human Resources Program-Evaluation Handbook* (Sage, 2003). He earned his Ph.D. from the Illinois Institute of Technology in 1985.

Nambury S. Raju, Ph.D., was a distinguished professor in the Institute of Psychology and a senior scientific advisor at the Center for Research and Service at the Illinois Institute of Technology, Chicago, Illinois, until his unexpected death in 2005. Prior to joining academia in 1978, he worked at Science Research Associates from 1961 to 1978, specializing in test development and validation. He had strong interests in personnel selection and psychometrics, especially in the areas of reliability, selection and validation, item bias, validity generalization/meta-analysis, and utility of organizational interventions. He served on the Department of Defense Advisory Committee on Military Personnel Testing from 1989 to 1992. He recently served on a National Academy of Science committee to evaluate the National Assessment of Educational Progress (NAEP). He also served on nine editorial boards, including *Educational and Psychological Measurement, Applied Psychological Measurement, Journal of Applied Psychology, Personnel Psychology, Psychological Bulletin, International Journal of Selection and Assessment,* and *Organizational Research Methods*. He had over 150 publications and presentations—including the book *The Human Resources Program-Evaluation Handbook* (Sage, 2003)—and was a Fellow of the Society for Industrial and Organizational Psychology and the American Psychological Association. He earned his Ph.D. from the Illinois Institute of Technology in 1974. In 2006, he was posthumously awarded the Distinguished Career Award from the Academy of Management's Research Methods Division for his contributions to the advancement of research methodology.

SHRM FOUNDATION
SOCIETY FOR HUMAN RESOURCE MANAGEMENT

The Society for Human Resource Management (SHRM) is the world's largest association devoted to human resource management. Representing more than 204,000 individual members, the Society's mission is to serve the needs of HR professionals by providing the most essential and comprehensive resources available. As an influential voice, the Society's mission is also to advance the human resource profession to ensure that HR is recognized as an essential partner in developing and executing organizational strategy. Founded in 1948, SHRM currently has more than five hundred affiliated chapters within the United States and members in more than one hundred countries. Visit SHRM Online at www.shrm.org.